O9-BTO-436

CALAMITIES

CRITICAL READING SERIES

21 Stories of Disasters That Touched the World—with Exercises for Developing Reading Comprehension and Critical Thinking Skills

Henry Billings
Melissa Billings

JAMESTOWN PUBLISHERS
a division of NTC/Contemporary Publishing Group
Lincolnwood, Illinois USA

ISBN 0-89061-111-4

Published by Jamestown Publishers,
a division of NTC/Contemporary Publishing Group, Inc.
4255 West Touhy Avenue
Lincolnwood (Chicago), Illinois 60646-1975, U.S.A.

8 9 0 VL 0 9 8 7 6 5 4 3 2 1

CONTENTS

To the Student 1
Sample Lesson: The Philadelphia Killer 4

UNIT ONE

1 Nightmare on Chemical Street: The Love Canal Story 14
2 The Sweatshop Inferno 22
3 Killer Tornado! 30
4 The Schoolyard Tragedy 38
5 The Crash of TWA Flight 800 46
6 A Dance with Death 54
7 In the Eye of the Storm 62

Compare and Contrast Chart 70
Words-per-Minute Table 71
Progress Graphs and Charts 72

UNIT TWO

8 Sabotage in the Desert 76
9 Poison on the Drugstore Shelf 84
10 Fire in the Subway 92
11 The World Series Earthquake 100

12 A Deadly Mistake 108

13 The North Sea Oil Rig Explosion 116

14 Baby Jessica: The Miracle of Midland 124

Compare and Contrast 132
Words-per-Minute Table 133
Progress Graphs and Charts 134

UNIT THREE

15 Oil, Oil Everywhere 138

16 Soccer Fans in a Death Trap 146

17 *Challenger:* The Final Countdown 154

18 The Great Mississippi Flood of 1993 162

19 Danger Behind Locked Doors 170

20 The World's Worst Accident: Massacre at Bhopal 178

21 The Oklahoma City Bombing 186

Compare and Contrast 194
Words-per-Minute Table 195
Progress Graphs and Charts 196

Picture Credits 199

To the Student

Webster's Dictionary defines a calamity as "an extraordinarily grave event marked by great loss and lasting distress and affliction."

What is the worst calamity that could happen to you? If it really happened, how would you act? Would you be brave and heroic or frightened and selfish? These are questions that we all ask ourselves at times. If we are truly fortunate, we will never find ourselves in the dire situations where our imaginations have taken us. The closest most of us ever come to these horrible events is observing them happening to other people. We read how other people deal with terrible calamities such as train wrecks, bombings, or mass poisonings and, in a small way, we put ourselves in their places. We're glad that the disaster hasn't happened to us, and, deep down, we know that it is just luck that keeps us safe while someone else suffers.

Each lesson in this book will introduce you to a famous calamity that has occurred during the 20th century. The details about each even were found in newspaper articles and magazines. For the most part, the victims of these calamities were powerless to stop them. They were simply in the wrong place at the wrong time. As you read each story, try to imagine how you would feel in that situation.

As you read and enjoy these articles, you will also be developing your reading skills. *Calamities* is for students who already read fairly well but who want to read faster and to increase their understanding of what they read. If you complete the 21 lessons—reading the articles and completing the exercises—you will surely increase your reading speed and improve your reading comprehension and critical thinking skills. Also, because these exercises include items of the types often found on state and national tests, learning how to complete them will prepare you for tests you may have to take in the future.

How to Use This Book

About the Book. *Calamities* contains three units, each of which includes seven lessons. Each lesson begins with an article about an unusual event, person, or group. The article is followed by a group of four reading comprehension exercises and a set of three critical thinking exercises. The reading comprehension exercises will help you understand the article. The critical thinking exercises will help you think about what you have read and how it relates to your own experience.

At the end of each lesson, you will also have the opportunity to give your personal response to some aspect of the article and then to assess how well you understood what you read.

The Sample Lesson. Working through the sample lesson, the first lesson in the book, with your class or group will demonstrate how a lesson is organized. The sample lesson explains how to complete the exercises and score your answers. The correct answers for the sample exercises and sample scores are printed in lighter type. In some cases, explanations of the correct answers are given. The explanations will help you understand how to think through these question types.

If you have any questions about how to complete the exercises or score them, this is the time to get the answers.

Working Through Each Lesson. Begin each lesson by looking at the photographs and reading the captions. Before you read, predict what you think the article will be about. Then read the article.

Sometimes your teacher may decide to time your reading. Timing helps you keep track of and increase your reading speed. If you have been timed, enter your reading time in the box at the end of the lesson. Then use the Words-per-Minute Table to find your reading speed, and record your speed on the Reading Speed graph at the end of the unit.

Next complete the Reading Comprehension and Critical Thinking exercises. The directions for each exercise will tell you how to mark your answers. When you have finished all four Reading Comprehension exercises, use the answer key provided by your teacher to check your work. Follow the directions after each exercise to find your score. Record your Reading Comprehension scores on the graph at the end of each unit. Then check your answers to the Author's Approach, Summarizing and Paraphrasing, and Critical Thinking exercises. Fill in the Critical Thinking chart at the end of each unit with your evaluation of your work and comments about your progress.

At the end of each unit you will also complete a Compare/Contrast chart. The completed chart will help you see what the articles have in common, and it will give you an opportunity to explore the way you think and feel about these terrible calamities.

SAMPLE LESSON

THE PHILADELPHIA KILLER

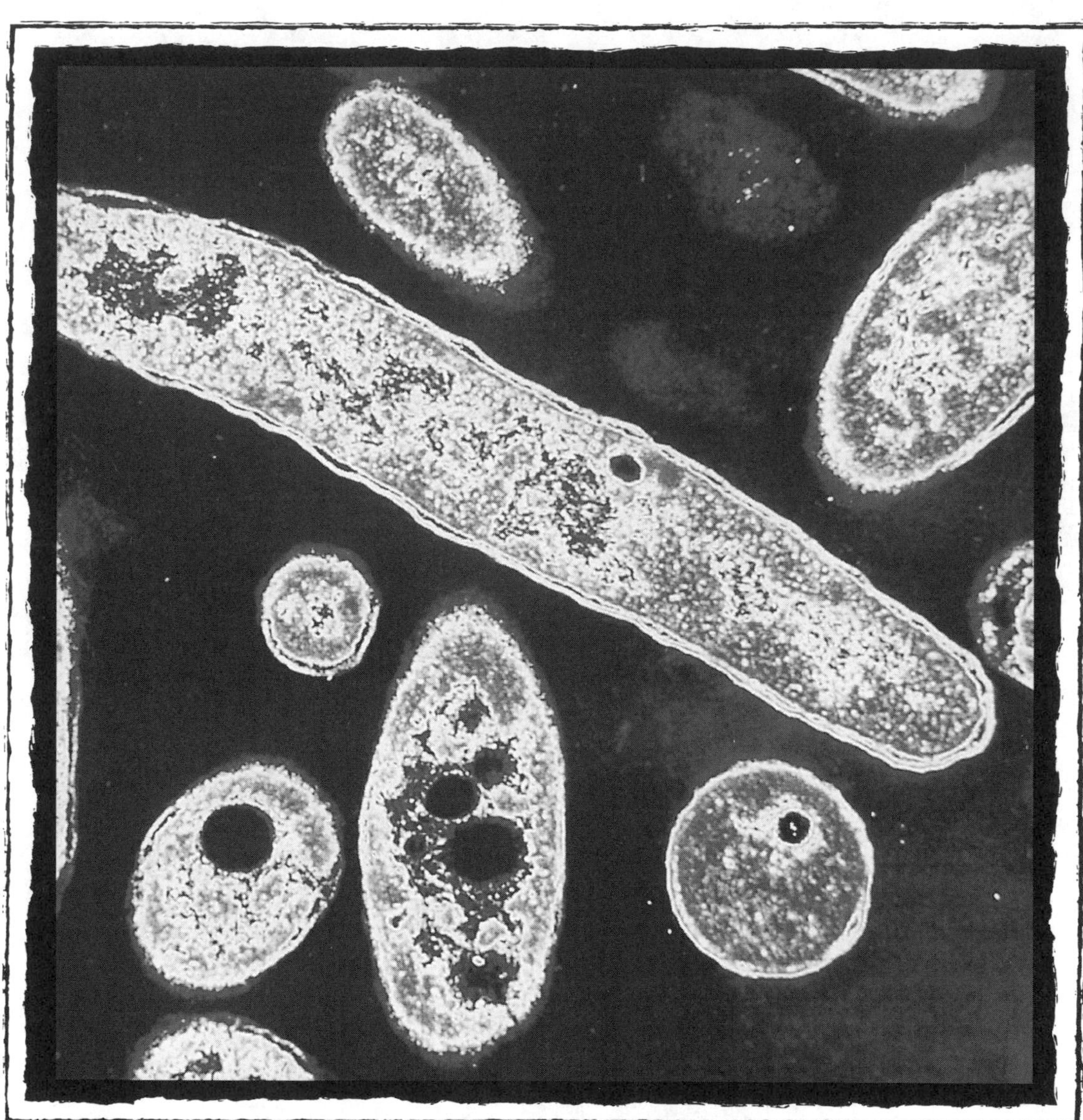

In June and July of 1976, American Legion members all over Pennsylvania were starting to get excited. Their state convention was coming up on July 21. Many Legion members had fought in World Wars I and II. Others had served in the Korean or Vietnam wars. All were planning to catch up with old friends at this year's meeting.

2 The American Legion is the largest veterans group in the United States. In 1976 the Pennsylvania branch of the Legion was holding its state meeting at the Bellevue Stratford Hotel in Philadelphia. The Legion members looked forward to speeches, parades, and fun. They planned dinners and parties. Many bought tickets for a baseball game between the Phillies and the Pirates.

3 The convention lasted from July 21 to July 24. It was a big success. The Pennsylvania members had a wonderful time in Philadelphia. They returned home tired and happy.

4 But the Philadelphia killer was about to strike.

5 Ray Brennan was the first victim. Brennan had retired from the air force

This bacterium, photographed through a microscope, is the cause of Legionnaires' disease.

several years earlier. He now worked as the bookkeeper of the American Legion Post 42 in Towanda, Pennsylvania. His sister Maize Travis remembers, "All he lived for was these conventions." But he came home from the July meeting completely worn out.

6 Brennan had suffered from heart problems for years. At home he complained of chest pains. Then he lost his appetite. He developed a high fever and started having trouble breathing. His sister recalls, "He didn't want to go to the hospital. We had to fight him all the way."

7 That same night, Brennan died. His lungs were full of fluid. Still, his family thought he'd suffered a heart attack. They were wrong.

8 Ray Brennan died on July 27. On July 30, three more Legion members died in hospitals around the state. By August 1, the death toll had risen to 10.

9 What did all these people have in common? All the victims had gone to the Philadelphia convention. All had suffered from the same symptoms. Each person had a very high fever, chest pains, and lungs filled with fluid.

10 The first person to notice a pattern was Dr. Ernest Campbell. Campbell worked at Bloomsburg State Health Center. He discovered that three patients at his hospital were showing the same symptoms. Then he learned that all three had gone to the convention.

11 Campbell was scared. He notified the state health department, and word of the strange disease began to spread. A killer disease was loose among Pennsylvania Legionnaires!

12 In tiny Williamstown (population 1,917), two leading citizens died within a day of each other. Earlier in the week one victim, John B. Ralph, had sponsored a dart contest at the local Legion hall. He had been the life of the party. On Thursday he went into the hospital. On Monday he was dead. His friend James Dolan had died the day before.

13 Dicko Dolan, leader of Williamstown's American Legion Post 239, said, "It just has everybody stunned. Fellows your age, your friends, are dead. I never expected anything so sudden." Dicko was James Dolan's cousin and John Ralph's best friend.

14 The people of Williamstown were terrified. They were afraid to go to the doctor who had treated the men. They were even afraid to sit next to the doctor's secretary at a Little League game.

15 Pennsylvania health officials called the Center for Disease Control (CDC) in Atlanta, Georgia. They asked for help. The Center for Disease Control studies

Harold W. Smith and Clarence Kirschner Seaman, photographed in 1978, survived both World War I and Legionnaires' disease.

epidemics. It sent specialists to Pennsylvania immediately.

16 CDC researchers began to interview patients. They inspected the Bellevue Stratford Hotel, headquarters of the convention. They checked the food and the ventilation system. They studied the neighborhood around the hotel. They tested patients for typhoid fever and swine flu. But they discovered nothing.

17 More Legion members came down with the frightening disease. Rumors began to spread. Word of a Pennsylvania epidemic made headlines all over the United States. Reporters for the *New York Times, Time Magazine*, and *Newsweek* wrote long articles about the Philadelphia killer.

18 Other kinds of rumors also spread. One woman claimed that the fever was part of a plot by the Taiwan government. She said that Taiwan citizens were angry at the United States for problems during the last Olympics.

19 Another person thought that someone disguised as a veteran had infected people at the convention. "Maybe he had a needle in his hand and just slapped a shoulder or shook hands," she told reporters.

20 More than 150 people fell ill with Legionnaires' disease. Twenty-nine people died. Doctors feared a widespread epidemic. They began to consult with President Gerald Ford about the nation's safety. Then suddenly, the number of illnesses slowed to a trickle. Finally they stopped.

21 But doctors kept running tests, hoping to learn more about the Philadelphia killer. Finally, in January 1977, Dr. Joseph E. McDade made a discovery. He learned that Legionnaires' disease is a form of pneumonia caused by a strange bacterium.

22 A bacterium is a tiny plant that can be seen only through a microscope. Some kinds of bacteria are helpful to people. But this one was a killer. Dr. McDade began to study other pneumonia epidemics. He decided that they, too, may have been caused by the deadly bacterium. However, he still couldn't answer one big question. How was the bacterium spread to the Legionnaires?

23 Even today, no one knows how Legionnaires' disease is spread. Some people still suspect the ventilation system at the Bellevue Stratford Hotel. But there is no solid evidence to prove that theory. Since 1976, other epidemics of Legionnaires' disease have broken out. But the Philadelphia killer remains a mystery.

If you have been timed while reading this article, enter your reading time below. Then turn to the Words-per-Minute Table on page 71 and look up your reading speed (words per minute). Enter your reading speed on the graph on page 72.

Reading Time: Sample Lesson

_______ : _______

Minutes *Seconds*

A Finding the Main Idea

One statement below expresses the main idea of the article. One statement is too general, or too broad. The other statement explains only part of the article; it is too narrow. Label the statements using the following key:

M—Main Idea **B—Too Broad** **N—Too Narrow**

B 1. Frightening things were happening to Legionnaires. [This statement is true, but it is *too broad*. The story is about one particular frightening thing—a killer disease.]

M 2. A disease that killed many Pennsylvania Legionnaires who attended a convention frightened people all over the United States. [This statement is the *main idea*. It tells you what the reading selection is about—a disease that killed Legionnaires. It also tells you that many people were frightened.]

N 3. Legionnaires' disease turned out to be a form of pneumonia. [This statement is true, but it is *too narrow*. It gives only one piece of information from the story.]

15 Score 15 points for a correct M answer.

10 Score 5 points for each correct B or N answer.

25 **Total Score:** Finding the Main Idea

B Recalling Facts

How well do you remember the facts in the article? Put an X in the box next to the answer that correctly completes each statement about the article.

1. Ernest Campbell was a
   - ☒ a. doctor at a state hospital.
   - ☐ b. victim of the strange disease.
   - ☐ c. reporter for the *New York Times*.

2. The Legion convention was held in
   - ☐ a. Atlanta.
   - ☐ b. Pittsburgh.
   - ☒ c. Philadelphia.

3. Members of the American Legion have all
   - ☒ a. served in the armed forces.
   - ☐ b. studied medicine.
   - ☐ c. suffered from a serious illness.

4. The bacterium was discovered by
   - ☐ a. Dicko Dolan.
   - ☒ b. Joseph E. McDade.
   - ☐ c. John B. Ralph.

5. The Center for Disease Control
   - ☐ a. discovered that the hotel food was poisoned.
   - ☒ b. studies strange diseases and epidemics.
   - ☐ c. showed no interest in Legionnaires' disease.

Score 5 points for each correct answer.

25 **Total Score:** Recalling Facts

C Making Inferences

When you combine your own experience and information from a text to draw a conclusion that is not directly stated in that text, you are making an inference. Below are five statements that may or may not be inferences based on information in the article. Label the statements using the following key:

C—Correct Inference **F—Faulty Inference**

C 1. The Pennsylvania Legionnaires were proud of their organization. [This is a *correct* inference. You are told in the story that Legion members were excited about their meeting. You also learned that one Legionnaire "lived for…these conventions."]

F 2. Dr. McDade believed that the ventilation system at the hotel had spread the bacteria. [This is a *faulty* inference. There is nothing in the story to indicate that Dr. McDade suspected the ventilation system.]

F 3. President Ford was not worried about the spread of Legionnaires' disease. [This is a *faulty* inference. In fact, the president talked to doctors about the nation's safety.]

C 4. Not all kinds of bacteria cause diseases. [This is a *correct* inference. The story says that some kinds of bacteria are helpful to people.]

F 5. Most of the people who died lived in large cities. [This is a *faulty* inference. The story mentions two deaths in Williamstown, a very small town.]

Score 5 points for each correct answer.

25 **Total Score:** Making Inferences

D Using Words Precisely

Each numbered sentence below contains an underlined word or phrase from the article. Following the sentence are three definitions. One definition is closest to the meaning of the underlined word. One definition is opposite or nearly opposite. Label those two definitions using the following key. Do not label the remaining definition.

C—Closest **O—Opposite or Nearly Opposite**

1. The convention lasted from July 21 to July 24.

____ a. illness
C b. large meeting
O c. individual assignment

2. Each person had a very high fever, chest pains, and lungs filled with fluid.

C a. liquid
____ b. aches
O c. solid material

3. Dicko Dolan…said, "It just has everybody stunned."

O a. bored
C b. shocked
____ c. laughing

4. The Center for Disease Control studies epidemics.

O a. illnesses that aren't contagious
____ b. important news
C c. diseases that spread to others

5. Then suddenly, the number of illnesses slowed to a trickle.

C a. small drip

O b. huge flow

____ c. small graph

15	Score 3 points for each correct C answer.
10	Score 2 points for each correct O answer.
25	**Total Score:** Using Words Precisely

Enter the four total scores in the spaces below, and add them together to find your Reading Comprehension Score. Then record your score on the graph on page 73.

Score	Question Type	Sample Lesson
25	Finding the Main Idea	
25	Recalling Facts	
25	Making Inferences	
25	Using Words Precisely	
100	**Reading Comprehension Score**	

Author's Approach

Put an X in the box next to the correct answer.

1. What does the author mean by the statement "He had been the life of the party"?

☐ a. He had still been alive at the party.

☐ b. He had died at the party.

☒ c. He had had a lot of energy at the party.

2. What is the author's purpose in writing "The Philadelphia Killer"?

☒ a. To inform the reader about a mysterious disease that struck members of the American Legion

☐ b. To express an opinion about the causes of Legionnaires' disease

☐ c. To convey the mood of fear caused by Legionnaires' disease

3. Choose the statement below that is the weakest argument for blaming the Bellevue Stratford Hotel for the Legionnaires' disease epidemic.

☒ a. Since the convention in 1976, other epidemics of the disease have broken out in other places.

☐ b. Immediately after a Legionnaires' convention at the hotel, many Legion members died, all showing the same symptoms.

☐ c. It is possible that the ventilation system at the hotel helped spread the disease.

4. How is the author's purpose for writing the article expressed in paragraph 18?

☐ a. The author claims that the disease was a plot by the Taiwan government.

☒ b. The author relates one of the strange rumors spread about the mysterious disease.

☐ c. The author discusses the possible hard feelings by Taiwanese against the U.S. during the last Olympics.

4 Number of correct answers

Record your personal assessment of your work on the Critical Thinking Chart on page 74.

Summarizing and Paraphrasing

Follow the directions provided for question 1. Put an X in the box next to the correct answer for question 2.

1. Complete the following one-sentence summary of the article using the lettered phrases from the phrase bank below. Write the letters on the lines.

Phrase Bank:

a. that some of the people who attended the convention suddenly and mysteriously died

b. the 1976 Legionnaires' state convention in Philadelphia

c. some theories and discoveries about the killer disease

The article about the Philadelphia killer begins with __b__, goes on to explain __a__, and ends with __c__.

2. Read the statement about the article below. Then read the paraphrase of that statement. Choose the reason that best tells why the paraphrase does not say the same thing as the statement.

Statement: Although Dr. Joseph McDade discovered that Legionnaires' disease is a form of pneumonia, no one has figured out how the disease spread to the Legion members at the Bellevue Stratford Hotel.

Paraphrase: Dr. McDade learned that Legionnaires' disease is a form of pneumonia.

☐ a. Paraphrase says too much.

☒ b. Paraphrase doesn't say enough.

☐ c. Paraphrase doesn't agree with the statement about the article.

2 Number of correct answers

Record your personal assessment of your work on the Critical Thinking Chart on page 74.

Critical Thinking

Put an X in the box next to the correct answer.

1. Which of the following statements from the article is an opinion rather than a fact?

☐ a. "Ray Brennan died on July 27."

☐ b. "The Center for Disease Control studies epidemics."

☒ c. "The Pennsylvania members had a wonderful time in Philadelphia."

2. From what Maize Travis said, you can conclude that her brother, Ray Brennan, had

☒ a. really looked forward to the state convention.

☐ b. dreaded going to the state convention.

☐ c. had a terrible time at the convention.

3. What was the effect of the epidemic in Williamstown, Pennsylvania?

☐ a. John Ralph sponsored a dart contest.

☒ b. People were afraid to go the doctor who had treated the men who died.

☐ c. People were relieved that only two of their citizens died.

4. What did you have to do to answer question 1?

☒ a. find an opinion (what someone thinks about something)

☐ b. find a fact (something that you can prove is true)

☐ c. find an effect (something that happened)

4 Number of correct answers

Record your personal assessment of your work on the Critical Thinking Chart on page 74.

Personal Response

What was most surprising or interesting to you about this article?

[Briefly identify and discuss a fact or detail in the article that interested you.]

Self-Assessment

Before reading this article, I already knew

[Describe your prior knowledge of the subject.]

Self-Assessment

To get the most out of the Critical Reading series program, you need to take charge of your own progress in improving your reading comprehension and critical thinking skills. Here are some of the features that help you work on those essential skills.

Reading Comprehension Exercises. Complete these exercises immediately after reading the article. They help you recall what you have read, understand the stated and implied main ideas, and add words to your working vocabulary.

Critical Thinking Skills Exercises. These exercises help you focus on the author's approach and purpose, recognize and generate summaries and paraphrases, and identify relationships between ideas.

Personal Response and Self-assessment. Questions in this category help you relate the articles to your personal experience and give you the opportunity to evaluate your understanding of the information in that lesson.

Compare and Contrast Charts. At the end of each unit you will complete a Compare and Contrast chart. The completed chart helps you see what the articles have in common and gives you an opportunity to explore your own ideas about the topics discussed in the articles.

The Graphs. The graphs and charts at the end of each unit enable you to keep track of your progress. Check your graphs regularly with your teacher. Decide whether your progress is satisfactory or whether you need additional work on some skills. What types of exercises are you having difficulty with? Talk with your teacher about ways to work on the skills in which you need the most practice.

UNIT ONE

NIGHTMARE ON CHEMICAL STREET
The Love Canal Story

Imagine that you live in a small, safe neighborhood in a medium-sized city. Imagine that you walk a short block to your local school. Imagine that you and your friends play on a wide grassy field on the weekends.

2 Sounds nice, doesn't it?

3 That's what Lois and Harry Gibbs thought when they bought their house on 101st Street in 1972. That's what Barbara and Jim Quimby thought when they bought the house Jim had grown up in, just a few blocks away. That's what more than 700 families believed when they moved into the pleasant neighborhood called Love Canal.

4 Love Canal is a section of Niagara Falls, New York. The city has many industries, and most residents work in local plants or factories. Many of the neighbors at Love Canal worked for chemical companies. They didn't make much money at their jobs, but they were proud of their work. They wanted a good, safe life for their families. And quiet Love Canal seemed like a great place to bring up kids.

5 But in the late 1970s, after several years of heavy rains, people started

Love Canal became a ghost town after people realized that their homes and the local school were sitting on the site of a toxic waste dump.

noticing strange things happening to their homes and lawns. Basement walls started oozing thick sludge. Rain puddles glowed bright yellow and purple. Trees and plants began to die. Strong chemical smells floated through the streets. And on the wide grassy field next to the school, rusted metal barrels began to rise to the surface.

6 Still, most people didn't pay much attention. They were busy going to work or school. They were busy leading normal lives.

7 But in 1978 Lois Gibbs read an article in the Niagara Falls *Gazette*. The article said that the local elementary school had been built on top of a chemical dump. Lois was shocked. Her five-year-old son went to that school. He already had some health problems. She didn't want them to get worse.

8 Lois tried to learn more about the chemical dump. She had never heard anyone mention it before. She read more newspaper articles. She talked to the school board and the city government. And she couldn't believe what she discovered about the history of Love Canal.

9 The canal was the idea of William T. Love. In 1892 he decided to build a canal to connect two parts of the Niagara River. But he ran out of money, so he gave up the project. He left behind Love Canal—a deep ditch one mile long and 15 yards wide.

10 In the late 1940s the canal was owned by Hooker Chemical & Plastics Corporation. The company decided to use the old waterway as a dumping place for toxic waste. Over the next 11 years, Hooker dumped about 20,000 tons of chemicals into the ditch. In 1953 the company covered up the barrels of chemicals with dirt. Then it sold the property to the Niagara Falls Board of Education for one dollar.

11 The board of education built a school right on top of the canal. Then it gave the rest of the land to the city. Soon small homes began to appear around the dump site. Hooker's chemical graveyard had been forgotten.

12 Lois Gibbs was scared and angry. Her family was in danger! Usually she was a quiet woman. She had devoted her life to taking care of her home and her children. She hated to speak in public. But she knew something had to be done. So with her neighbors she formed the Love Canal Homeowners Association.

13 Association members forced the state of New York to pay attention to the problems at Love Canal. They asked the state to clean up the area. But the state was slow in acting. It was hard for the government to believe that something was really wrong.

14 Meanwhile, the homeowners were finding more frightening evidence about the danger of Love Canal. They took a neighborhood health survey. They discovered that many residents were suffering from severe health problems. There were several people fighting cancer. Some people had leukemia or kidney problems. Children often developed strange burns and rashes after playing in their yards.

15 In Barbara and Jim Quimby's family, everyone was sick. Both Barbara and Jim had spent their entire lives in the neighborhood. Since her childhood, Barbara had suffered from lung problems. In her 20s doctors told her that she had a hernia and an ulcer. She underwent a gallbladder operation. Those illnesses are common in elderly people. They are very rare in a young woman.

16 Jim had terrible problems with migraine headaches. His sister had died of a bone marrow disease when she was only 16. His father had skin cancer.

A resident of Love Canal, who eventually left his home, offers to sell the chemicals that are leaking into his basement.

17 The Quimbys' eldest daughter was born retarded and had eye and tooth problems. Their youngest daughter had been rushed to the hospital several times with breathing problems.

18 But the Quimbys, like most residents, couldn't leave Love Canal. As Barbara said, "If we left here, we'd have to pay rent as well as our mortgage. We don't have that kind of money.... We have 2,000 dollars in savings. How long would that last? We hate this house. We really do. But we can't afford a down payment on a new one until we get the money for this one. So we're stuck...."

19 The Love Canal Homeowners Association wanted the United States government to declare the area a federal disaster. Then New York State would receive enough money to buy the houses around Love Canal.

20 But the state and the federal government also had pressure from the other side. Some members of the local government didn't want to give Niagara Falls a bad name. The mayor even told the homeowners, "You are hurting Niagara Falls with your publicity. There is no problem here."

21 Meanwhile, health problems continued to show up. In one year, 15 children were born. Only two were normal. The others were born dead or had birth defects.

22 Then the Environmental Protection Agency (EPA) revealed that many residents had suffered from another terrible side effect. Tests showed that some people had blood cells that contained broken chromosomes.

23 Chromosomes (CROHM-uh-sohmz) are small parts of cells. They contain information about traits that will be passed on from parent to child.

24 People with broken chromosomes are more at risk of developing serious illnesses, such as cancer. So it's no wonder that people around Love Canal were terrified. They had once believed that the neighborhood was a great place to raise kids. Now they felt as if they were killing their own children. In 1980, after two long years of work, the Love Canal Homeowners Association finally won its battle. The federal government agreed to help New York State buy the homes closest to the dump site and relocate the residents. The decision meant that about 240 families could use the money from the state to purchase new homes in a safer place.

25 But it was too late for many people. Newborn babies had already died. Others had been born with club feet or extra toes. Some had permanent health problems, such as ulcers or epilepsy. A few were retarded.

26 Adults were dying of cancer or suffering from lung damage. Some people were afraid to have children. They didn't know what their chromosomes would pass on to the next generation.

27 The government made an attempt to clean up the area. But the chemicals were too dangerous to handle. And many of them had already leaked into the ground. So Love Canal was covered with a thick layer of clay. Homes that once edged the grassy field were torn down. The school was closed. And the canal was surrounded by a fence.

28 Some houses in the area are still standing. New York State is starting to sell those houses. And once again people are moving into the neighborhood—even former residents.

29 One potential home buyer said, "They must have cleaned it [Love Canal] up pretty well. It's probably one of the safest places to live in Niagara Falls by now."

30 The government hopes it has solved the problems at Love Canal. But rusted barrels of chemicals still lie beneath that layer of clay. Will the tragedy at Love Canal happen all over again?

31 Who knows for sure?

If you have been timed while reading this article, enter your reading time below. Then turn to the Words-per-Minute Table on page 71 and look up your reading speed (words per minute). Enter your reading speed on the graph on page 72.

Reading Time: Lesson 1

________ : ________

Minutes *Seconds*

A Finding the Main Idea

One statement below expresses the main idea of the article. One statement is too general, or too broad. The other statement explains only part of the article; it is too narrow. Label the statements using the following key:

M—Main Idea **B—Too Broad** **N—Too Narrow**

_____ 1. Chemical dumps and toxic-waste sites are very dangerous to people.

_____ 2. Many residents at Love Canal suffered from serious illnesses such as leukemia and kidney disease.

_____ 3. The chemical dump at Love Canal created many problems for local residents.

_____ Score 15 points for a correct M answer.

_____ Score 5 points for each correct B or N answer.

_____ **Total Score:** Finding the Main Idea

B Recalling Facts

How well do you remember the facts in the article? Put an X in the box next to the answer that correctly completes each statement about the article.

1. Lois Gibbs was
   - ☐ a. a reporter for the Niagara Falls *Gazette*.
   - ☐ b. a resident of the Love Canal neighborhood.
   - ☐ c. the mayor of Niagara Falls, New York.
2. Who dumped the chemicals into Love Canal?
   - ☐ a. Hooker Chemical & Plastics Corporation
   - ☐ b. William T. Love
   - ☐ c. the Niagara Falls Board of Education
3. The Quimby family
   - ☐ a. suffered from many serious illnesses.
   - ☐ b. worked for Hooker Chemical & Plastics Corporation.
   - ☐ c. were not concerned about the effects of Love Canal.
4. Chromosomes are parts of cells that
   - ☐ a. are not affected by chemicals and toxic waste.
   - ☐ b. affected the eating and sleeping habits of the homeowners.
   - ☐ c. tell about traits that can be passed on from parents to children.
5. In an attempt to clean up Love Canal, the government
   - ☐ a. removed all the barrels of chemicals.
   - ☐ b. covered the canal with a thick layer of clay.
   - ☐ c. destroyed all traces of the canal.

Score 5 points for each correct answer.

_____ **Total Score:** Recalling Facts

C Making Inferences

When you combine your own experience and information from a text to draw a conclusion that is not directly stated in that text, you are making an inference. Below are five statements that may or may not be inferences based on information in the article. Label the statements using the following key:

C—Correct Inference **F—Faulty Inference**

_______ 1. Hooker Chemical & Plastics Corporation did not know about the chemicals in the canal.

_______ 2. The Quimby family suffered from the effects of the chemicals.

_______ 3. As soon as the residents complained about Love Canal, the government took action.

_______ 4. People with broken chromosomes are less likely to have serious health problems.

_______ 5. The tragedy at Love Canal might happen again.

Score 5 points for each correct answer.

_______ **Total Score:** Making Inferences

D Using Words Precisely

Each numbered sentence below contains an underlined word or phrase from the article. Following the sentence are three definitions. One definition is closest to the meaning of the underlined word. One definition is opposite or nearly opposite. Label those two definitions using the following key. Do not label the remaining definition.

C—Closest **O—Opposite or Nearly Opposite**

1. The company decided to use the old waterway as a dumping place for <u>toxic</u> waste.

_______ a. healthful

_______ b. unused

_______ c. poisonous

2. They discovered that many residents were suffering from <u>severe</u> health problems.

_______ a. serious

_______ b. unimportant

_______ c. painful

3. But the Quimbys, like most <u>residents</u>, couldn't leave Love Canal.

_______ a. employees

_______ b. visitors

_______ c. inhabitants

4. "You are hurting Niagara Falls with your <u>publicity</u>."

_______ a. lifestyle

_______ b. attracting public interest

_______ c. keeping something private

5. The others [babies] were born dead or had birth <u>defects</u>.

_______ a. memories

_______ b. perfection

_______ c. flaws

_______ Score 3 points for each correct C answer.

_______ Score 2 points for each correct O answer.

_______ **Total Score:** Using Words Precisely

Enter the four total scores in the spaces below, and add them together to find your Reading Comprehension Score. Then record your score on the graph on page 73.

Score	Question Type	Lesson 1
_______	Finding the Main Idea	
_______	Recalling Facts	
_______	Making Inferences	
_______	Using Words Precisely	
_______	**Reading Comprehension Score**	

Author's Approach

Put an X in the box next to the correct answer.

1. Which of the following statements from the article best describes the way Lois Gibbs chose to live her life before the dangers of Love Canal became well known?

☐ a. "But in 1978 Lois Gibbs read an article in the Niagara Falls *Gazette*."

☐ b. "She talked to the school board and the city government."

☐ c. "She had devoted her life to taking care of her home and her children."

2. From the statements below, choose those that you believe the author would agree with.

☐ a. Love Canal is a perfectly safe neighborhood now.

☐ b. The state and federal governments should have acted more quickly to help the residents of Love Canal.

☐ c. It is too soon to tell whether Love Canal is safe.

3. Choose the statement below that is the weakest argument for claiming that Love Canal is a safe place to live.

☐ a. Love Canal was covered with a thick layer of clay.

☐ b. Barrels of chemicals still lie beneath the ground.

☐ c. The government made an attempt to clean up the area.

4. In this article, "Some members of the local government didn't want to give Niagara Falls a bad name" means

☐ a. they were afraid that the bad publicity would ruin Niagara Falls's reputation as an appealing tourist spot.

☐ b. some members objected to changing the area's name.

☐ c. some government officials didn't believe that anything was wrong.

_________ Number of correct answers

Record your personal assessment of your work on the Critical Thinking Chart on page 74.

Summarizing and Paraphrasing

Follow the directions provided for question 1. Put an X in the box next to the correct answer for question 2.

1. Look for the important ideas and events in paragraphs 10 and 11. Summarize those paragraphs in one or two sentences.

____

____

____

2. Read the statement about the article below. Then read the paraphrase of that statement. Choose the reason that best tells why the paraphrase does not say the same thing as the statement.

Statement: The Hooker Chemical & Plastics Corporation buried their toxic waste in the ditch known as Love Canal but didn't realize the harmful effects the chemicals would have on future residents of the area.

Paraphrase: The chemicals in Love Canal were left there by the Hooker Chemical & Plastics Corporation.

☐ a. Paraphrase says too much.

☐ b. Paraphrase doesn't say enough.

☐ c. Paraphrase doesn't agree with the statement about the article.

_________ Number of correct answers

Record your personal assessment of your work on the Critical Thinking Chart on page 74.

Critical Thinking

Put an X in the box next to the correct answer for questions 1, 2, and 5. Follow the directions provided for the other questions.

1. Which of the following statements from the article is an opinion rather than a fact?

☐ a. "'[Love Canal is] probably one of the safest places to live in Niagara Falls by now.'"

☐ b. "Love Canal is a section of Niagara Falls, New York."

☐ c. "In the late 1940s the canal was owned by Hooker Chemical & Plastics Corporation."

CRITICAL THINKING

2. From what the article told about the Quimbys, you can predict that they

- ☐ a. chose to move back into the neighborhood after it was cleaned up.
- ☐ b. never moved away from Love Canal.
- ☐ c. moved away as soon as the government bought their home.

3. Choose from the letters below to correctly complete the following statement. Write the letters on the lines.

On the positive side, ________, but on the negative side ________.

a. many families had already become seriously ill
b. Niagara Falls received a great deal of publicity
c. the government helped some Love Canal residents relocate

4. Read paragraph 9. Then choose from the letters below to correctly complete the following statement. Write the letters on the lines.

According to paragraph 9, ________ because ________.

a. he ran out of money
b. William T. Love gave up his idea of building a canal that would connect two parts of the Niagara River
c. the ditch was one mile long and 15 yards wide

5. If you were president of a chemical corporation, how could you use the information in the article to protect the health of people around your business?

- ☐ a. Dump chemical waste in a nearby ditch and cover it with dirt.
- ☐ b. Place chemical waste in barrels and sell the land to a school.
- ☐ c. Seal chemical waste tightly and store it far away from all forms of life.

________ Number of correct answers

Record your personal assessment of your work on the Critical Thinking Chart on page 74.

✓

Personal Response

What would you have done if you had lived in Love Canal and you discovered that it had been built on toxic wastes?

____

____

____

____

Self-Assessment

A word or phrase in the article that I do not understand is

____

____

____

____

THE SWEATSHOP INFERNO

At the turn of the 20th century, New York City was teeming with immigrants. All had come to the United States looking for a better life. But instead of finding riches, many immigrants found horrible living conditions. City slums were filthy and overcrowded, and jobs were scarce. Many people died of hunger and disease.

2 Even though millions of Americans were living in misery, the United States economy was flourishing. Factories poured out all kinds of manufactured goods. Some plants made machine parts, while others produced steel. And textile mills worked night and day, making everything from thread to finished clothing.

3 Many of New York City's immigrant women and girls worked at the Triangle Shirtwaist Factory on Greene Street. They made shirtwaists, a kind of blouse popular with women in the early 1900s. Every day at least 600 employees reported to work at the factory. Five hundred of them were women, and 125 were young girls. Many could barely speak English.

4 On March 25, 1911, employees at the Triangle Shirtwaist Factory went to work as usual, even though it was a Saturday.

In the late 1800s and the early 1900s, many children worked in the sweatshops of the garment industry.

Several other companies located in the same building were also open. However, at noon those businesses closed for the day, and all their employees went home. Those workers were lucky. They didn't have to run for their lives when a deadly fire roared through the factory shortly before 5:00 P.M., the normal quitting time.

5 The factory was known as a sweatshop. Employees labored long hours for meager wages—as little as 25 cents a day. They worked in unhealthy and dangerous conditions. Children were employed full time to do adult jobs. And there were no child-labor laws to protect them. Some sweatshops hired children who were as young as five or six.

6 Employees at the Triangle Shirtwaist Factory worked in a building that was 10 stories high. It had just one tiny fire escape that led into a courtyard. There were stairways inside, but the owners often locked the stair doors to prevent theft. None of the employees could leave the factory unless a man on the first floor sent up a freight elevator.

7 Crowded freight elevators brought workers up to the factory's three floors. The big rooms were packed with sewing machines, and workers had to squeeze through narrow aisles and step over belts and machinery as they moved around the factory.

8 The air was full of floating bits of lint and thread. The floor was littered with cloth scraps, many of them soaked with oil that had dripped from the machines. But workers were used to breathing the dusty lint and slipping on the scraps.

9 At 4:30 P.M. on March 25, some workers began to put on their coats and hats so that they would be ready to leave at 5:00. Saturday was payday, and most employees were tucking pay envelopes into purses, pockets, or stockings. Some were talking about their plans for Saturday night. And everyone was looking forward to a day off on Sunday.

10 At 4:45, a fire suddenly broke out on the eighth floor. No one knows exactly what started the fire, but some people suspect a spark from one of the sewing machines. Max Rother, a tailor, heard women yelling "fire" across the room. He saw a line of clothes in flames above their heads. He tried to put the fire out with pails of water. But the burning clothes started to fall.

11 The fire spread rapidly through the room, igniting more shirtwaists that hung from the ceiling as well as the oily scraps on the floor. In moments the room was an inferno, and the fire had spread up to the next floor.

12 Workers panicked. Screaming and crying, they raced for the exit doors, only to find them locked. One woman broke a glass door with a sewing machine, and a few workers managed to escape down the staircase. Others frantically rang the bell for the freight elevator.

13 Elevator operator Joseph Zito made 20 trips that day but never rescued anyone above the eighth floor. Every time he reached that floor there were more women waiting. They pushed, shoved, and fought their way into the elevator, desperate to flee. Some fainted on the way down. When Zito saw the flames in the elevator shaft, he made one last trip. The women left behind must have known he couldn't help them anymore. They started to jump on top of the elevator cage as it was lowered. Some slid down the elevator cables. "Oh, it was horrible," said Zito. "I will never get the sight out of my mind."

14 With nowhere else to go, factory workers rushed to the windows that overlooked Greene Street. Onlookers below saw hundreds of desperate women and girls leaning from the windows. Then one young girl jumped. Suddenly dozens of women and girls followed her, leaping from heights eight or nine stories above the sidewalk.

A garment industry sweatshop in New York around 1910

15 Some women crashed through glass awnings. Others tangled themselves in telegraph lines. A 13-year-old girl hung from a window ledge for several minutes. Then when flames licked at her fingers, she dropped to the street. A young couple appeared at a ninth-story window. The two kissed and embraced. Then they jumped to their deaths.

16 Onlookers pleaded with those still trapped not to jump. But their calls were ignored.

17 Nearly all the workers who jumped from the windows were killed in the fall. But those trapped inside were no better off. Rosie Safran survived the fire, and this is what she remembers:

> Some girls were screaming, some were beating the door with their fists, some were trying to tear it open.... I got to the street and watched the upper floors burning, and the girls hanging by their hands and then dropping as the fire reached up to them. There they were dead on the sidewalk. It was an awful, awful sight, especially to me who had so many friends among the girls and young men who were being roasted alive or dashed to death.

18 The owners of the company, Isaac Harris and Max Blanck, were also in the building at the time of the fire. They rented the upper floors of the building. Blanck had been entertaining his two children and their governess when the family heard the cries of fire. Harris and the Blanck family escaped over the roof of another building. Nearby university students helped some employees also escape that way, but few of the workers knew about the route. Most were desperately trying to get to the street.

19 Fire engines from all parts of the city roared through the streets to the burning factory. When firefighters arrived, bodies were already piling up on the sidewalk. They had to step over them to set up their equipment. They worked quickly to extend their ladders up the side of the building. It was then they made a terrible discovery. The ladders only reached the sixth floor, and the fire had started on the eighth. Helpless, the firefighters could only watch as the women and young girls screamed for help on the top floors of the building.

20 Firefighters then hurried to set up safety nets to catch the women as they fell. But the nets weren't strong enough. They tore easily. Bodies were still hitting the pavement.

21 The fire chief said at the scene, "This is just the calamity I have been predicting." He said he tried to get the owners of factories to install more fire escapes and sprinkler systems. He knew many buildings were unsafe. But his fire protection plans were opposed. Factory owners thought outside fire escapes were unsightly.

22 At least 146 people died in the shirtwaist factory blaze. Fifty bodies were found on the ninth floor alone. They were huddled near the staircase and the elevator shaft. Many victims were burned too badly to be identified.

23 The owners of the factory went on trial for murder. But they were acquitted because jurors did not believe that Harris and Blanck had intended to kill anyone. Families were outraged at the verdict, but most jurors did not feel sympathetic. They thought the factory was well managed, and they had no interest in safety conditions for workers.

24 The fire at the Triangle Shirtwaist Factory did shock many concerned citizens. Those people forced the city of New York to make changes in the fire codes. And around the country, stronger labor unions helped improve job safety for factory workers.

25 More than anything else, the tragedy on Greene Street helped to establish child-labor laws in the United States.

If you have been timed while reading this article, enter your reading time below. Then turn to the Words-per-Minute Table on page 71 and look up your reading speed (words per minute). Enter your reading speed on the graph on page 72.

Reading Time: Lesson 2

________ : ________

Minutes *Seconds*

A Finding the Main Idea

One statement below expresses the main idea of the article. One statement is too general, or too broad. The other statement explains only part of the article; it is too narrow. Label the statements using the following key:

M—Main Idea **B—Too Broad** **N—Too Narrow**

_______ 1. Rosie Safran worked at the Triangle Shirtwaist Factory.

_______ 2. A tragic fire in New York helped to change labor and fire laws around the country.

_______ 3. New York City sweatshops had terrible working conditions.

_______ Score 15 points for a correct M answer.

_______ Score 5 points for each correct B or N answer.

_______ **Total Score:** Finding the Main Idea

B Recalling Facts

How well do you remember the facts in the article? Put an X in the box next to the answer that correctly completes each statement about the article.

1. In the early 1900s many companies

☐ a. paid close attention to fire codes.
☐ b. hired children for factory work.
☐ c. offered high wages to immigrants.

2. Shirtwaists are a kind of

☐ a. blouse.
☐ b. vest.
☐ c. overcoat.

3. The fire started

☐ a. on the ground floor.
☐ b. in the building next door.
☐ c. on the eighth floor.

4. The owners of the company

☐ a. were in the building.
☐ b. had recently sold the factory.
☐ c. were vacationing in upstate New York.

5. Firefighters made an awful discovery when they realized

☐ a. they didn't have any safety nets.
☐ b. the fire had been set on purpose.
☐ c. their ladders only reached the sixth floor.

Score 5 points for each correct answer.

_______ **Total Score:** Recalling Facts

C Making Inferences

When you combine your own experience and information from a text to draw a conclusion that is not directly stated in that text, you are making an inference. Below are five statements that may or may not be inferences based on information in the article. Label the statements using the following key:

C—Correct Inference **F—Faulty Inference**

_______ 1. All immigrants are born in the United States.

_______ 2. A textile factory makes or uses cloth.

_______ 3. The workers had trouble moving around the factory.

_______ 4. Firefighters had no trouble rescuing the workers.

_______ 5. Everyone sympathized with the factory workers.

Score 5 points for each correct answer.

_______ **Total Score:** Making Inferences

D Using Words Precisely

Each numbered sentence below contains an underlined word or phrase from the article. Following the sentence are three definitions. One definition is closest to the meaning of the underlined word. One definition is opposite or nearly opposite. Label those two definitions using the following key. Do not label the remaining definition.

C—Closest **O—Opposite or Nearly Opposite**

1. City slums were filthy and overcrowded, and jobs were scarce.

_______ a. clean

_______ b. far away

_______ c. dirty

2. Even though millions of Americans were living in misery, the United States economy was flourishing.

_______ a. growing well

_______ b. failing

_______ c. confusing

3. Employees labored long hours for meager wages—as little as 25 cents a day.

_______ a. daily

_______ b. scanty

_______ c. excessive

4. Others frantically rang the bell for the freight elevator.

_______ a. in a very upset way

_______ b. sadly

_______ c. calmly

5. But they were acquitted because jurors did not believe that Harris and Blanck had intended to kill anyone.

_______ a. found guilty

_______ b. found innocent

_______ c. praised

_______ Score 3 points for each correct C answer.

_______ Score 2 points for each correct O answer.

_______ **Total Score:** Using Words Precisely

Enter the four total scores in the spaces below, and add them together to find your Reading Comprehension Score. Then record your score on the graph on page 73.

Score	Question Type	Lesson 2
_______	Finding the Main Idea	
_______	Recalling Facts	
_______	Making Inferences	
_______	Using Words Precisely	
_______	**Reading Comprehension Score**	

Author's Approach

Put an X in the box next to the correct answer.

1. The main purpose of the first paragraph is to

☐ a. describe the living conditions for immigrants in the early 20th century.

☐ b. compare living conditions in the United States with those in other parts of the world.

☐ c. inform the reader about the immigrants' unrealistic expectations.

2. From the statement "Factory owners thought outside fire escapes were unsightly," you can conclude that the author wants the reader to think that

☐ a. fire escapes at the turn of the century were especially ugly.

☐ b. the factory owners placed the fire escapes inside.

☐ c. the factory owners cared more about the appearance of their companies than about their employees' safety.

3. What does the author imply by saying "But workers were used to breathing the dusty lint and slipping on the scraps"?

☐ a. The workers didn't think that their working conditions were so bad.

☐ b. The workers were strong but clumsy.

☐ c. The workers had put up with bad working conditions for a long time.

4. The author probably wrote this article in order to
- ☐ a. tell the reader about a deadly fire in a New York City factory around the turn of the century.
- ☐ b. persuade the reader never to work in a factory.
- ☐ c. create a mood of terror.

_________ Number of correct answers

Record your personal assessment of your work on the Critical Thinking Chart on page 74.

Summarizing and Paraphrasing

Put an X in the box next to the correct answer.

1. Below are summaries of the article. Choose the summary that says all the most important things about the article but in the fewest words.
- ☐ a. The fire at the Triangle Shirtwaist Factory killed many people because the workers were trapped inside the building.
- ☐ b. Unsafe working conditions in the Triangle Shirtwaist Factory led to a fire that trapped and killed many of the women and young girls who worked there. Although the owners of the factory were found innocent of any wrongdoing, the tragedy eventually led to changes in job safety laws.
- ☐ c. The women and young girls who worked in the Triangle Shirtwaist Factory were trapped in the building during the fire. The stair doors were locked to prevent theft, and the building had only one small fire escape. Company owners Isaac Harris and Max Blanck were acquitted of the murder charges leveled against them. But laws were soon passed that helped improve job safety for factory workers.

2. Choose the sentence that correctly restates the following sentence from the article:

   "The fire spread rapidly through the room, igniting more shirtwaists that hung from the ceiling as well as the oily scraps on the floor."
- ☐ a. The fire started when the oily scraps on the floor and the shirtwaists caught fire.
- ☐ b. The fire caused an explosion when it reached the shirtwaists hanging from the ceiling and the oily scraps of cloth on the floor.
- ☐ c. The fire in the room grew quickly, fed by the shirtwaists hanging from the ceiling and the oily scraps of cloth on the floor.

_________ Number of correct answers

Record your personal assessment of your work on the Critical Thinking Chart on page 74.

Critical Thinking

Put an X in the box next to the correct answer for questions 1, 4, and 5. Follow the directions provided for the other questions.

1. From the article, you can predict that if the factory owners had not locked the stair doors,
- ☐ a. many more thefts would have occurred.
- ☐ b. fewer employees would have died in the fire.
- ☐ c. the fire would have spread to the stairs.

CRITICAL THINKING

2. Choose from the letters below to correctly complete the following statement. Write the letters on the lines.

   In the article, _________ and _________ are different.

   a. working conditions for Max Blanck

   b. working conditions for Joseph Zito

   c. working conditions for Isaac Harris

3. Think about cause-effect relationships in the article. Fill in the blanks in the cause-effect chart, drawing from the letters below.

Cause	Effect
Their ladders only reached the sixth floor.	____________
Zito saw flames in the elevator shaft.	____________
____________	The factory owners were acquitted.

   a. Jurors didn't believe that the owners meant to hurt anyone.

   b. The firefighters couldn't rescue workers on the top floors.

   c. He stopped making trips to try to rescue the workers.

4. If you were a factory owner, how could you use the information in the article to ensure your workers' safety?

   ☐ a. Lock the stair doors to prevent theft.

   ☐ b. Provide elevators that work only when someone on the first floor sends them up.

   ☐ c. Install sprinklers and several fire escapes in your building.

5. What did you have to do to answer question 2?

   ☐ a. draw a conclusion (a sensible statement based on the text and your experience)

   ☐ b. find an effect (something that happened)

   ☐ c. find a contrast (how things are different)

_________ Number of correct answers

Record your personal assessment of your work on the Critical Thinking Chart on page 74.

Personal Response

Would you recommend this article to other students? Explain.

____

____

____

Self-Assessment

One of the things I did best when reading this article was

____

____

____

I believe I did this well because

____

____

____

KILLER TORNADO!

This funnel cloud of a Force 5 tornado touched down in Jarrell, Texas, in 1997.

Ray Westphal saw the tornado approach the small town of Jarrell, 38 miles north of Austin, Texas. It didn't seem like much when he first noticed it. But then it got ugly. "It looked about two inches tall at first," remembered Westphal. "Then it started taking up the entire horizon. As it got closer, building tops were flying around. It was picking cars right up into the air, flinging them everywhere."

2 Another man was driving away from the tornado in his pickup truck. Out the window he could see a black swirling cloud hundreds of feet across. The cloud itself, the man said, was full of "pieces of tin, plywood, boards, flying cows, cornstalks, bits of trees, everything you could imagine."

3 Over the years, Texans have seen more than their fair share of tornadoes. In fact, Jarrell had been hit by twisters before. On May 17, 1989, a tornado ripped through the town. That storm left one person dead and 28 injured. It damaged or destroyed nearly 50 homes. But this tornado was worse, much worse. In fact, the tornado

that struck on May 27, 1997, was one of the worst in Texas history.

4 Westphal and the truck driver were not the only ones to see the storm coming. Weather forecasters saw it, too. Radio and TV reports warned the people along the storm's path that a Force 5 tornado was headed their way. (This is the highest rating a twister can get. Such a rating is extremely rare. It means that winds will reach at least 260 miles per hour) The people of Jarrell who heard the warnings tried to find a place to hide. Unfortunately, there weren't many good places. Few of the homes in Jarrell had basements or underground storm cellars.

5 Tornadoes weave a narrow path of destruction. But within that narrow path, the devastation can be absolute. Homes on one side of the road can suffer little or no damage, while those on the other side of the road get blown away. There is no telling exactly where a tornado will hit until it is too late. People have to do what seems reasonable and then just hope for the best.

6 With a Force 5 storm, the chances of surviving a direct hit are slim at best. The power of such a tornado is hard to imagine. It will lift houses off their foundations. It will blow cars around like toys and strip the bark off trees. A Force 5 storm will suck the asphalt from paved roads, vegetation out of the ground, and even the hair off a cow's back.

7 The tornado moved slowly as it approached the town from the north. It wasn't advancing more than 20 miles per hour. "That sky was black as night, just boiling," said Bud Taylor who watched the storm from the Speedway Inn. "[It] seemed like it set there for 10 minutes making up its mind which way to go."

8 Maria Ruiz thought the tornado was headed toward her trailer home. She knew that if her trailer were to be hit, she would

High winds and heavy rains followed the tornado. Here, a truck drives through swinging stop lights and downed electrical wires.

have no chance of surviving the storm. So Ruiz took her two sons—Michael, age 14, and John, age 15—to their family friends, the Moehrings. She felt her family would be safer in that home because it was sturdier. Sadly, the tornado hit the house with its full force, killing everyone inside. As chance would have it, the storm missed the Ruizes' trailer.

9 Fate smiled on some people. Virginia Davidson knows she was lucky to survive the wrath of the storm. "I thought for sure I was going to die, and I was just hoping it would happen very fast." She had been working in the yard when she saw the tornado coming. Davidson ran inside her house, jumped into the bathtub, and pulled a blanket over her head. The storm blew her house to smithereens. It moved the bathtub several hundred feet. Although she was tossed out of the tub and badly bruised, Davidson survived.

10 Juanita Peterson also survived by hiding in her bathroom. She huddled there with her daughter, her daughter-in-law, and two young grandchildren. "People tell you [tornadoes] don't take long to pass through," Peterson later said. "But when you're lying in a bathtub covering two little babies, it seems like forever."

11 The twister spun just west of the downtown area. It then smacked straight into the Double Creek neighborhood. This was where the tornado did its worst damage. The siren at the volunteer fire station had sounded a warning 10 minutes before the storm struck. But Double Creek is about two miles from the fire station. Many residents just didn't hear it. Their little neighborhood was completely destroyed.

12 The tornado lasted about 15 minutes. Then it started to rain and turn dark. Fearfully, rescue workers surveyed the damage. "All we found was dead cows, dead horses, and dead people," said Dennis Jaroszewski. "As you looked and found more and more bodies, you just said, 'Isn't this enough?'"

13 This tornado was a real killer. It left 27 dead and destroyed 50 homes. The storm caused roughly $20 million in damages. "It was like someone dropped a bomb," said LaDonna Peterson, whose house was flattened. Referring to her home, she said it was "like a vacuum cleaner just sucked it away."

14 Most tornadoes leave an area littered with debris. This one was different, however. It was so strong that houses were blown far away. It was as though they had simply disappeared. There was no debris; nothing was left but the bare earth.

15 Governor George W. Bush, who rushed to the scene, summed up the storm's power: "It's hard to believe you're looking at a patch of earth where life was literally sucked out of it."

If you have been timed while reading this article, enter your reading time below. Then turn to the Words-per-Minute Table on page 71 and look up your reading speed (words per minute). Enter your reading speed on the graph on page 72.

Reading Time: Lesson 3

________ : ________

Minutes *Seconds*

A Finding the Main Idea

One statement below expresses the main idea of the article. One statement is too general, or too broad. The other statement explains only part of the article; it is too narrow. Label the statements using the following key:

M—Main Idea **B—Too Broad** **N—Too Narrow**

_______ 1. The tornado is one of the most destructive types of storms.

_______ 2. Virginia Davidson and Juanita Peterson survived the tornado by hiding in their bathrooms.

_______ 3. A devastating tornado struck a small Texas town, killing 27 people and causing terrible damage.

_______ Score 15 points for a correct M answer.

_______ Score 5 points for each correct B or N answer.

_______ **Total Score:** Finding the Main Idea

B Recalling Facts

How well do you remember the facts in the article? Put an X in the box next to the answer that correctly completes each statement about the article.

1. The winds of a Force 5 tornado can reach speeds of at least

☐ a. 20 miles per hour.
☐ b. 100 miles per hour.
☐ c. 260 miles per hour.

2. When a powerful tornado strikes, a good place to hide is in a

☐ a. trailer.
☐ b. basement or underground storm cellar.
☐ c. car.

3. As the twister approached, Maria Ruiz thought her family would be safer in

☐ a. her friends' house.
☐ b. a bathtub.
☐ c. her own home.

4. Many people living in the Double Creek neighborhood weren't aware of the twister's approach because

☐ a. the fire station didn't sound a warning.
☐ b. the tornado missed that area.
☐ c. they hadn't heard the warning.

5. The tornado that struck Jarrell

☐ a. left the area littered with debris.
☐ b. sucked houses away leaving behind only bare earth.
☐ c. lasted about 15 hours.

Score 5 points for each correct answer.

_______ **Total Score:** Recalling Facts

C Making Inferences

When you combine your own experience and information from a text to draw a conclusion that is not directly stated in that text, you are making an inference. Below are five statements that may or may not be inferences based on information in the article. Label the statements using the following key:

C—Correct Inference **F—Faulty Inference**

_______ 1. Houses directly hit by a Force 5 tornado are completely destroyed.

_______ 2. No one can predict the exact path of a tornado.

_______ 3. A good place to hide from a tornado is under a tree.

_______ 4. The people of Jarrell, Texas, have never received instructions about how to survive a tornado.

_______ 5. Bathrooms offer more protection than other rooms in a house during a tornado.

Score 5 points for each correct answer.

_______ **Total Score:** Making Inferences

D Using Words Precisely

Each numbered sentence below contains an underlined word or phrase from the article. Following the sentence are three definitions. One definition is closest to the meaning of the underlined word. One definition is opposite or nearly opposite. Label those two definitions using the following key. Do not label the remaining definition.

C—Closest **O—Opposite or Nearly Opposite**

1. But within that narrow path, the devastation can be absolute.

_______ a. renewal

_______ b. terror

_______ c. destruction

2. She felt her family would be safer in that home because it was sturdier.

_______ a. stronger

_______ b. weaker

_______ c. farther away

3. Virginia Davidson knows she was lucky to survive the wrath of the storm.

_______ a. path

_______ b. fury

_______ c. calm

4. The storm blew her house to smithereens.

_______ a. moved her house across the street

_______ b. allowed her house to remain whole

_______ c. broke her house into small fragments

5. She <u>huddled</u> there with her daughter, her daughter-in-law, and two young grandchildren.

_____ a. crowded together

_____ b. fell asleep

_____ c. moved apart

_____ Score 3 points for each correct C answer.

_____ Score 2 points for each correct O answer.

_____ **Total Score:** Using Words Precisely

Enter the four total scores in the spaces below, and add them together to find your Reading Comprehension Score. Then record your score on the graph on page 73.

Score	Question Type	Lesson 3
_____	Finding the Main Idea	
_____	Recalling Facts	
_____	Making Inferences	
_____	Using Words Precisely	
_____	**Reading Comprehension Score**	

Author's Approach

Put an X in the box next to the correct answer.

1. The author uses the first sentence of the article to

☐ a. inform the reader about the tornado approaching Jarrell.

☐ b. inform the reader about Ray Westphal.

☐ c. compare Jarrell and Austin, Texas.

2. What does the author mean by the statement "A Force 5 storm will suck the asphalt from paved roads, vegetation out of the ground, and even the hair off a cow's back"?

☐ a. A Force 5 storm doesn't hurt people.

☐ b. Cows don't know how to hide from a Force 5 storm.

☐ c. A Force 5 storm has tremendous power.

3. What is the author's purpose in writing "Killer Tornado!"?

☐ a. To express an opinion about the courage of the people in Jarrell, Texas

☐ b. To inform the reader about the destruction caused by a powerful tornado

☐ c. To emphasize the similarities between a tornado and a bomb

4. The author tells this story mainly by

☐ a. retelling several people's personal experiences of the twister that struck Jarrell.

☐ b. comparing the May 1997 twister in Jarrell to other tornadoes that have struck the town.

☐ c. telling different stories about tornadoes that have hit Texas in recent years.

_____ Number of correct answers

Record your personal assessment of your work on the Critical Thinking Chart on page 74.

Summarizing and Paraphrasing

Follow the directions provided for question 1. Put an X in the box next to the correct answer for question 2.

1. Reread paragraph 9 in the article. Below, write a summary of the paragraph in no more than 25 words.

____

____

____

____

Reread your summary and decide whether it covers the important ideas in the paragraph. Next, decide how to shorten the summary to 15 words or less without leaving out any essential information. Write this summary below.

____

____

____

2. Read the statement about the article below. Then read the paraphrase of that statement. Choose the reason that best tells why the paraphrase does not say the same thing as the statement.

Statement: Many people from the Double Creek neighborhood who were hurt or killed by the twister might have been spared if they had heard the siren sound the warning.

Paraphrase: Most people from the Double Creek neighborhood survived the tornado because they heard the siren sound the warning.

☐ a. Paraphrase says too much.

☐ b. Paraphrase doesn't say enough.

☐ c. Paraphrase doesn't agree with the statement about the article.

_______ Number of correct answers

Record your personal assessment of your work on the Critical Thinking Chart on page 74.

Critical Thinking

Follow the directions provided for questions 1, 3, and 4. Put an X in the box next to the correct answer for the other questions.

1. For each statement below, write O if it expresses an opinion and write F if it expresses a fact.

_______ a. Because of its tornadoes, Jarrell is the most dangerous town in Texas.

_______ b. Tornadoes are more devastating than earthquakes.

_______ c. A Force 5 tornado is the most destructive type.

2. From the article, you can predict that if Maria Ruiz and her family had stayed in their home,

- ☐ a. they would have been killed anyway.
- ☐ b. they would have survived.
- ☐ c. the Moehrings would have survived.

3. Choose from the letters below to correctly complete the following statement. Write the letters on the lines.

In the article, ________ and ________ are alike.

a. Bud Taylor's hiding place during the twister

b. Virginia Davidson's hiding place during the twister

c. Juanita Peterson's hiding place during the twister

4. Read paragraph 11. Then choose from the letters below to correctly complete the following statement. Write the letters on the lines.

According to paragraph 11, ________ because ________.

a. the siren at the local fire station sounded a warning 10 minutes before the tornado struck

b. the tornado hit Double Creek directly

c. the tornado did its worst damage in the Double Creek neighborhood

5. What did you have to do to answer question 3?

- ☐ a. find an opinion (what someone thinks about something)
- ☐ b. find a comparison (how things are the same)
- ☐ c. find a cause (why something happened)

________ Number of correct answers

Record your personal assessment of your work on the Critical Thinking Chart on page 74.

Personal Response

How do you think you would feel if you heard that a tornado was heading for your area?

____

____

____

____

Self-Assessment

While reading the article, I found it easiest to

____

____

____

____

THE SCHOOLYARD TRAGEDY

Aberfan. A coal-mining village surrounded by green meadows and a wide valley. A town of narrow streets and old houses. A peaceful place where everyone is a friend.

2 Aberfan is nestled in the Cambrian Mountains of Wales in the United Kingdom. Anyone driving through the village notices its haunting landmark—a man-made black mountain of sludge.

3 For generations the men of Aberfan have wrestled coal from the pit near the village. Every day the men go down into the mine. Every day their wives and children worry they will never see their husbands and fathers again.

4 The people of Aberfan have always been prepared for death. They have heard the mine's sirens in times of disaster. They have often watched stretchers come up from the pit, loaded with men's bodies. Everyone knows the dangers—miners can be poisoned by underground gas or crushed by collapsing walls. They can also suffer from black lung, a serious health problem caused by breathing coal dust.

This aerial photo of Aberfan shows the destruction caused by the slag-heap avalanche. The school is in the foreground of the photo.

5 What the little town of Aberfan did not know was that a mining disaster could strike its women and children.

6 For nearly 100 years, men worked the coal mine near Aberfan, piling the waste on a hillside. Villagers could see the waste heap that had built up near the entrance to the mine. The waste was mostly rock and slag, which is coal that cannot be used for burning.

7 The tip, as people called the slag heap, loomed over the town. Everyone talked about it. Over the years the tip grew and grew, until it reached a height of more than 100 feet.

8 The villagers knew that the tip was dangerous. For years they complained to the National Coal Board that someday the tip would collapse, engulfing Pantaglas School. But the board decided to do nothing. The members claimed it would be too expensive to move the mountain of rubble. The coal board made that decision in 1947. In 1966 the tip was almost 20 years older, and higher than ever.

9 In late October, heavy rains had soaked southeastern Wales. Black streams of coal dust washed into Moy Road, a street in the center of Aberfan. The dust formed a thick, sticky mud in the playground of the Pantaglas School. But students and teachers were used to the black mud, and no one paid any more attention than usual.

10 On the morning of October 21, most of the miners were headed underground. A few noticed that the tip had begun to crumble overnight. They spoke to the mine's manager. He told the miners not to add anymore waste to the heap that day. But he didn't send any warning to the village below.

11 At 9:00 A.M. most of the children had gathered in the school playground. It was the last day of school before vacation, and students were excited. A few older children still hung around in Moy Road, wasting time before school.

12 Raymond Collins, age 14, had just left his house when something made him turn back. He ran to his front door, perhaps to speak to his mother. No one will ever know his real reason.

13 At 9:20 A.M., the 90-year-old tip that shadowed the village slipped 600 feet down a hill. The avalanche swept through the center of Aberfan, straight down Moy Road.

14 In seconds the Pantaglas School was nearly obliterated. Moy Road had vanished. Eight houses were crushed flat. Then a water main burst, flooding the entire neighborhood.

15 The tragedy was unbelievable. Townspeople grabbed miners' shovels and other tools to help search for survivors. Mothers and fathers clawed at the debris.

16 For days, rescue workers struggled to find living children beneath the rubble of the Pantaglas School. But nearly everyone was dead. The children who hadn't been

Rescuers dig through the debris to rescue school children who had been on the school playground and were trapped by the avalanche.

killed instantly were drowned after the broken water main flooded the area.

17 When workers thought they were finished, they heard a tiny voice from inside the heap of sludge. "My name is Margret. My name is Margret," cried a little girl. The rescue workers promised the child they would save her. But when they finally found Margret, she had died.

18 A few children swept along in the ruins of the school survived. But 116 were killed, nearly all the school-age children in the village. Twenty-eight adults were also killed, mostly women working as housewives or teachers.

19 George Williams, the town barber, was grateful he overslept for work that morning. As he approached his shop on Moy Road, he hear a roar coming from the mountain. He guessed it was the tip. Williams was soon stuck in the sludge up to his waist. "If I had been on time, I would have had it," he said.

20 No one in town was untouched by the accident. Everyone lost a wife or a child, a nephew or a grandchild, a cousin or a best friend. John Collins, an engineer, lost his entire family. "I found my wife in two pieces, my little Peter smothered in the school, and my Raymond crushed at what used to be our front door."

21 Collins's father spent most of his life in the mines. He helped pile the slag that killed his grandchildren.

22 Lord Robens, head of the National Coal Board, visited Aberfan soon after the disaster. "There will be money for all," he promised. But grieving families shouted insults at him. "You murdered our children." "Write on the death certificate 'Buried alive by the National Coal Board!'"

23 The funerals took place over several days. The dead were buried on a green hillside overlooking the town. People from all over the world sent flowers for the graves. But the memories themselves belonged to the people of Aberfan. "For little Dai from his auntie," said one card. At a child's grave, a man quietly dropped a ragged teddy bear on top of a coffin.

24 A year after the accident, Aberfan had still not recovered. Most of the rubble had been cleaned up. Some of the houses had been rebuilt. But people like John Collins could not go back to their new homes. "I spent one night there," he said, "but I couldn't stand being alone, so I went back to my dad's cottage...."

25 Aberfan had plenty of money to rebuild the village. Huge gifts of cash had come from around the world, and the National Coal Board had given thousands of dollars to each parent. But the lives of the villagers could not be rebuilt. They had no one to work for. People had looked to their children for hope, but most of the children were gone. The tragedy also caused arguments among neighbors. Parents who had lost their children had a hard time dealing with families who had not.

26 Aberfan may never get over this disaster. As John Collins said, "We watched a generation of babies grow, and they were wiped out."

If you have been timed while reading this article, enter your reading time below. Then turn to the Words-per-Minute Table on page 71 and look up your reading speed (words per minute). Enter your reading speed on the graph on page 72.

Reading Time: Lesson 4

________ : ________

Minutes *Seconds*

Finding the Main Idea

One statement below expresses the main idea of the article. One statement is too general, or too broad. The other statement explains only part of the article; it is too narrow. Label the statements using the following key:

M—Main Idea **B—Too Broad** **N—Too Narrow**

_______ 1. The sudden movement of a huge slag heap killed many people in Aberfan, Wales.

_______ 2. The slag pile had been built near the mine's entrance.

_______ 3. Mining disasters are common in Wales.

_______ Score 15 points for a correct M answer.

_______ Score 5 points for each correct B or N answer.

_______ **Total Score:** Finding the Main Idea

B Recalling Facts

How well do you remember the facts in the article? Put an X in the box next to the answer that correctly completes each statement about the article.

1. On the morning of the disaster the manager told the miners
- ☐ a. to send a warning to the village below.
- ☐ b. not to add any more waste to the slag pile.
- ☐ c. to remove as much of the pile as possible.

2. The people in Aberfan
- ☐ a. asked the coal board to remove the tip.
- ☐ b. never worried about the tip.
- ☐ c. did not know what the tip was made of.

3. Most of the people killed in the disaster were
- ☐ a. teachers.
- ☐ b. children.
- ☐ c. miners.

4. A little girl named Margret
- ☐ a. died before she was rescued.
- ☐ b. was rescued alive by workers.
- ☐ c. was never found.

5. The tragedy at Aberfan
- ☐ a. was not noticed by the rest of the world.
- ☐ b. received much attention around the world.
- ☐ c. angered the Welsh police force.

Score 5 points for each correct answer.

_______ **Total Score:** Recalling Facts

Making Inferences

When you combine your own experience and information from a text to draw a conclusion that is not directly stated in that text, you are making an inference. Below are five statements that may or may not be inferences based on information in the article. Label the statements using the following key:

C—Correct Inference **F—Faulty Inference**

______ 1. Since the accident, Aberfan has become the largest, busiest city in Wales.

______ 2. The people of Aberfan did not know that coal mining could be dangerous.

______ 3. The coal board made a mistake when it decided not to move the tip.

______ 4. Everyone in Aberfan was affected by the disaster.

______ 5. Aberfan recovered quickly from the tragedy.

Score 5 points for each correct answer.

______ **Total Score:** Making Inferences

D Using Words Precisely

Each numbered sentence below contains an underlined word or phrase from the article. Following the sentence are three definitions. One definition is closest to the meaning of the underlined word. One definition is opposite or nearly opposite. Label those two definitions using the following key. Do not label the remaining definition.

C—Closest **O—Opposite or Nearly Opposite**

1. Everyone knows the dangers—miners can be poisoned by underground gas or crushed by collapsing walls.

______ a. falling

______ b. rising

______ c. ancient

2. [The villagers] complained to the National Coal Board that someday the tip would collapse, engulfing the school.

______ a. burying

______ b. exposing to air and light

______ c. ruining

3. The members claimed it would be too expensive to move the mountain of rubble.

______ a. shiny stones

______ b. broken, worthless pieces

______ c. perfect, valuable fragments

4. In seconds the Pantaglas School was nearly obliterated.

______ a. constructed

______ b. destroyed

______ c. emptied

5. But grieving families shouted insults at him.

_______ a. remaining

_______ b. joyous

_______ c. mourning

_______ Score 3 points for each correct C answer.

_______ Score 2 points for each correct O answer.

_______ **Total Score:** Using Words Precisely

Enter the four total scores in the spaces below, and add them together to find your Reading Comprehension Score. Then record your score on the graph on page 73.

Score	Question Type	Lesson 4
_______	Finding the Main Idea	
_______	Recalling Facts	
_______	Making Inferences	
_______	Using Words Precisely	
_______	**Reading Comprehension Score**	

Author's Approach

Put an X in the box next to the correct answer.

1. Which of the following statements from the article best describes Aberfan since the disaster?

☐ a. "Aberfan may never get over this disaster."

☐ b. "A town of narrow streets and old houses."

☐ c. "A peaceful place where everyone is a friend."

2. What does the author imply by saying "But the lives of the villagers could not be rebuilt"?

☐ a. No amount of money could replace the villagers' dead friends and family members.

☐ b. The village had been completely destroyed in the accident.

☐ c. The villagers all decided to move away after the accident.

3. The author probably wrote this article in order to

☐ a. convince readers to stay away from Aberfan.

☐ b. persuade readers to oppose the National Coal Board.

☐ c. inform the reader about the tragic mining disaster that devastated Aberfan.

_______ Number of correct answers

Record your personal assessment of your work on the Critical Thinking Chart on page 74.

Summarizing and Paraphrasing

Follow the directions provided for questions 1 and 2. Put an X in the box next to the correct answer for question 3.

1. Complete the following one-sentence summary of the article using the lettered phrases from the phrase bank below. Write the letters on the lines.

Phrase Bank:

a. a description of Aberfan and its slag heap

b. what happened when the heap swept through the village

c. Aberfan's attempts to deal with the terrible loss

The article about the tragedy in Aberfan begins with ________, goes on to explain ________, and ends with ________.

2. Reread paragraph 10 in the article. Below, write a summary of the paragraph in no more than 25 words.

____

____

____

____

Reread your summary and decide whether it covers the important ideas in the paragraph. Next, decide how to shorten the summary to 15 words or less without leaving out any essential information. Write this summary below.

____

____

____

3. Read the statement about the article below. Then read the paraphrase of that statement. Choose the reason that best tells why the paraphrase does not say the same thing as the statement.

Statement: After the tragedy, the people of Aberfan blamed the National Coal Board for refusing to remove the waste heap and insulted board members when they offered money to the grieving families.

Paraphrase: Aberfan survivors were angry with the National Coal Board for not removing the tip.

☐ a. Paraphrase says too much.

☐ b. Paraphrase doesn't say enough.

☐ c. Paraphrase doesn't agree with the statement about the article.

________ Number of correct answers

Record your personal assessment of your work on the Critical Thinking Chart on page 74.

Critical Thinking

Put an X in the box next to the correct answer for questions 1 and 4. Follow the directions provided for the other questions.

1. From the article, you can predict that if the mine's manager had warned the village that the tip was beginning to crumble,

☐ a. people would have ignored the warning.

☐ b. fewer people would have been killed.

☐ c. the men working at the mine would have been killed.

2. Choose from the letters below to correctly complete the following statement. Write the letters on the lines.

   In the article, ________ and ________ are alike.

   a. John Collins's fate
   b. Peter Collins's fate
   c. Margret's fate

3. Read paragraph 19. Then choose from the letters below to correctly complete the following statement. Write the letters on the lines.

   According to paragraph 19, ________ because ________.

   a. George Williams overslept for work that morning
   b. George Williams heard a roar coming from the mountain
   c. George Williams survived the accident

4. What did you have to do to answer question 1?

☐ a. find a cause (why something happened)
☐ b. find a comparison (how things are the same)
☐ c. make a prediction (what might happen next)

________ Number of correct answers

Record your personal assessment of your work on the Critical Thinking Chart on page 74.

Personal Response

Why do you think John Collins didn't want to live in his new home?

____

____

____

____

Self-Assessment

I'm proud of how I answered question # ________ in section ________ because

____

____

____

____

THE CRASH OF TWA FLIGHT 800

Jack O'Hara hated to fly. A TV producer for ABC Sports, he often drove to his assignments to avoid taking a plane. But in July 1996, he was asked to cover the Tour de France bicycle race. Since he could not drive across the Atlantic Ocean, O'Hara *had* to fly. As a bonus, ABC gave him two extra tickets. One was for his wife, Janet, and the other was for his 13-year-old daughter, Caitlin.

2 Jacques and Connie Charbonnier, on the other hand, loved to fly. For 21 years they had flown on TWA's Flight 800 between New York and Paris. Jacques was the flight service manager. Connie was the senior flight attendant. They enjoyed showing the ropes to new members of the crew. So they were happy to hear that staffer Jill Ziemkiewicz would be joining them for her first New York-to-Paris flight. Ziemkiewicz, too, was pleased. "[She was] so happy about being taken under their wing," said a colleague.

3 Frenchman Marcel Dadi did not think about flying one way or the other. He was too excited. A guitarist, Dadi had just been

Having placed a rose in the sand on a Fire Island beach, a woman mourns the loss of friends who were part of the flight crew of TWA Flight 800.

inducted into the country music Walkway of Stars in Nashville, Tennessee. He was the first person from France to be so honored. "This was the greatest honor Marcel could ever have wished for," said his sister Martine Fournier. "He was at a peak of happiness."

4 The O'Haras, Charbonniers, Ziemkiewicz, and Dadi all boarded the same plane on July 17, 1996. They were on TWA Flight 800. In all, the flight carried 230 passengers and crew members. There were 21 students from a high school French club in Pennsylvania. They were off to see Paris for the first time. There was a young exchange student going home. And there was a mother who planned to tour old French castles with her daughter. She had overcome her fear of flying to make the trip.

5 After a delay of more than an hour, the plane bound for Paris took off from New York's JFK Airport. It was 8:19 P.M. The huge 747 climbed slowly through the night sky. It headed east over the Atlantic Ocean just south of Long Island. Everything looked good. There was no sign of trouble. At 8:30 P.M. the pilot got his final instructions from the control tower.

6 In the busy air space near New York City, other planes were in the sky at the same time. Just after 8:30, the pilot of Eastwind Airlines Flight 507 saw something alarming. "We just saw an explosion up ahead out here at about 16,000 feet,..." he radioed. "It blew up in the air and then we saw two fireballs go down to the water. There was smoke coming up from that."

7 The pilot of an Italian airliner also saw the explosion. So, too, did a pilot from Virgin Atlantic. A pilot for United Airlines flew directly over the site. He reported that the wreckage was "still burning down there.... It's bright red. There is smoke coming out."

8 The control tower tried to reach the pilot of Flight 800 to find out if he had seen the explosion. There was no reply. Again, the tower tried to radio Flight 800. And again, there was no answer. A few minutes later, the grim realization began to sink in.

9 "I think that was him," said one unidentified pilot.

10 "I think so," answered the control tower.

11 "God bless him," whispered the pilot.

12 National Guard helicopter pilot Chris Baur was in the area at the time. He saw an orange fireball in the distance. It looked to him as though there had been two explosions and then "a waterfall of flames" spiraling down. At first, Baur thought that maybe two planes had collided. Then he moved in for a closer look. He spotted a young man in blue jeans floating face down in the water. Baur thought briefly about turning the chopper

Victims are remembered in a memorial on the first anniversary of the crash of Flight 800.

over to his co-pilot and jumping into the water. A second look, however, convinced him that it would be a needless risk and a waste of time. The man was already dead.

13 Moments later, the awful truth became clear. The young man was not alone. Baur's flight engineer spotted many other bodies amid the debris. Flight 800 had exploded. All 230 people on board had been killed. Jack O'Hara had died, along with his wife and daughter. So, too, had the Charbonniers, Jill Ziemkiewicz, Marcel Dadi, and all the rest.

14 Recovering the bodies was grim work. East Moriches was the town closest to the crash. People from the town rushed out in boats to see if there were any survivors. Soon people from as far away as Massachusetts joined the search. All they found, though, were dead bodies. Some of the victims were still strapped in their seats. Some had had their clothes completely blown off in the blast.

15 It was hard for many searchers to keep calm in the face of such a tragedy. Said Randy Penney, "I tried not to get a good look at them, at their faces. I didn't have time to think about what I was seeing—we were out there looking for survivors. And by about 3:00 A.M., it became apparent there were none."

16 Grieving family members and friends wanted to know who or what had caused the explosion. So, too, did everyone else. At first, most people suspected a terrorist attack. After all, it would not have been the first time an airliner was brought down by a bomb. In 1988, a bomb had blown up a Pan Am 747 plane over Scotland. A total of 270 people had died in that explosion. Or perhaps terrorists had used a rocket of some kind. A madman could have attacked the plane with a small handheld rocket launcher.

17 Other people thought the disaster might have been caused by a freak of nature. For instance, a meteor could have hit the plane. The explosion could also have been caused by a mechanical failure. But the reputation of the Boeing 747 was so good that most experts at first dismissed that notion.

18 Finding the real answer, of course, was not easy. The pieces of the plane were scattered over a wide zone. They were in ocean water that was 120 to 200 feet deep. It took a year and a half to recover the pieces and study them. At last, the experts announced their findings. The verdict surprised many people. TWA Flight 800 had not been targeted by terrorists. The tragedy was not caused by either a bomb or a rocket. And the plane hadn't been hit by a meteor.

19 It turned out that the explosion was the result of a mechanical failure after all. The 26-year-old plane's central fuel tank had exploded. Somehow an electrical spark ignited a mixture of air and fuel. What exactly caused the spark remains a mystery, however.

20 The families and friends of the victims were grateful for information about the cause of the crash. But the fact remained that their loved ones were gone. Sadly, no amount of information could change that.

If you have been timed while reading this article, enter your reading time below. Then turn to the Words-per-Minute Table on page 71 and look up your reading speed (words per minute). Enter your reading speed on the graph on page 72.

Reading Time: Lesson 5

_______ : _______

Minutes *Seconds*

A Finding the Main Idea

One statement below expresses the main idea of the article. One statement is too general, or too broad. The other statement explains only part of the article; it is too narrow. Label the statements using the following key:

M—Main Idea **B—Too Broad** **N—Too Narrow**

_____ 1. A mechanical failure caused TWA Flight 800 to explode, killing all of its passengers and crew members.

_____ 2. Jack O'Hara and his family were among the passengers who died on TWA Flight 800.

_____ 3. TWA Flight 800 was a Boeing 747, which has a reputation for being a safe, reliable airplane.

_____ Score 15 points for a correct M answer.

_____ Score 5 points for each correct B or N answer.

_____ **Total Score:** Finding the Main Idea

B Recalling Facts

How well do you remember the facts in the article? Put an X in the box next to the answer that correctly completes each statement about the article.

1. The senior flight attendant on Flight 800 was
   - ☐ a. Jill Ziemkiewicz.
   - ☐ b. Connie Charbonnier.
   - ☐ c. Jacques Charbonnier.
2. The pilot of Eastwind Airlines Flight 507
   - ☐ a. saw Flight 800 explode in the air.
   - ☐ b. radioed the pilot of Flight 800 to find out what he had seen.
   - ☐ c. saw a man floating face down in the water.
3. The town closest to the crash site was
   - ☐ a. East Moriches.
   - ☐ b. Long Island.
   - ☐ c. Nashville.
4. The pieces of the plane
   - ☐ a. were collected and studied quickly.
   - ☐ b. were never found.
   - ☐ c. took a year and a half to recover and study.
5. The explosion of TWA Flight 800 was caused by
   - ☐ a. a meteor.
   - ☐ b. a terrorist bomb.
   - ☐ c. an electrical spark in the central fuel tank.

Score 5 points for each correct answer.

_____ **Total Score:** Recalling Facts

C Making Inferences

When you combine your own experience and information from a text to draw a conclusion that is not directly stated in that text, you are making an inference. Below are five statements that may or may not be inferences based on information in the article. Label the statements using the following key:

C—Correct Inference **F—Faulty Inference**

_______ 1. The families of the victims didn't blame TWA for the tragic accident.

_______ 2. Flight 800 exploded soon after it took off from JFK Airport.

_______ 3. The flight was delayed because TWA officials knew that something was wrong with the airplane.

_______ 4. Mechanical failure is a common occurrence on the Boeing 747.

_______ 5. The passengers and crew members on board Flight 800 had no warning that anything was wrong.

Score 5 points for each correct answer.

_______ **Total Score:** Making Inferences

D Using Words Precisely

Each numbered sentence below contains an underlined word or phrase from the article. Following the sentence are three definitions. One definition is closest to the meaning of the underlined word. One definition is opposite or nearly opposite. Label those two definitions using the following key. Do not label the remaining definition.

C—Closest **O—Opposite or Nearly Opposite**

1. A guitarist, Dadi had just been inducted into the country music Walkway of Stars in Nashville, Tennessee.

_______ a. rejected by
_______ b. admitted into
_______ c. interviewed by

2. A few minutes later, the grim realization began to sink in.

_______ a. depressing
_______ b. sudden
_______ c. cheerful

3. At first, Baur thought that maybe two planes had collided.

_______ a. communicated with each other
_______ b. missed each other
_______ c. crashed into each other

4. A second look, however, convinced him that it would be a needless risk and a waste of time.

_______ a. safe activity
_______ b. peril
_______ c. job

5. Somehow an electrical spark ignited a mixture of air and fuel.

_____ a. extinguished

_____ b. combined

_____ c. set on fire

_____ Score 3 points for each correct C answer.

_____ Score 2 points for each correct O answer.

_____ **Total Score:** Using Words Precisely

Enter the four total scores in the spaces below, and add them together to find your Reading Comprehension Score. Then record your score on the graph on page 73.

Score	Question Type	Lesson 5
_____	Finding the Main Idea	
_____	Recalling Facts	
_____	Making Inferences	
_____	Using Words Precisely	
_____	**Reading Comprehension Score**	

Author's Approach

Put an X in the box next to the correct answer.

1. The main purpose of the first paragraph is to

☐ a. inform the reader about Jack O'Hara's assignment in France.

☐ b. compare driving to flying.

☐ c. introduce some of the passengers on board TWA Flight 800.

2. In this article, "[Jacques and Connie Charbonnier] enjoyed showing the ropes to new members of the crew" means they

☐ a. knew a great deal about their jobs and enjoyed sharing their knowledge.

☐ b. were fairly new at their jobs and appreciated some help.

☐ c. were known for their knowledge of the ropes kept on Flight 800 and wanted to show them to the new crew members.

3. Choose the statement below that best describes the author's position in paragraph 20.

☐ a. Knowing what caused the explosion will not bring the victims back to life.

☐ b. TWA tried to cover up the real cause of the explosion.

☐ c. The families and friends of the victims were relieved to hear that the explosion was not caused by a terrorist bomb.

_____ Number of correct answers

Record your personal assessment of your work on the Critical Thinking Chart on page 74.

Summarizing and Paraphrasing

Follow the directions provided for questions 1 and 2. Put an X in the box next to the correct answer for question 3.

1. Look for the important ideas and events in paragraphs 14 and 15. Summarize those paragraphs in one or two sentences.

____

____

____

2. Complete the following one-sentence summary of the article using the lettered phrases from the phrase bank below. Write the letters on the lines.

Phrase Bank:

a. what those who witnessed the explosion or aided in the search effort saw
b. a description of some of the passengers on board the plane
c. the experts' conclusion that a mechanical failure caused the explosion

The article about TWA Flight 800 begins with _________, goes on to explain _________, and ends with _________.

3. Choose the best one-sentence paraphrase for the following sentence from the article:
"It looked to him as though there had been two explosions and then 'a waterfall of flames' spiraling down."

- ☐ a. He thought he saw two explosions blow up beside a waterfall.
- ☐ b. He thought he saw flames flowing and twisting down from the two explosions.
- ☐ c. He thought the two explosions had been caused by a wall of flames.

_________ Number of correct answers

Record your personal assessment of your work on the Critical Thinking Chart on page 74.

Critical Thinking

Put an X in the box next to the correct answer for questions 1 and 4. Follow the directions provided for the other questions.

1. From the events in the article, you can predict that the following will happen next:

- ☐ a. TWA and other airlines will carefully check the fuel tanks in all of their airplanes.
- ☐ b. TWA will cancel all of its flights to France.
- ☐ c. TWA will accuse terrorists of causing the explosion on Flight 800.

2. Choose from the letters below to correctly complete the following statement. Write the letters on the lines.

   In the article, _________ and _________ were different.

   a. Jack O'Hara's attitude toward flying
   b. Jacques Charbonnier's attitude toward flying
   c. Connie Charbonnier's attitude toward flying

3. Choose from the letters below to correctly complete the following statement. Write the letters on the lines.

   According to the article, an electrical spark caused _________ to _________, and the effect was _________.

   a. the plane's fuel tank
   b. everyone on board the plane died
   c. explode

4. How is the explosion of Flight 800 an example of a calamity?

- [ ] a. The passengers on the flight died tragically and left behind many family members and friends to mourn their loss.
- [ ] b. Experts took a long time to determine the cause of the explosion.
- [ ] c. Experts claimed that the explosion was not due to a bomb or some kind of rocket.

5. Which paragraphs from the article provide evidence that supports your answer to question 2?

____

_________ Number of correct answers

Record your personal assessment of your work on the Critical Thinking Chart on page 74.

Personal Response

What new question do you have about this topic?

____

____

____

____

Self-Assessment

Before reading this article, I already knew

____

____

____

____

A DANCE WITH DEATH

John Davis can't shake the guilt. It was his idea to go to that hotel dance. If only he had picked another place...

2 It was a Friday night in mid-July. John and Judy Davis felt like celebrating before they left for their vacation. John suggested the Hyatt Regency Hotel where they could dance to big band music, popular in the 1930s and 40s. The Davises asked their best friends, Larry and Suzanne Watson, to join them. John remembered telling them that it might be their last chance that summer to go to a tea dance.

3 The Hyatt in Kansas City, Missouri, is an elegant 40-story hotel. And like other hotels in the Hyatt chain, it has a spectacular atrium lobby. Sky bridges suspended from the ceiling span across the soaring atrium. Guests cross the bridges to go to their rooms or to attend meetings on the other side of the building. Walled in by glass, the four-story atrium was the perfect setting for the hotel's popular tea dances. The dances were held every Friday from five to eight o'clock.

4 On July 17, 1981, about 2,000 people dressed in evening gowns and tuxedos filled the Hyatt lobby. They danced, drank, and talked as the Steve Miller

The lobby of the Hyatt Regency Hotel in Kansas City after the catwalks collapsed

Orchestra played jazz tunes. When the Davises and their friends arrived shortly before 7:00 P.M., there was a dance contest going on. They saw people dancing on two of the narrow sky bridges. Other people were on the bridges watching the crowd below. John made his way to the bar next to the dance floor to get some drinks. Suddenly he heard a snapping sound like a gunshot. The noise silenced the crowd. Everyone looked up. In seconds, the fourth-floor bridge buckled in the middle and crashed onto the second-floor span. Then with a loud roar, the two bridges dropped to the lobby. (The third-floor bridge, which was 15 feet farther from the glass wall, did not collapse.)

5 People on the skywalks went flying in all directions. Some tried to hang on to the railings but couldn't. As the remaining sections of the bridges ripped from the walls, chunks of concrete, glass, and steel rained on the lobby. Huge dust clouds and gas fumes filled the air. The scene was horrifying. One witness said it looked like a bomb exploded. Hundreds of people were pinned under slabs of concrete, and many were dead. All over the room dancers were piled on top of one another. And the chaos worsened when water pipes burst, flooding the lobby floor.

6 When the shower of debris stopped, the screams could be heard. Many people needed immediate medical attention. Others called out the names of their loved ones and friends. Karyl Hill lay in a fetal position with her friend's head resting on her shoulder. She heard him moan and touched his neck to feel for a pulse. "I felt him die," she said. John Davis found himself on the floor. His leg was pinned, and he could see a pool of blood. He didn't know where his wife and friends were.

7 Rescue units arrived at the Hyatt within minutes of the disaster. They found some survivors wandering in the lobby dazed and bleeding. With blowtorches, chain saws, and jackhammers, rescuers struggled to free those trapped. But they had to move concrete boulders and twisted beams. Because the concrete was so heavy, progress was slow. Construction cranes were brought in to remove the

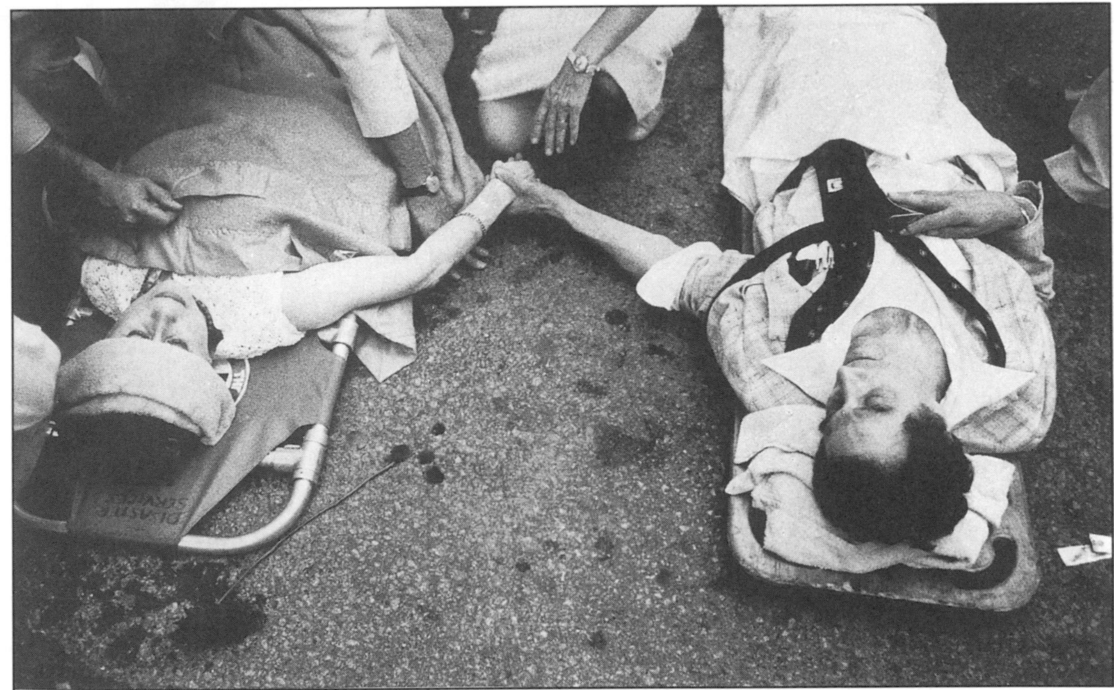

Two victims of the Hyatt Regency disaster hold hands as they wait for medical treatment.

skywalks. They were lifted inch by inch to guard against any sudden movement. One firefighter said he saw people lying everywhere. "Some were begging me to get them out," he said. In some places, the debris was six feet deep.

8 About 1,000 police, doctors, firefighters, and bystanders joined the rescue effort. Doctors set up a makeshift hospital on the sidewalk outside the hotel. In the lobby, medical teams gave emergency blood transfusions. Bystanders not only helped to comfort the injured but also helped to move debris. Twenty-five ambulances and a helicopter made repeated trips to local hospitals. As more bodies were recovered, an exhibit hall at the hotel became a temporary morgue.

9 Rescue teams worked tirelessly at the scene for 13 hours. Every time they found a survivor, they cheered. The discovery of another body brought only silence. A police sergeant said he didn't think the nightmare would ever end. He saw too many black bags containing bodies. "I must have asked... a million times that night: 'Is this the last one?'"

10 Ten survivors were trapped until 6:00 A.M. They were the last ones found alive. A little later, cranes lifted another huge piece of concrete. Thirty-one bodies were underneath.

11 The Hyatt disaster killed 114 people and injured more than 200. Judy Davis and Larry and Suzanne Watson were among the dead. John Davis, who suffered a broken back, was interviewed at the hospital the day after. He hadn't been told yet about his wife and two friends.

12 Hyatt officials closed the year-old hotel and began their own investigation. They ordered that the third-floor walkway be torn down. Building experts examined that bridge and the wreckage looking for clues. They had been told that shortly before the collapse, the bridges were swaying and shaking. Some officials suggested that the bridges couldn't handle the extra weight and movement of the dancers.

13 Six months after the disaster, the National Bureau of Standards issued a report. It found that the design of the walkways was flawed. For some reason, the original design had been changed during construction. The second-floor bridge was supposed to be suspended from steel rods attached to the ceiling. Instead, the rods were attached to the fourth-floor skywalk. That change made the fourth-floor bridge bear too much weight. "It was a small detail," said Dr. Edward Pfrang, who led the investigation. "And yet it killed more people than any other building failure in the United States." Pfrang also said the dancers' movement did not cause the bridge collapse.

14 In October 1981 the Hyatt Regency reopened its doors. The skywalks had been rebuilt, but they were now supported by pillars instead of steel rods. The survivors, meanwhile, filed lawsuits against the Hyatt company. By 1983 they had been awarded $86 million in damages. And more lawsuits were pending.

15 It was a difficult recovery for many. Besides physical pain, tea dance victims had also suffered emotional scars. Survivors like John Davis felt guilt. Others experienced anger, loss of appetite, and insomnia.

16 Chuck Hayes and his wife, Jayne, were standing under the skywalks when the walks collapsed. "If I allow my mind to wander," said Chuck, "it wanders back to that night.... I can see the walkways falling, the concrete, everything hitting us." Jayne suffered a broken leg, internal injuries, broken hips, and broken ribs. She spent nearly four months in the hospital. Chuck, who was released after her, had crushed bones in both legs. And two vertebrae in his back had been shattered. Chuck made it home in time for Thanksgiving. Ever since the Hyatt disaster, he has been giving thanks.

If you have been timed while reading this article, enter your reading time below. Then turn to the Words-per-Minute Table on page 71 and look up your reading speed (words per minute). Enter your reading speed on the graph on page 72.

Reading Time: Lesson 6

________ : ________

Minutes *Seconds*

A Finding the Main Idea

One statement below expresses the main idea of the article. One statement is too general, or too broad. The other statement explains only part of the article; it is too narrow. Label the statements using the following key:

M—Main Idea **B—Too Broad** **N—Too Narrow**

_______ 1. Hundreds of people were killed or injured when the sky bridges at the Kansas City Hyatt Hotel collapsed.

_______ 2. It is unwise to change the design of a building at the last moment, as the Hyatt Hotel disaster proves.

_______ 3. John Davis's wife and friends were killed when the sky bridges at the Hyatt Hotel collapsed.

_______ Score 15 points for a correct M answer.

_______ Score 5 points for each correct B or N answer.

_______ **Total Score:** Finding the Main Idea

B Recalling Facts

How well do you remember the facts in the article? Put an X in the box next to the answer that correctly completes each statement about the article.

1. The sky bridges collapsed at the Hyatt Regency Hotel in
   - ☐ a. Atlanta, Georgia.
   - ☐ b. Dallas, Texas.
   - ☐ c. Kansas City, Missouri.
2. At the time of the collapse, the lobby was crowded because
   - ☐ a. there was a tea dance.
   - ☐ b. there was a business convention.
   - ☐ c. the hotel had just reopened.
3. The collapse began
   - ☐ a. in the hotel ballroom.
   - ☐ b. with the fourth-floor sky bridge.
   - ☐ c. with the second-floor walkway.
4. The disaster worsened when
   - ☐ a. rescue vehicles couldn't get to the accident.
   - ☐ b. water pipes burst, flooding the floor.
   - ☐ c. fires broke out in the lobby.
5. The original design of the sky bridges
   - ☐ a. was changed during construction.
   - ☐ b. was faulty and caused the collapse.
   - ☐ c. did not allow for dancing on the walkways.

Score 5 points for each correct answer.

_______ **Total Score:** Recalling Facts

C Making Inferences

When you combine your own experience and information from a text to draw a conclusion that is not directly stated in that text, you are making an inference. Below are five statements that may or may not be inferences based on information in the article. Label the statements using the following key:

C—Correct Inference **F—Faulty Inference**

______ 1. The sky bridges might not have collapsed if the original design had been followed.

______ 2. The collapse was caused by the guests who danced on the bridges.

______ 3. No one knows why the sky bridges collapsed.

______ 4. Before the accident, the Hyatt Regency was a popular spot in Kansas City.

______ 5. Many of the survivors of the Hyatt collapse still suffer from physical and emotional pain.

Score 5 points for each correct answer.

______ **Total Score:** Making Inferences

D Using Words Precisely

Each numbered sentence below contains an underlined word or phrase from the article. Following the sentence are three definitions. One definition is closest to the meaning of the underlined word. One definition is opposite or nearly opposite. Label those two definitions using the following key. Do not label the remaining definition.

C—Closest **O—Opposite or Nearly Opposite**

1. And the <u>chaos</u> worsened when water pipes burst, flooding the lobby floor.

______ a. perfect order

______ b. confusion

______ c. dance

2. They found some survivors wandering in the lobby <u>dazed</u> and bleeding.

______ a. alert

______ b. contented

______ c. stunned

3. Doctors set up a <u>makeshift</u> hospital on the sidewalk outside the hotel.

______ a. temporary

______ b. permanent

______ c. small

4. Rescue teams worked <u>tirelessly</u> at the scene for 13 hours.

______ a. without any help

______ b. without tiring

______ c. wearily

5. Others experienced anger, loss of appetite, and <u>insomnia</u>.

_____ a. wakefulness

_____ b. happiness

_____ c. drowsiness

_____ Score 3 points for each correct C answer.

_____ Score 2 points for each correct O answer.

_____ **Total Score:** Using Words Precisely

Enter the four total scores in the spaces below, and add them together to find your Reading Comprehension Score. Then record your score on the graph on page 73.

Score	Question Type	Lesson 6
_____	Finding the Main Idea	
_____	Recalling Facts	
_____	Making Inferences	
_____	Using Words Precisely	
_____	**Reading Comprehension Score**	

Author's Approach

Put an X in the box next to the correct answer.

1. The author uses the first sentence of the article to

☐ a. inform the reader that John Davis was responsible for the disaster.

☐ b. describe John Davis's emotions after the disaster.

☐ c. express an opinion about John Davis.

2. What does the author mean by the statement "As more bodies were recovered, an exhibit hall at the hotel became a temporary morgue"?

☐ a. Bodies were placed in the exhibit hall so that people could see them.

☐ b. People were taken to the exhibit hall to die.

☐ c. Dead bodies were placed in one of the hotel's exhibit halls.

3. In this article, "Survivors like John Davis felt guilt" means the survivors

☐ a. blamed themselves for the flaws in the building.

☐ b. felt bad that they had lived when so many others had died.

☐ c. were relieved that they had lived.

4. The author tells this story mainly by

☐ a. returning several times to John Davis's experiences throughout the disaster.

☐ b. relating the experiences of the Hyatt Hotel staff.

☐ c. comparing the disaster at the Hyatt with similar tragedies.

_____ Number of correct answers

Record your personal assessment of your work on the Critical Thinking Chart on page 74.

Summarizing and Paraphrasing

Follow the directions provided for questions 1 and 2. Put an X in the box next to the correct answer for question 3.

1. Look for the important ideas and events in paragraphs 4 and 5. Summarize those paragraphs in one or two sentences.

____

____

____

2. Reread paragraph 13 in the article. Below, write a summary of the paragraph in no more than 25 words.

____

____

____

____

Reread your summary and decide whether it covers the important ideas in the paragraph. Next, decide how to shorten the summary to 15 words or less without leaving out any essential information. Write this summary below.

____

____

____

3. Choose the best one-sentence paraphrase for the following sentence from the article:

   "Bystanders not only helped to comfort the injured but also helped to move debris."

☐ a. Bystanders helped remove debris but did not help those who had been injured.

☐ b. Some people stood by while others helped dig through the rubble.

☐ c. Those who were not victims of the disaster helped by calming the injured and removing some of the wreckage.

_______ Number of correct answers

Record your personal assessment of your work on the Critical Thinking Chart on page 74.

Critical Thinking

Put an X in the box next to the correct answer for question 1. Follow the directions provided for the other questions.

1. From the article, you can predict that if John Davis had stayed with his wife and friends, he

☐ a. would have been killed.

☐ b. wouldn't have been hurt at all.

☐ c. might have been able to save the others.

2. Choose from the letters below to correctly complete the following statement. Write the letters on the lines.

   On the positive side, ________, but on the negative side ________.

   a. Chuck and Jayne Hayes survived the Hyatt disaster
   b. Chuck and Jayne Hayes suffered many injuries
   c. Chuck Hayes made it home for Thanksgiving, but Jane did not

3. Choose from the letters below to correctly complete the following statement. Write the letters on the lines.

   According to the article, ________ caused ________ to collapse, and the effect was ________.

   a. the fourth-floor skywalk
   b. 114 people were killed and more than 200 were injured
   c. too much weight

4. In which paragraph did you find the information or details to answer question 2?

   ____

________ Number of correct answers

Record your personal assessment of your work on the Critical Thinking Chart on page 74.

Personal Response

I wonder why

____

____

____

____

Self-Assessment

I was confused on question # ________ in section __________ because

____

____

____

____

IN THE EYE OF THE STORM

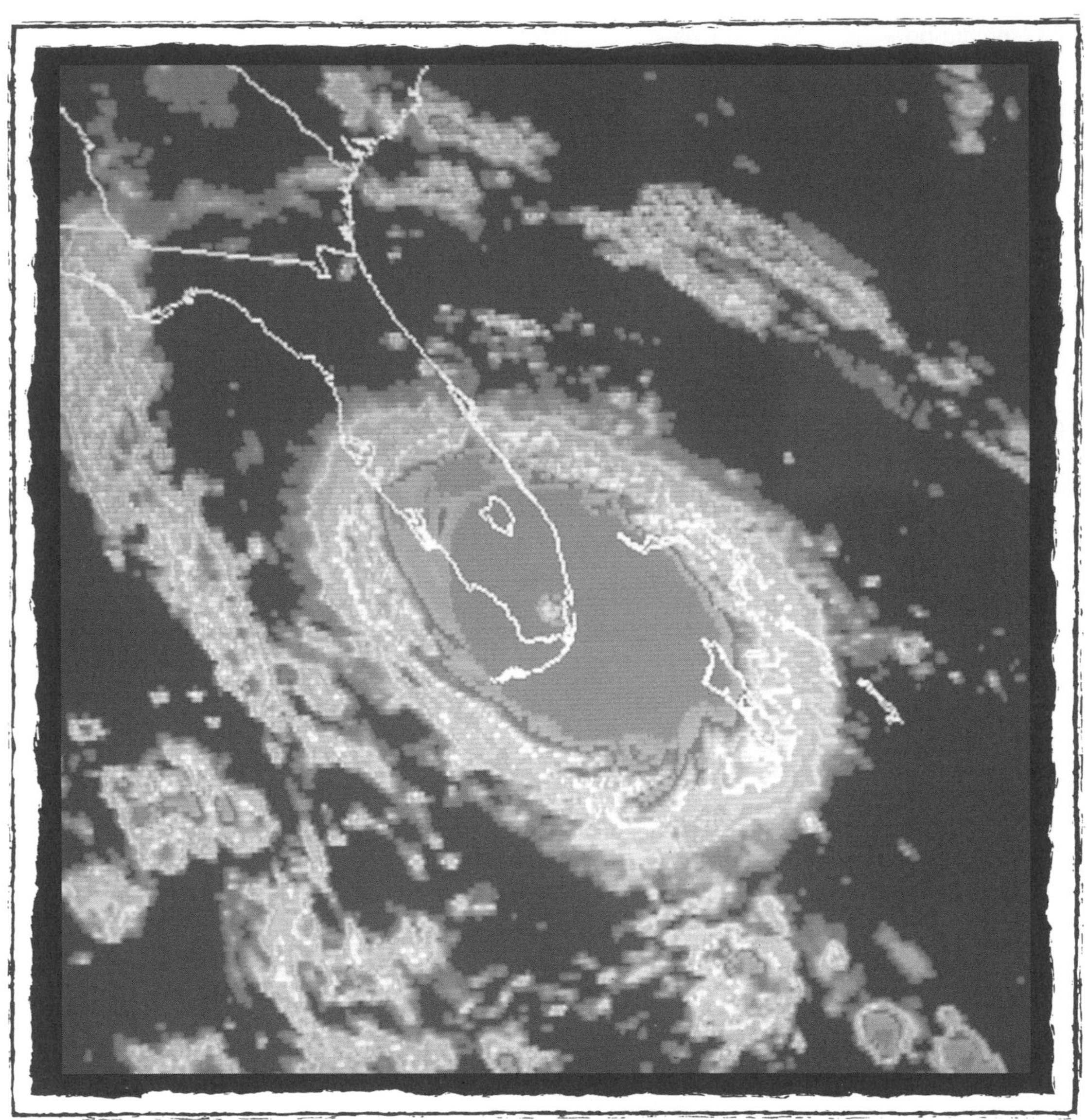

From West Africa a patch of thunderstorms moved over the Atlantic. The summer storm seemed unusually strong. Over the next few days, the storm became even more powerful. Then the swirling mass developed an evil eye. Weather forecasters plotting the monster's path named it Hurricane Andrew.

2 In Miami, Florida, TV meteorologist Bryan Norcross was also watching Andrew. He didn't like the looks of the storm. "I knew that soon someone within the sound of my voice was going to have a hurricane—and maybe a bad one." Norcross was right.

3 By Sunday, August 23, 1992, Andrew's winds grew to 150 miles per hour. The Bahamas would be Andrew's first victim. Late that night the hurricane struck the island, killing four people and damaging homes and property. Norcross went on the air and warned the residents of South Florida that they were next. Andrew would be the third-strongest hurricane to hit the United States this century. Many people had already started to evacuate, clogging roads and highways. Norcross told them to keep driving out of town or head to emergency shelters.

This satellite photo shows Hurricane Andrew swirling over the state of Florida.

4 Tom McEvoy, a Coral Gables police officer, decided to wait out the hurricane at home with his family. Many other residents also ignored the warnings and refused to evacuate. They either had nowhere else to go, or they didn't fear the storm. Instead, they taped and boarded up their windows and pruned trees. They stocked up on bottled water, and some bought portable generators. All the while, they stayed tuned to Bryan Norcross. His broadcast marathon would be their salvation.

5 Early Monday morning the National Hurricane Center in Dade County knew Andrew had come ashore. The center had been expecting it for days. Director Bob Sheets, who alerted the country about Andrew, thought the center was prepared. But about 1:00 A.M. forecasters felt the entire building shake. Then the center's electricity went out, and the air conditioner broke. With a wind gust of 164 miles per hour, the storm tore the center's radar dish right off the roof. The dish disappeared into Andrew's massive jaw.

6 Farther south, the McEvoys woke up to screaming winds. The family fled downstairs as a window in the living room blew out. Soon windows all over the house were exploding. Rain came whipping through. In fear, Tom McEvoy led his family from room to room, trying to find someplace safe. The four of them ended up jammed into a bathroom with their two dogs. Throughout the night, they cried and prayed as Andrew took their house apart.

7 Jo and Bruce Powers, their children, Jo's sister, and neighbors hid in bathrooms too. For two frightening hours they listened as Andrew swirled around the Powers' house. Savage winds tried to rip the bathroom door off, so Bruce pressed his 200-pound frame against the door and braced one foot on the sink. Water was pouring in around the medicine cabinet, and the tub was pulling away from the wall. Tiles from the roof sometimes flew under the bathroom door.

8 Chris Heagan and his family crouched in a closet during the storm. "You haven't lived through anything until you find a trailer flying into your house," Chris said. Huge chunks of metal from the trailer sliced through the walls of the Heagan's home.

9 During Andrew's rampage, one very nervous woman phoned Bryan Norcross. Norcross was now broadcasting from his "Bunker," a concrete storeroom at the TV station. "Bryan, we have two doors that blew out on one side of the house. Should we open windows on the other side to alleviate pressure?" Norcross gave the woman and many other anxious callers the same advice: Find a safe place and stay put.

10 Hurricane Andrew raced wildly across southern Florida. At times the winds reached 200 miles per hour. Andrew destroyed almost everything in its path.

A man sits in the remains of his living room after winds from Hurricane Andrew caused a tree to crash into his home.

When residents finally emerged from their hiding places, they said their neighborhoods looked like they had been hit by an atomic bomb.

11 More than 80,000 homes were flattened or severely damaged. Another 55,000 were still standing but needed major repairs. Residents found themselves without electricity, phones, water, bathrooms, food, shelter, or transportation. Dazed and fearful, they stood amid the rubble in the hot summer sun.

12 Two days after leaving Florida, Andrew slammed into Louisiana, killing 15 people. Most of the storm damage occurred in marshland and small towns.

13 Not much escaped Andrew's 60-mile wide rampage in Florida. In the Everglades, 70,000 acres of mangrove trees were destroyed. At a small airport, 275 small planes were mangled. Animals at Miami's Metrozoo escaped after fences were blown apart. Many birds were crushed in their cages. All over Dade County boats were battered and stacked in piles.

14 Andrew hit the blue-collar community of Homestead the hardest. Debris is all that is left of homes, schools, businesses, and the Homestead Air Force Base. Outside her mobile home, Mildred Gray talked about the total destruction. "I still can't believe what my eyes are seeing," she said. The manager of the mobile home park told Gray he planned to bulldoze the ruined park in two weeks. There wasn't much to save.

15 With so many people left homeless, military units set up tent cities. It was the only way to shelter and feed Andrew's victims. Some residents, however, wouldn't leave their damaged homes. Armed troops walked the streets, trying to persuade them to go to shelters. Troops also helped residents clean up debris and patrolled neighborhoods to prevent looting.

16 Andrew claimed 43 lives in Florida. Twelve-year-old Naomi Browning was killed when a beam fell on her in her bedroom. Robert Ramos, 49, and others were killed by flying debris. Many people were crushed in their homes. Officials say that if the eye of the storm had struck Miami, the death toll would have been much higher.

17 Hurricane Andrew was the most costly natural disaster to hit the United States. Insurance companies paid at least $20 billion in damages. Some residents rebuilt their homes and businesses. Rebuilding their lives, however, may take more time. People like Noemy Calderon still panic whenever they see storm clouds gather. At the sound of thunder, children cry and dogs whimper.

18 Chris Heagan said there are no words to describe the fear he felt that Monday morning. Andrew the monster will live in his memory.

If you have been timed while reading this article, enter your reading time below. Then turn to the Words-per-Minute Table on page 71 and look up your reading speed (words per minute). Enter your reading speed on the graph on page 72.

Reading Time: Lesson 7

_______ : _______

Minutes *Seconds*

A Finding the Main Idea

One statement below expresses the main idea of the article. One statement is too general, or too broad. The other statement explains only part of the article; it is too narrow. Label the statements using the following key:

M—Main Idea **B—Too Broad** **N—Too Narrow**

_____ 1. Hurricane Andrew ripped through South Florida causing widespread destruction.

_____ 2. Bryan Norcross helped South Florida survive the devastating hurricane.

_____ 3. Hurricanes can be dangerous storms causing both death and destruction.

_____ Score 15 points for a correct M answer.

_____ Score 5 points for each correct B or N answer.

_____ **Total Score:** Finding the Main Idea

B Recalling Facts

How well do you remember the facts in the article? Put an X in the box next to the answer that correctly completes each statement about the article.

1. Hurricane Andrew's first victim was

☐ a. South Florida.
☐ b. the Bahamas.
☐ c. Louisiana.

2. Insurance companies paid damages as high as

☐ a. $20 billion.
☐ b. $20,000.
☐ c. $20 million.

3. Many people weathered the brutal storm

☐ a. at Homestead Air Force Base.
☐ b. inside Bryan Norcross's "Bunker."
☐ c. by hiding in closets and bathrooms.

4. Troops patrolled the neighborhoods in order to

☐ a. estimate storm damage.
☐ b. prevent looting.
☐ c. locate missing zoo animals.

5. The death toll would have been higher if the storm's eye had hit

☐ a. Miami.
☐ b. the Everglades.
☐ c. Homestead.

Score 5 points for each correct answer.

_____ **Total Score:** Recalling Facts

C Making Inferences

When you combine your own experience and information from a text to draw a conclusion that is not directly stated in that text, you are making an inference. Below are five statements that may or may not be inferences based on information in the article. Label the statements using the following key:

C—Correct Inference **F—Faulty Inference**

_______ 1. Meteorologist Bryan Norcross helped to save lives.

_______ 2. Forecasters couldn't predict that Hurricane Andrew would be a strong storm.

_______ 3. The military was prepared to deal with the needs of hurricane victims.

_______ 4. Most survivors were unaffected by the hurricane.

_______ 5. The Bahamas suffered as much damage as South Florida.

Score 5 points for each correct answer.

_______ **Total Score:** Making Inferences

D Using Words Precisely

Each numbered sentence below contains an underlined word or phrase from the article. Following the sentence are three definitions. One definition is closest to the meaning of the underlined word. One definition is opposite or nearly opposite. Label those two definitions using the following key. Do not label the remaining definition.

C—Closest **O—Opposite or Nearly Opposite**

1. Weather forecasters <u>plotting</u> the monster's path named it Hurricane Andrew.

_______ a. ignoring

_______ b. mapping or charting out carefully

_______ c. underestimating

2. Many people had already started to <u>evacuate</u>, clogging roads and highways.

_______ a. return

_______ b. panic

_______ c. leave

3. They stocked up on bottled water, and some bought <u>portable</u> generators.

_______ a. easily carried

_______ b. immovable

_______ c. efficient

4. "Should we open windows on the other side to <u>alleviate</u> pressure?"

_______ a. relieve

_______ b. measure

_______ c. increase

5. At a small airport, 275 planes were mangled.

_______ a. grounded

_______ b. repaired

_______ c. damaged

_______ Score 3 points for each correct C answer.

_______ Score 2 points for each correct O answer.

_______ **Total Score:** Using Words Precisely

Enter the four total scores in the spaces below, and add them together to find your Reading Comprehension Score. Then record your score on the graph on page 73.

Score	Question Type	Lesson 7
_______	Finding the Main Idea	
_______	Recalling Facts	
_______	Making Inferences	
_______	Using Words Precisely	
_______	**Reading Comprehension Score**	

Author's Approach

Put an X in the box next to the correct answer.

1. The main purpose of the first paragraph is to

☐ a. describe the beginnings of Hurricane Andrew.

☐ b. tell the reader that weather forecasters give names to hurricanes.

☐ c. compare Hurricane Andrew to a thunderstorm.

2. Which of the following statements from the article best describes the area that was affected by Hurricane Andrew?

☐ a. "The summer storm seemed unusually strong."

☐ b. "Not much escaped Andrew's 60-mile rampage in Florida."

☐ c. "Andrew would be the third-strongest hurricane to hit the United States this century."

3. What does the author imply by saying "When residents finally emerged from their hiding places, they said their neighborhoods looked like they had been hit by an atomic bomb"?

☐ a. The residents' homes and neighborhoods had been completely destroyed by the hurricane.

☐ b. Some people, not realizing that a hurricane had swept through, assumed that their area had been bombed.

☐ c. When people came out of hiding, they were hit by flying debris.

4. Choose the statement below that best describes the author's position in paragraph 17.

☐ a. Since Andrew was a natural disaster, insurance companies shouldn't have had to pay so much money in damages.

☐ b. The residents in areas hit by Andrew have completely recovered from the hurricane.

☐ c. Some people may never get over the fear inspired by Hurricane Andrew.

_________ Number of correct answers

Record your personal assessment of your work on the Critical Thinking Chart on page 74.

Summarizing and Paraphrasing

Put an X in the box next to the correct answer.

1. Below are summaries of the article. Choose the summary that says all the most important things about the article but in the fewest words.

☐ a. Even though people were warned about Hurricane Andrew, some people decided not to evacuate their homes. When the hurricane swept through, many of these people hid in their bathrooms. After the storm passed, they emerged to find terrible destruction.

☐ b. Hurricane Andrew is the most costly natural disaster ever to hit the United States.

☐ c. Hurricane Andrew caused terrible destruction wherever it struck. The people who chose to stay in their homes during the storm felt its full force. The deadly hurricane is the most costly natural disaster to ever hit the United States.

2. Choose the sentence that correctly restates the following sentence from the article:

"Savage winds tried to rip the bathroom door off, so Bruce pressed his 200-pound frame against the door and braced one foot on the sink."

☐ a. Bruce tried to rip the bathroom door off by leaning against it and pushing off the sink.

☐ b. When terrible winds tried to tear off the bathroom door, Bruce huddled by the door under the sink.

☐ c. Bruce fought the terrible winds by leaning against the bathroom door and planting his foot firmly on the sink.

_________ Number of correct answers

Record your personal assessment of your work on the Critical Thinking Chart on page 74.

Critical Thinking

Put an X in the box next to the correct answer for questions 1, 3, and 4. Follow the directions provided for the other questions.

1. From what the article told about Tom McEvoy's experience during Andrew, you can predict that he will

☐ a. evacuate his family the next time a hurricane is about to strike.

☐ b. hide his family in the bathroom again during other hurricanes.

☐ c. build bigger bathrooms in his reconstructed home.

2. Choose from the letters below to correctly complete the following statement. Write the letters on the lines.

   In the article, _________ and _________ are different.

   a. Jo Powers's hiding place during the hurricane
   b. Tom McEvoy's hiding place during the hurricane
   c. Chris Heagan's hiding place during the hurricane

3. What was the cause of tent cities being set up in Florida?

☐ a. Many people were left homeless by Hurricane Andrew.
☐ b. Some residents wouldn't leave their damaged homes.
☐ c. Looters stole what was left in damaged homes.

4. Of the following theme categories, which would this story fit into?

☐ a. The weather is unpredictable.
☐ b. Accurate weather forecasting insures our safety during bad weather.
☐ c. People are helpless against the power of nature.

5. Which paragraphs from the article provide evidence that supports your answer to question 2?

____

_________ Number of correct answers

Record your personal assessment of your work on the Critical Thinking Chart on page 74.

Personal Response

Begin the first 5–8 sentences of your own article about the devastation caused by a terrible hurricane. It may tell of a real experience or one that is imagined.

____

____

____

____

Self-Assessment

Before reading this article, I already knew

____

____

____

____

Compare and Contrast

Think about the articles you have read in Unit One. Pick the four articles that described the most frightening calamities. Write the titles of the articles in the first column of the chart below. Use information you learned from the articles to fill in the empty boxes in the chart.

Title	What caused this calamity?	Which of the people touched by this calamity would you least like to be? Explain why.	Could this calamity happen to you? Explain why or why not.

The calamity that I fear most is ______________________________ because ______________________________

____

____

Words-per-Minute Table

Unit One

Directions: If you were timed while reading an article, refer to the Reading Time you recorded in the box at the end of the article. Use this words-per-minute table to determine your reading speed for that article. Then plot your reading speed on the graph on page 72.

Minutes and Seconds

Lesson	Sample	1	2	3	4	5	6	7	*Seconds*
No. of Words	936	1366	1429	964	1140	1186	1181	1047	
1:30	624	911	953	643	760	791	787	698	**90**
1:40	562	820	857	578	684	712	709	628	**100**
1:50	511	745	779	526	622	647	644	571	**110**
2:00	468	683	715	482	570	593	591	524	**120**
2:10	432	630	660	445	526	547	545	483	**130**
2:20	401	585	612	413	489	508	506	449	**140**
2:30	374	546	572	386	456	474	472	419	**150**
2:40	351	512	536	362	428	445	443	393	**160**
2:50	330	482	504	340	402	419	417	370	**170**
3:00	312	455	476	321	380	395	394	349	**180**
3:10	296	431	451	304	360	375	373	331	**190**
3:20	281	410	429	289	342	356	354	314	**200**
3:30	267	390	408	275	326	339	337	299	**210**
3:40	255	373	390	263	311	323	322	286	**220**
3:50	244	356	373	251	297	309	308	273	**230**
4:00	234	342	357	241	285	297	295	262	**240**
4:10	225	328	343	231	274	285	283	251	**250**
4:20	216	315	330	222	263	274	273	242	**260**
4:30	208	304	318	214	253	264	262	233	**270**
4:40	201	293	306	207	244	254	253	224	**280**
4:50	194	283	296	199	236	245	244	217	**290**
5:00	187	273	286	193	228	237	236	209	**300**
5:10	181	264	277	187	221	230	229	203	**310**
5:20	176	256	268	181	214	222	221	196	**320**
5:30	170	248	260	175	207	216	215	190	**330**
5:40	165	241	252	170	201	209	208	185	**340**
5:50	160	234	245	165	195	203	202	179	**350**
6:00	156	228	238	161	190	198	197	175	**360**
6:10	152	222	232	156	185	192	192	170	**370**
6:20	148	216	226	152	180	187	186	165	**380**
6:30	144	210	220	148	175	182	182	161	**390**
6:40	140	205	214	145	171	178	177	157	**400**
6:50	137	200	209	141	167	174	173	153	**410**
7:00	134	195	204	138	163	169	169	150	**420**
7:10	131	191	199	135	159	165	165	146	**430**
7:20	128	186	195	131	155	162	161	143	**440**
7:30	125	182	191	129	152	158	157	140	**450**
7:40	122	178	186	126	149	155	154	137	**460**
7:50	119	174	182	123	146	151	151	134	**470**
8:00	117	171	179	121	143	148	148	131	**480**

Plotting Your Progress: Reading Speed

Unit One

Directions: If you were timed while reading an article, write your words-per-minute rate for that article in the box under the number of the lesson. Then plot your reading speed on the graph by putting a small X on the line directly above the number of the lesson, across from the number of words per minute you read. As you mark your speed for each lesson, graph your progress by drawing a line to connect the X's.

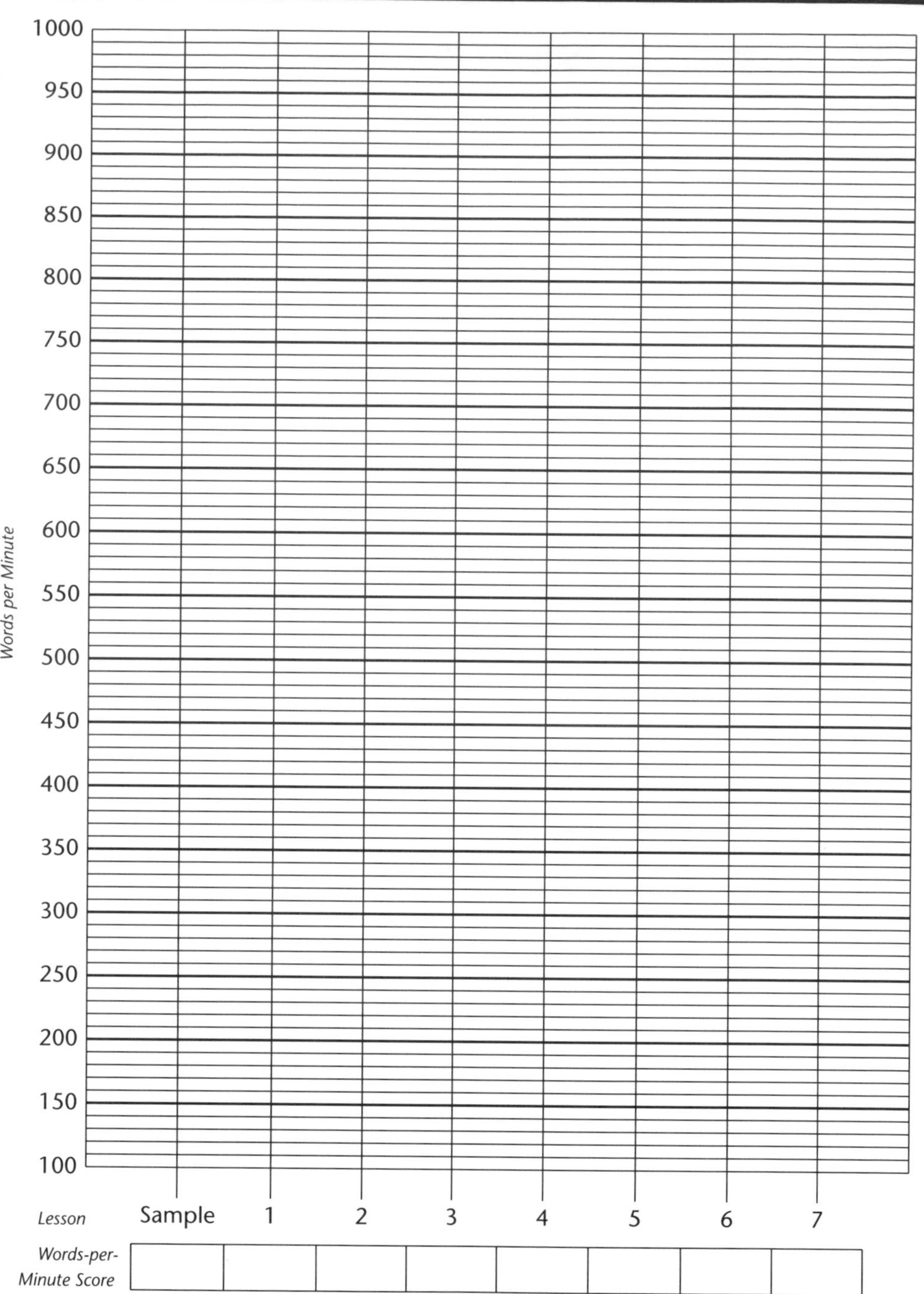

Plotting Your Progress: Reading Comprehension

Unit One

Directions: Write your Reading Comprehension score for each lesson in the box under the number of the lesson. Then plot your score on the graph by putting a small X on the line directly above the number of the lesson and across from the score you earned. As you mark your score for each lesson, graph your progress by drawing a line to connect the X's.

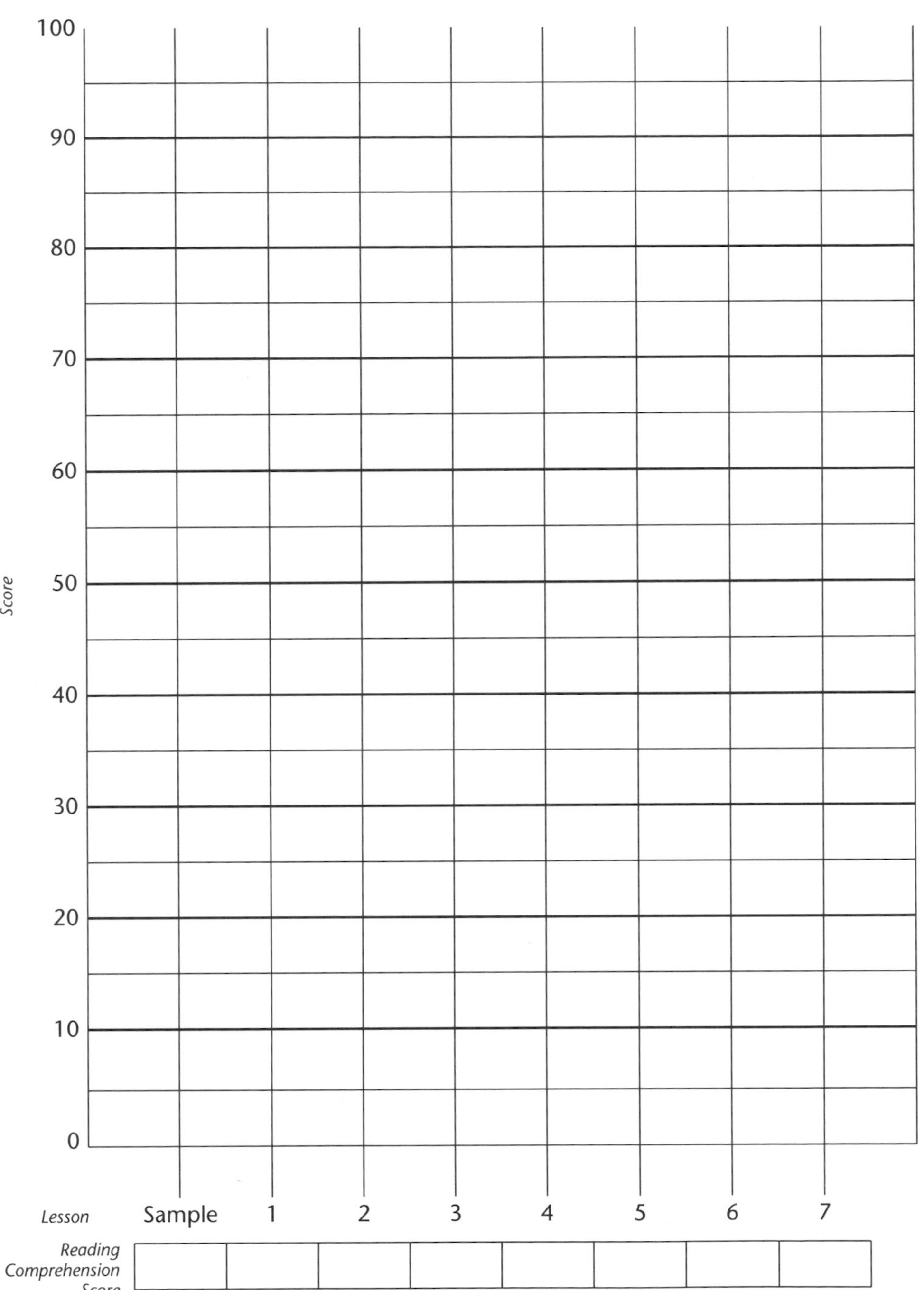

Plotting Your Progress: Critical Thinking

Unit One

Directions: Work with your teacher to evaluate your responses to the Critical Thinking questions for each lesson. Then fill in the appropriate spaces in the chart below. For each lesson and each type of Critical Thinking question, do the following: Mark a minus sign (–) in the box to indicate areas in which you feel you could improve. Mark a plus sign (+) to indicate areas in which you feel you did well. Mark a minus-slash-plus sign (–/+) to indicate areas in which you had mixed success. Then write any comments you have about your performance, including ideas for improvement.

Lesson	Author's Approach	Summarizing and Paraphrasing	Critical Thinking
Sample			
1			
2			
3			
4			
5			
6			
7			

UNIT TWO

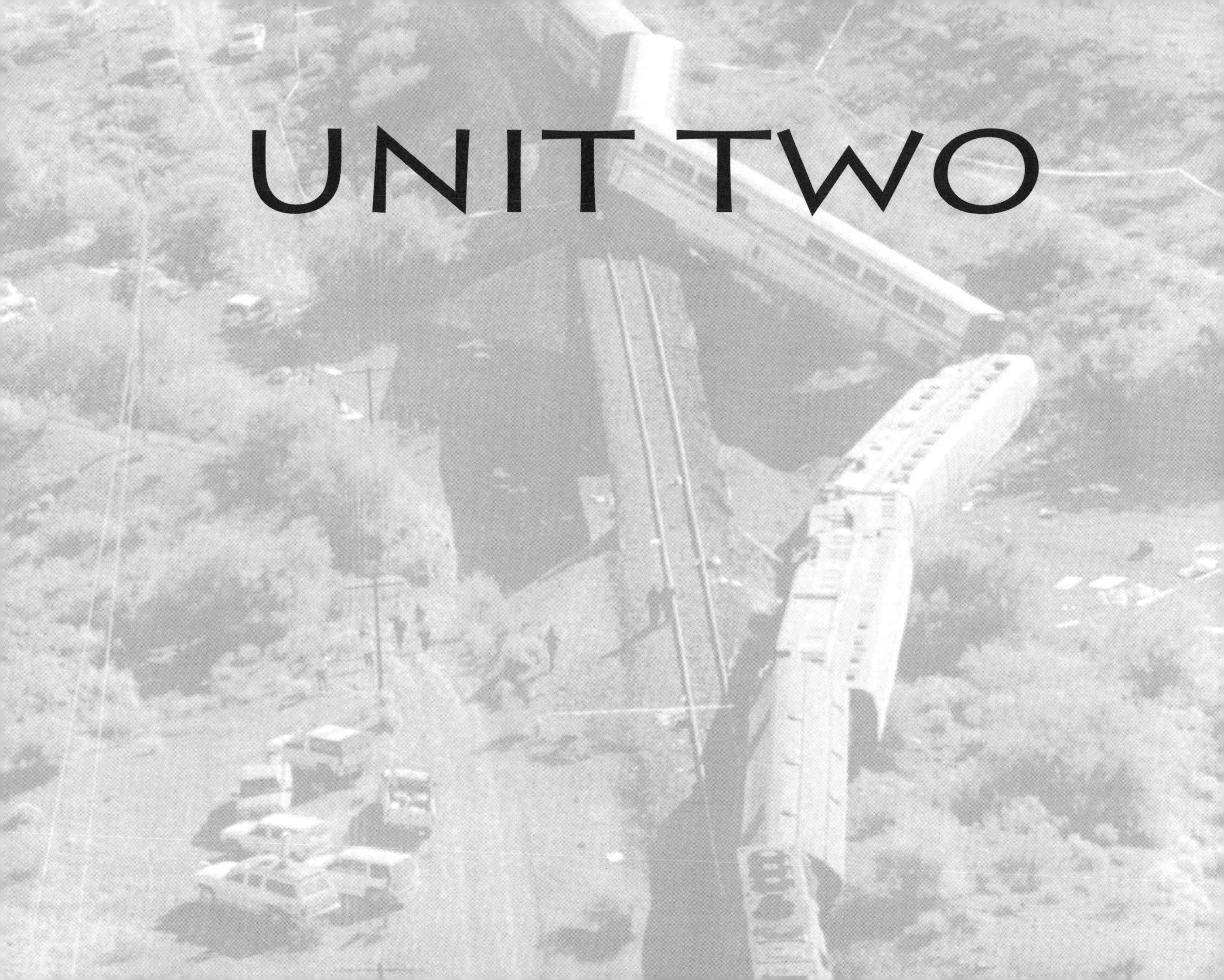

SABOTAGE IN THE DESERT

It was about 1:20 A.M. on October 9, 1995. Amtrak's 12-car *Sunset Limited* train was headed toward Los Angeles. There were 268 people aboard, including 20 crew members. The lights on the track flashed green. The train was going about 50 miles per hour. It was just 27 miles east of Hyder, Arizona.

2 Suddenly, just as the *Sunset Limited* crossed a trestle, it jerked violently. The two diesel locomotives made it to the other side of the bridge, but the rest of the train didn't. The cars jumped off the track. One of them tumbled 30 feet down to a desert ravine. Three more cars dangled off the trestle like a string of giant paper clips.

3 This wasn't an accident. This was sabotage. Someone had deliberately pulled up 29 spikes and removed 4 bolts from the track. That someone hoped to kill as many people on the train as possible. He or she pulled the spikes and bolts from the trestle so that the cars would tumble into the ravine, maximizing the deaths and injuries. In this, at least, the killer failed. Although about 70 people were hurt,

The Sunset Limited *hangs off the track in a dry stream bed in the desert outside Phoenix, Arizona. Inset: In a similar tragedy 56 years earlier, tracks had been tampered with causing the derailment of the* City of San Francisco.

some badly, only one person died. Investigators called that a miracle.

4 "Someone obviously intended to have the train drop off the ravine," said Thomas M. Downs, the president of Amtrak. "They could have easily killed a large number of passengers."

5 Sheriff Joe Arpaio concurred. "It's an act of God that more people weren't killed."

6 Clearly, the saboteur knew what he or she was doing. The villain made sure that the train's engineer had no warning of danger. The saboteur rewired the track connection so that all the lights remained green. (Usually, a broken track will cause red lights along the track to flash. That warns the engineer in case a flood or a rock slide knocks out the tracks.)

7 Whoever the killer was had picked the perfect spot—along a blind, right-hand turn. Even if the engineer had seen the damaged tracks, he wouldn't have had time to stop the train. Also, the saboteur picked a very remote location. That remoteness meant that it would take a long time for rescue workers to arrive on the scene. In fact, no rescuers reached the wreck until an hour after the derailment.

8 The people on the *Sunset Limited* did what they could to rescue the injured, but there was nothing they could do for Mitchell Bates. A sleeping car attendant, Bates had worked for the railroad for 20 years. David Lee Flowe was the last person to see him alive. He asked Bates to be certain to wake him up so he wouldn't miss his stop. "Don't you worry about a thing," responded Bates.

9 The crash occurred when most passengers and crew members were sleeping. Crew member Darryl Taylor was in bed in the dormitory car, along with Bates and several others. A loud screech startled everyone. "It felt like the train took a bunny hop," Taylor said, "and I went flying through the air and smashed against a window."

10 Although injured, Taylor kept his wits about him. He and some other crew members grabbed sledgehammers from the emergency cases. They climbed onto the roof of the cars and began smashing windows to save hurt or elderly people who were trapped inside their rooms. "Some of us dropped down into the cars and tied sheets around the injured," he said. "Then we pulled them up through the windows. We rescued 75 to 80 people that way."

11 While he was working, Taylor suddenly remembered Bates. He hadn't seen him since the crash. So he and some others returned to the dormitory car to look for their friend. "I broke the glass in his room because the door was locked shut," said Taylor. Inside they found Mitchell Bates crumpled beneath his mattress. "His body was bent, and his head was smashed," recalled Taylor. "We were yelling, 'Wake up! Please wake up!' I sat by the door and cried."

12 Taylor and his fellow rescuers had pulled most of the people out of their

Rescue workers carry an injured woman from the wreckage of the Sunset Limited.

rooms and onto the roof when the police and medical help at last arrived by helicopter. What they found was a scene of bloody carnage. "It was horrible," said Dennis Dowell, a sheriff's deputy. "People were groaning and screaming and yelling for help. The tops of the fallen cars were littered with bodies, bloodied and injured."

13 Officials soon began to consider who might have committed the crime and why. Was it a copycat crime? Agents for the FBI who investigated the crash thought it could be. That was why they woke John Signor out of bed early that morning. He was the editor and also a contributing writer for the magazine, *SP Trainline*. (*SP* stands for Southern Pacific.) Just a week earlier, Signor had published one of his own articles entitled "Tragedy at Harney." The article was about the tragic derailment of *The City of San Francisco* train on August 12, 1939, near Harney, Nevada. The sabotaged train had tumbled off the track and into a canyon, killing 24 people. The police never found who committed that crime.

14 Now, 56 years later, a similar derailment had occurred. Many of the details were the same. At Harney, someone had removed a small section of track in a remote area on a curve before a bridge. Also, the alarm system was bypassed in the same way.

15 Had the article inspired some lunatic with a grudge against the railroad? The FBI asked Signor to help them find suspects. He gave them a list of all the people who subscribed to the magazine. The magazine had only about 1,800 readers. They were mostly railroad buffs or former employees of the Southern Pacific railroad. As with the Harney tragedy, however, police failed to find the person who caused the crash of the *Sunset Limited.*

If you have been timed while reading this article, enter your reading time below. Then turn to the Words-per-Minute Table on page 133 and look up your reading speed (words per minute). Enter your reading speed on the graph on page 134.

Reading Time: Lesson 8

________ : ________

Minutes *Seconds*

A Finding the Main Idea

One statement below expresses the main idea of the article. One statement is too general, or too broad. The other statement explains only part of the article; it is too narrow. Label the statements using the following key:

M—Main Idea **B—Too Broad** **N—Too Narrow**

_______ 1. Mitchell Bates was the only person who died when the *Sunset Limited* derailed.

_______ 2. Sabotage by an unknown person caused the derailment of the *Sunset Limited*, which killed one person and injured many others.

_______ 3. Any train derailment can cause damage, injury, or even death.

_______ Score 15 points for a correct M answer.

_______ Score 5 points for each correct B or N answer.

_______ **Total Score:** Finding the Main Idea

B Recalling Facts

How well do you remember the facts in the article? Put an X in the box next to the answer that correctly completes each statement about the article.

1. The *Sunset Limited* train was headed for
- ☐ a. Hyder, Arizona.
- ☐ b. Los Angeles, California.
- ☐ c. Harney, Nevada.

2. The saboteur rewired the track connection so that
- ☐ a. all the lights on the track remained red.
- ☐ b. all the lights on the track remained green.
- ☐ c. the train would blow up.

3. Darryl Taylor and others used sheets to
- ☐ a. signal for help.
- ☐ b. break windows on the train.
- ☐ c. pull passengers out of the train cars.

4. The police and medical help arrived by
- ☐ a. helicopter.
- ☐ b. train.
- ☐ c. ambulance.

5. John Signor
- ☐ a. was an FBI agent.
- ☐ b. was considered a suspect in the *Sunset Limited* crime.
- ☐ c. wrote an article about a similar crime.

Score 5 points for each correct answer.

_______ **Total Score:** Recalling Facts

C Making Inferences

When you combine your own experience and information from a text to draw a conclusion that is not directly stated in that text, you are making an inference. Below are five statements that may or may not be inferences based on information in the article. Label the statements using the following key:

C—Correct Inference **F—Faulty Inference**

_______ 1. Darryl Taylor and the other rescuers acted heroically after the *Sunset Limited* derailed.

_______ 2. The saboteur was probably disappointed that only one person died in the crash.

_______ 3. The passengers had no warning before the train crashed.

_______ 4. A former employee of the Southern Pacific railroad sabotaged the *Sunset Limited.*

_______ 5. If Darryl Taylor had found Mitchell Bates earlier, Bates would have lived.

Score 5 points for each correct answer.

_______ **Total Score:** Making Inferences

D Using Words Precisely

Each numbered sentence below contains an underlined word or phrase from the article. Following the sentence are three definitions. One definition is closest to the meaning of the underlined word. One definition is opposite or nearly opposite. Label those two definitions using the following key. Do not label the remaining definition.

C—Closest **O—Opposite or Nearly Opposite**

1. This was <u>sabotage</u>.

_______ a. support

_______ b. mystery

_______ c. destructive mischief

2. Someone had <u>deliberately</u> pulled up 29 spikes and removed 4 bolts from the track.

_______ a. automatically

_______ b. carelessly

_______ c. intentionally

3. He or she pulled the spikes and bolts from the trestle so that the cars would tumble into the ravine, <u>maximizing</u> the deaths and injuries.

_______ a. increasing

_______ b. decreasing

_______ c. reporting on

4. What they found was a scene of bloody <u>carnage</u>.

_______ a. accident

_______ b. slaughter

_______ c. revival

5. Had the article inspired some lunatic with a grudge against the railroad?

_____ a. admiration for

_____ b. fantasy about

_____ c. resentment against

_____ Score 3 points for each correct C answer.

_____ Score 2 points for each correct O answer.

_____ **Total Score:** Using Words Precisely

Enter the four total scores in the spaces below, and add them together to find your Reading Comprehension Score. Then record your score on the graph on page 135.

Score	Question Type	Lesson 8
_____	Finding the Main Idea	
_____	Recalling Facts	
_____	Making Inferences	
_____	Using Words Precisely	
_____	**Reading Comprehension Score**	

Author's Approach

Put an X in the box next to the correct answer.

1. What is the author's purpose in writing "Sabotage in the Desert"?

☐ a. To express an opinion about the dangers of train travel

☐ b. To tell the reader about the sabotage of the *Sunset Limited*

☐ c. To emphasize the similarities between the *Sunset Limited* crash and the crash of *The City of San Francisco*

2. Which of the following statements from the article best describes Darryl Taylor's response to the disaster?

☐ a. "Although injured, Taylor kept his wits about him."

☐ b. "While he was working, Taylor suddenly remembered Bates."

☐ c. "Crew member Darryl Taylor was in bed in the dormitory car, along with Bates and several others."

3. What does the author imply by saying "The people on the *Sunset Limited* did what they could to rescue the injured, but there was nothing they could do for Mitchell Bates"?

☐ a. Bates refused their help.

☐ b. Bates didn't need any help.

☐ c. Bates was dead.

4. How is the author's purpose for writing the article expressed in paragraph 13?

☐ a. The author describes a train crash that killed 24 people.

☐ b. The author informs the reader that John Signor was the editor of *SP Trainline.*

☐ c. The author informs the reader that the sabotage of the *Sunset Limited* may have been a copycat crime.

_____ Number of correct answers

Record your personal assessment of your work on the Critical Thinking Chart on page 136.

Summarizing and Paraphrasing

Follow the directions provided for questions 1 and 2. Put an X in the box next to the correct answer for question 3.

1. Complete the following one-sentence summary of the article using the lettered phrases from the phrase bank below. Write the letters on the lines.

Phrase Bank:

a. the rescue efforts of Darryl Taylor and others
b. a description of the train's crash and sabotage
c. the theory that it may have been a copycat crime

The article about the *Sunset Limited* begins with _________, goes on to explain _________, and ends with _________.

2. Reread paragraph 10 in the article. Below, write a summary of the paragraph in no more than 25 words.

____

____

____

____

Reread your summary and decide whether it covers the important ideas in the paragraph. Next, decide how to shorten the summary to 15 words or less without leaving out any essential information. Write this summary below.

____

____

____

3. Choose the best one-sentence paraphrase for the following sentence from the article:

"He or she pulled the spikes and bolts from the trestle so that the cars would tumble into the ravine, maximizing the deaths and injuries."

☐ a. The person sabotaged the trestle so that the train cars would fall into the ravine and more people would be killed and injured.
☐ b. The person sabotaged the trestle so that cars driving by would fall into the ravine and kill and injure more people.
☐ c. The person sabotaged the trestle to reduce the number of dead and injured people.

_________ Number of correct answers

Record your personal assessment of your work on the Critical Thinking Chart on page 136.

Critical Thinking

Put an X in the box next to the correct answer for questions 1 and 3. Follow the directions provided for the other questions.

1. From what Darryl Taylor said, you can predict that he
☐ a. hadn't known Mitchell Bates very well.
☐ b. was a good friend of Mitchell Bates.
☐ c. hadn't liked Mitchell Bates.

2. Using what is told about the sabotage of the *Sunset Limited* and *The City of San Francisco* in the article, name three ways the derailment of the *Sunset Limited* is similar to and three ways it is different from the derailment of *The City of San Francisco*. Cite the paragraph number(s) where you found details in the article to support your conclusions.

Similarities

Differences

3. What was the cause of the train's derailment?

- ☐ a. The train crossed a trestle.
- ☐ b. Someone had pulled up spikes and removed bolts from the track.
- ☐ c. The train tumbled down a ravine.

4. In which paragraph did you find the information or details to answer question 3?

______ Number of correct answers

Record your personal assessment of your work on the Critical Thinking Chart on page 136.

Personal Response

What was most surprising or interesting to you about this article?

Self-Assessment

I can't really understand how

POISON ON THE DRUGSTORE SHELF

Four years after the original Tylenol poisonings, tragedy struck again. Here, a manager at a Walgreen's drugstore in Chicago removes packages of Tylenol from the shelves. A New York woman died of cyanide poisoning after taking the pain reliever.

On a morning in early October 1982, Adam Janus, age 27, woke up with a pain in his chest. The pain wasn't too severe, but it bothered him. He went out to a local store and bought a bottle of Extra-Strength Tylenol capsules. He returned to his house in Arlington Heights, Illinois, where he took at least one capsule. An hour later he collapsed. His family rushed him to the hospital, watching in horror as doctors struggled to revive him. But their efforts made no difference. Adam's heart and lungs had stopped working. Dr. Thomas Kim, one of the doctors who had tried to save Adam, was shocked at the young man's death. "He suffered sudden death without warning," said Dr. Kim. "It was most unusual."

2 Adam's family was overwhelmed by his unexpected death. That evening they sat together at the Janus home. No one was feeling very well, and someone offered to buy a bottle of aspirin. But Stanley Janus, Adam's younger brother,

pointed out the bottle of Tylenol in the kitchen. He and his wife Theresa each took at least one capsule. Five hours after his older brother's death, Stanley Janus was pronounced dead. Theresa died two days later.

3 In nearby Elk Grove Village, 12-year-old Mary Kellerman was suffering from a cold. She took a Tylenol and died. Mary Reiner of Winfield had recently returned from the hospital with her new baby. She also took a Tylenol and died. Paula Prince, a flight attendant, was found dead in her apartment in Chicago. In the bathroom was an open bottle of Tylenol.

4 By the end of the week, seven people in the Chicago area had died after taking Tylenol. Each person had swallowed a capsule loaded with cyanide (SYE-uh-nide), an extremely dangerous poison.

5 Apparently, the killer had taken apart a number of Tylenol capsules. Then he or she had inserted huge quantities of cyanide into the red half of the capsules before putting them back together again. After adding the poison, the killer had returned the contaminated bottles of medicine to store shelves. As Winfield's police chief said, "Apparently a very sophisticated and very malicious person is at large who had to spend a lot of time and effort on this terrible plan."

6 Even though the seven victims were all from the Chicago area, people around the country panicked. Cyanide in drugstore medicine! Who would die next? Johnson & Johnson, the company that makes Tylenol, stopped all production and asked store owners to remove the capsules from their shelves. Police stations and hospitals were filled with people convinced they had been poisoned. A Chicago hospital received 700 calls in one day. But Dr. William Robertson, director of the Poison Control Center in Seattle, had some advice for callers. He said, "If it was going to be a lethal dose, you wouldn't have time to call."

7 Illinois's attorney general began a nationwide search for the killer. Police all over the country looked into old and new cases, hoping to find a promising lead. In California, Pennsylvania, and Wyoming, they found similar poisoning cases. But some were clearly unrelated, and others were "copycat" cases set up by people interested in attention.

8 Still, the copycat killers were dangerous in their own right. As Halloween approached, some cities and towns banned trick-or-treating. Citizens were afraid that children would be hurt. And in fact, three children in Chicago got sick after eating chocolate bars. People were afraid to buy anything from the store. Food and drug manufacturers began to realize that they had to make safer packages in order to stay in business.

9 In mid-October a letter showed up at the office of McNeil Consumer Products. McNeil is a branch of Johnson & Johnson—the branch that manufactures Tylenol. The letter demanded one million dollars, payable to a mailbox at a Chicago bank. The letter threatened more

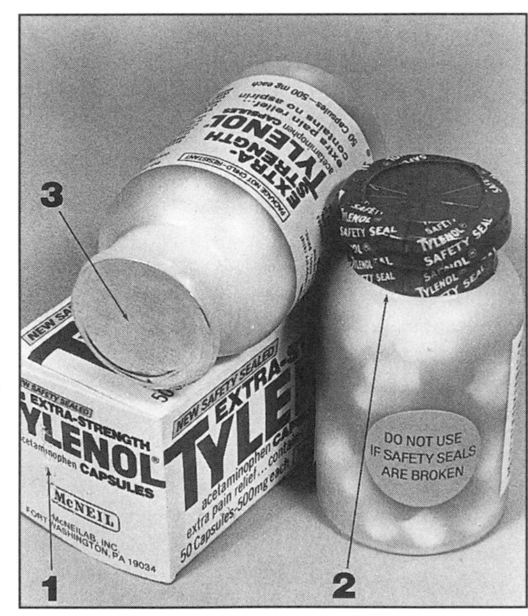

Tamper resistant packaging was developed as a result of the Tylenol poisonings.

poisonings if the company refused to send the money.

10 The extortion letter was eventually linked to James and LeAnn Lewis—also known as Robert and Nancy Richardson. FBI agents soon learned about James Lewis's frightening past. Kansas City police recognized him as a tax accountant who was once charged in the killing of an elderly man. He was also accused of attacking his mother with an ax, and he had been hospitalized twice for mental health problems. In 1974 his five-year-old daughter had died after heart surgery, and a police officer who knew Lewis claimed he had always blamed Johnson & Johnson for the girl's death.

11 But when the FBI entered the Lewises' apartment in Chicago, they found no trace of the couple. They tracked the pair to New York City, where more than 100 FBI agents searched for them.

12 In November the *Chicago Tribune* received a letter signed by Robert Richardson—an alias often used by James Lewis. The letter said, "My wife and I have not committed the Chicago-area Tylenol murders." And records showed that the Lewises had been in New York when the tainted Tylenol first appeared on shelves in Chicago.

13 James Lewis was finally arrested in December when a librarian at a branch of the New York Public Library recognized his face. He went to trial, accused of trying to extort money from Johnson & Johnson. Lewis was convicted of that charge and sent to prison. But he was never charged with the Tylenol murders. And most FBI officials think he probably did not commit them.

14 Although the Tylenol killer was never found, the tragedy did change the ways in which food and medicine are packaged. Bottles and boxes now have special safety seals. Pills are often enclosed in individual plastic packs.

15 Still, better packaging does not guarantee safety. In 1986 Diane Elsroth bought a bottle of Tylenol. Minutes later she was dead, killed by cyanide that had been inserted into the capsules. The box was brand-new. The package had three separate safety seals. But the killer had somehow managed to get past those seals to add poison to the capsules.

16 In the end, there is nothing anyone can do to make packages completely safe. But food and drug companies are doing their best to make sure that their products are as tamperproof as possible.

If you have been timed while reading this article, enter your reading time below. Then turn to the Words-per-Minute Table on page 133 and look up your reading speed (words per minute). Enter your reading speed on the graph on page 134.

Reading Time: Lesson 9

_______ : _______

Minutes *Seconds*

A Finding the Main Idea

One statement below expresses the main idea of the article. One statement is too general, or too broad. The other statement explains only part of the article; it is too narrow. Label the statements using the following key:

M—Main Idea **B—Too Broad** **N—Too Narrow**

_____ 1. Adam Janus bought contaminated Tylenol at a local store.

_____ 2. Several people died after a killer put cyanide into Tylenol capsules.

_____ 3. Contaminated food and drugs caused a nationwide panic.

_____ Score 15 points for a correct M answer.

_____ Score 5 points for each correct B or N answer.

_____ **Total Score:** Finding the Main Idea

B Recalling Facts

How well do you remember the facts in the article? Put an X in the box next to the answer that correctly completes each statement about the article.

1. The first Tylenol deaths took place in
   - ☐ a. 1986.
   - ☐ b. 1982.
   - ☐ c. 1963.
2. The seven people who died all lived in
   - ☐ a. Seattle suburbs.
   - ☐ b. California, Pennsylvania, or Wyoming.
   - ☐ c. the Chicago area.
3. James Lewis was convicted of
   - ☐ a. trying to extort money from Johnson & Johnson.
   - ☐ b. murdering at least seven people.
   - ☐ c. stealing manufacturing secrets from Johnson & Johnson.
4. Lewis also used the alias
   - ☐ a. Robert Richardson.
   - ☐ b. Richard Smith.
   - ☐ c. Ralph Robertson.
5. Because of the Tylenol scare, food and drug companies
   - ☐ a. stopped making painkillers.
   - ☐ b. made packaging safer.
   - ☐ c. boycotted Johnson & Johnson products.

Score 5 points for each correct answer.

_____ **Total Score:** Recalling Facts

Making Inferences

When you combine your own experience and information from a text to draw a conclusion that is not directly stated in that text, you are making an inference. Below are five statements that may or may not be inferences based on information in the article. Label the statements using the following key:

C—Correct Inference **F—Faulty Inference**

_____ 1. The Janus family suffered a terrible tragedy.

_____ 2. The Tylenol killer was a careful, intelligent person.

_____ 3. The copycat cases did not worry the police.

_____ 4. The FBI had no trouble tracking down the Lewises.

_____ 5. The Tylenol case influenced the ways in which companies now package their products.

Score 5 points for each correct answer.

_____ **Total Score:** Making Inferences

D Using Words Precisely

Each numbered sentence below contains an underlined word or phrase from the article. Following the sentence are three definitions. One definition is closest to the meaning of the underlined word. One definition is opposite or nearly opposite. Label those two definitions using the following key. Do not label the remaining definition.

C—Closest **O—Opposite or Nearly Opposite**

1. After adding the poison, the killer had returned the contaminated bottles of medicine to store shelves.

_____ a. poisoned

_____ b. purified

_____ c. opened

2. As Winfield's police chief said, "Apparently a…very malicious person is at large who had to spend a lot of time and effort on this terrible plan."

_____ a. kindly

_____ b. courageous

_____ c. spiteful

3. In November the *Chicago Tribune* received a letter signed by Robert Richardson—an alias often used by James Lewis.

_____ a. a real name

_____ b. a fake name

_____ c. a last name

4. He went to trial, accused of trying to extort money from Johnson & Johnson.

_______ a. blackmail

_______ b. counterfeit

_______ c. earn legally

5. Lewis was convicted of that charge and sent to prison.

_______ a. declared innocent

_______ b. questioned about

_______ c. found guilty

_______ Score 3 points for each correct C answer.

_______ Score 2 points for each correct O answer.

_______ **Total Score:** Using Words Precisely

Enter the four total scores in the spaces below, and add them together to find your Reading Comprehension Score. Then record your score on the graph on page 135.

Score	Question Type	Lesson 9
_______	Finding the Main Idea	
_______	Recalling Facts	
_______	Making Inferences	
_______	Using Words Precisely	
_______	**Reading Comprehension Score**	

Author's Approach

Put an X in the box next to the correct answer.

1. What is the author's purpose in writing "Poison on the Drugstore Shelf"?

☐ a. To encourage the reader not to use any medicine

☐ b. To inform the reader about the tainted Tylenol scare in the 1980s

☐ c. To convey a mood of fear

2. Choose the statement below that is the weakest argument for charging James Lewis and his wife with the Tylenol murders.

☐ a. They sent a letter to Johnson & Johnson threatening more poisonings if the company wouldn't pay them one million dollars.

☐ b. Lewis blamed Johnson & Johnson for his five-year-old daughter's death.

☐ c. Lewis and his wife had been in New York when the poisoned Tylenol appeared on drugstore shelves in Chicago.

3. How is the author's purpose for writing the article expressed in paragraph 15?

☐ a. The author inspires fear of all drugstore medicine.

☐ b. The author says that current ways of packaging medicine are not good enough.

☐ c. The author tells the reader about another case of Tylenol poisoning.

_______ Number of correct answers

Record your personal assessment of your work on the Critical Thinking Chart on page 136.

Summarizing and Paraphrasing

Follow the directions provided for questions 1 and 2. Put an X in the box next to the correct answer for question 3.

1. Look for the important ideas and events in paragraphs 1 and 2. Summarize those paragraphs in one or two sentences.

____

____

____

2. Complete the following one-sentence summary of the article using the lettered phrases from the phrase bank below. Write the letters on the lines.

Phrase Bank:

a. the cause of those deaths
b. several mysterious deaths in the Chicago area
c. the search for the killer and efforts to improve packaging

The article about the Tylenol tampering scare begins with _________, goes on to explain _________, and ends with _________.

3. Choose the best one-sentence paraphrase for the following sentence from the article:

"James Lewis was finally arrested in December when a librarian at a branch of the New York Public Library recognized his face."

☐ a. In December, a librarian in a New York library recognized Lewis and had him arrested.
☐ b. A librarian in New York City arrested Lewis in December.
☐ c. A librarian who knew James Lewis arrested him in a branch of the New York Public Library.

_________ Number of correct answers

Record your personal assessment of your work on the Critical Thinking Chart on page 136.

Critical Thinking

Follow the directions provided for questions 1, 3, and 4. Put an X in the box next to the correct answer for the other questions.

1. For each statement below, write O if it expresses an opinion and write F if it expresses a fact.

_______ a. Food and drug companies could do more to make their products tamperproof.

_______ b. Prescription medicine is safer than medicines found on drugstore shelves.

_______ c. James Lewis was convicted of trying to extort money from Johnson & Johnson.

2. From the events in the article, you can predict that the following will happen next :

☐ a. Food and drug companies will eliminate tamperproof seals because they do not guarantee safety.
☐ b. Food and drug companies will continue to take steps to make their products safe.
☐ c. The production of Tylenol and other drugstore medicines will be permanently halted.

3. Choose from the letters below to correctly complete the following statement. Write the letters on the lines.

   On the positive side, _________, but on the negative side _________.

   a. bottles and boxes now have special safety seals
   b. copycat crimes occurred after the Tylenol murders
   c. poison was added to Tylenol capsules enclosed in a sealed box

4. Think about cause-effect relationships in the article. Fill in the blanks in the cause-effect chart, drawing from the letters below.

Cause	Effect
Adam Janus took a Tylenol capsule.	__________
__________	James Lewis was arrested.
Tylenol was tainted with cyanide.	__________

   a. Drug companies began to enclose their products in bottles and boxes with special safety seals.
   b. He died.
   c. He tried to extort money from Johnson & Johnson.

5. What did you have to do to answer question 2?

☐ a. find an opinion (what someone thinks about something)
☐ b. find a cause (why something happened)
☐ c. make a prediction (what might happen next)

_________ Number of correct answers

Record your personal assessment of your work on the Critical Thinking Chart on page 136.

Personal Response

I disagree with the author because

____

____

____

____

Self-Assessment

One good question about this article that was not asked would be

____

____

____

____

and the answer is

____

____

____

____

LESSON 10

FIRE IN THE SUBWAY

A 1985 report had it right. The London subway—known as the Tube—was a potential firetrap. The report was written by the Passenger Transport Review Group. It declared that the city's subway system did not meet even minimal safety standards. The report said the subway should have automatic sprinklers. There should be smoke detectors and fire doors. Flammable building materials should be cleaned up. Subway workers ought to receive better fire emergency training.

2 When the report came out, no one paid much attention to it. Its suggestions were totally ignored. In fact, to save money, the cleaning crew at King's Cross station was cut from 14 workers to two. The cuts did not seem to concern subway officials. After all, the 124-year-old Tube had a fine safety record. Since the end of World War II, only four people had died in subway fires. John Cope, Director of Underground Operations, boasted, "Our fire prevention procedures are among the most stringent anywhere. There is more of a danger crossing the road outside the station than there is down here [in the subway]."

3 On November 17, 1987, Cope's words came back to haunt him. At 7:29 P.M., as the evening rush hour slowed down, a fire broke out at King's Cross subway stop. This was London's busiest station. Five subway lines and a major railroad converge here.

4 The blaze started under a wooden escalator. The top of the escalator was 20 feet below ground. At that level were the exit doors and the circular ticket concourse.

5 Deborah Wren, a 19-year-old secretary, got off her subway train and headed up the escalator. "When I got a quarter of the way up the escalator, I could smell burning," she said. "I got further up and I could see the red flames underneath [the escalator treads.]" Wren shoved her way past people to warn a subway official.

The charred remains of the King's Cross subway station show the extent of the fire damage.

Firefighters clean up around the King's Cross subway station.

"Excuse me," she told him, "I think there's a fire on the escalator."

6 But it was too late. At the bottom of the escalator, dozens of people pushed their way onto the moving stairs. They didn't see the fire up ahead of them. The fire, which started about halfway up the escalator, quickly spread upward. The ticket concourse soon became a burning inferno. Yet the escalator continued to deliver more and more people into the thick of the blaze. Panic-stricken, people trapped in the concourse tried either to race through the flames toward the exit doors or go back down the escalator. Going back down, however, was nearly impossible because so many people were still coming up the death belt.

7 The heat in the ticket concourse was incredible. It turned the metal ticket-vending machines into molten lumps. Roof tiles melted, and the concrete floor cracked. The turnstiles turned black. Some of the passengers trapped in the concourse were burned beyond recognition. Many of those who made it to the exits were badly burned. Survivors later told of passengers with their clothes and hair aflame as they desperately crawled their way toward the exits.

8 The scene in the subway was utter bedlam. "Everyone was so confused," said passenger Mark Silver. "People were shouting and screaming and panicking."

9 There was no obvious exit route for those who were trapped. The smoke made matters worse. "There was thick, black, choking smoke everywhere," said Doug Patterson, a subway guard. "It was impossible to see anything."

10 The fire caused an electrical blackout, so there were no lights to guide people through the smoke. Even the subway attendants and the firefighters who rushed to the scene were not sure what to do. At first, they directed passengers to go up the escalator because they couldn't see that it was burning at the other end. "The ceiling above was on fire and debris was falling down, but the escalator was still moving," said Andrew Lea, who managed to get off the flaming stairs.

11 For a short while, subway trains kept stopping, dumping more passengers out onto the smoke-filled platform. Later, the trains were instructed not to stop. As they rolled through King's Cross station with their doors closed, people on the platform frantically banged on the car windows in the vain hope of being rescued.

12 It took firefighters several hours to douse the blaze. By then the damage had been done. The fire was by far the worst disaster in the history of the London subway. Thirty people, including one firefighter, died in the flames. Eighty others were badly burned. "It's a major tragedy, and our heart just goes out to all those who are involved and their families," said Sir Keith Bright, the chairman of the London Regional Transport. "I feel absolutely shattered by what has happened."

13 People had two contradictory feelings about the disaster. On the one hand, they reasoned that it could have been a lot worse. The fire could have broken out an hour or so earlier when the station would really have been packed with commuters. About 32,000 passengers an hour move through King's Cross at the peak of the rush hour. Then the death toll would have been much higher.

14 On the other hand, many people believed that the fire would have been far less tragic if only the subway had followed just one of the suggestions outlined in the 1985 report. Automatic sprinklers, for instance, would have saved many lives. According to Michael Doherty, deputy chief of the London Fire Brigade, "[With sprinklers,] we would not have had the outcome we have had." But there were no sprinklers, and in the aftermath of the fire, Londoners found their faith in the safety of the Tube shattered.

If you have been timed while reading this article, enter your reading time below. Then turn to the Words-per-Minute Table on page 133 and look up your reading speed (words per minute). Enter your reading speed on the graph on page 134.

Reading Time: Lesson 10

________ : ________

Minutes *Seconds*

A Finding the Main Idea

One statement below expresses the main idea of the article. One statement is too general, or too broad. The other statement explains only part of the article; it is too narrow. Label the statements using the following key:

M—Main Idea **B—Too Broad** **N—Too Narrow**

_______ 1. Deborah Wren told a subway official that the escalator was on fire, but the warning came too late.

_______ 2. Before the fire in King's Cross station, the London Tube had had an excellent safety record.

_______ 3. A fire in London's busy King's Cross Tube station trapped commuters in a deadly inferno.

_______ Score 15 points for a correct M answer.

_______ Score 5 points for each correct B or N answer.

_______ **Total Score:** Finding the Main Idea

B Recalling Facts

How well do you remember the facts in the article? Put an X in the box next to the answer that correctly completes each statement about the article.

1. The suggestions made by the Passenger Transport Review Group were
   - ☐ a. largely ignored.
   - ☐ b. taken very seriously.
   - ☐ c. proved to be unnecessary.

2. The fire at the King's Cross subway stop started
   - ☐ a. in the ticket concourse.
   - ☐ b. in a subway train.
   - ☐ c. under the escalator.

3. There were no lights to help guide people in the station because
   - ☐ a. the thick, black smoke darkened the lights.
   - ☐ b. the fire caused an electrical blackout.
   - ☐ c. they hadn't been installed.

4. At first, the firefighters who rushed to the scene
   - ☐ a. led people to the exits.
   - ☐ b. helped people onto subway trains.
   - ☐ c. directed people to go up the escalator.

5. The subway fire killed
   - ☐ a. 30 people.
   - ☐ b. 80 people.
   - ☐ c. 124 people.

Score 5 points for each correct answer.

_______ **Total Score:** Recalling Facts

C Making Inferences

When you combine your own experience and information from a text to draw a conclusion that is not directly stated in that text, you are making an inference. Below are five statements that may or may not be inferences based on information in the article. Label the statements using the following key:

C—Correct Inference **F—Faulty Inference**

_______ 1. Fewer people would have died in the fire if the subway directors had followed the suggestions made by the safety report.

_______ 2. The subway attendants had been well trained and knew what procedures to follow in a fire.

_______ 3. Everyone in the ticket concourse remained calm during the fire.

_______ 4. Fires in London's subway system occur frequently.

_______ 5. For a while after the fire, many Londoners were afraid to take the Tube.

Score 5 points for each correct answer.

_______ **Total Score:** Making Inferences

D Using Words Precisely

Each numbered sentence below contains an underlined word or phrase from the article. Following the sentence are three definitions. One definition is closest to the meaning of the underlined word. One definition is opposite or nearly opposite. Label those two definitions using the following key. Do not label the remaining definition.

C—Closest **O—Opposite or Nearly Opposite**

1. The London subway—known as the Tube—was a potential firetrap.

_______ a. impossible

_______ b. likely

_______ c. powerful

2. John Cope, Director of Underground Operations, boasted, "Our fire prevention procedures are among the most stringent anywhere."

_______ a. complex

_______ b. casual

_______ c. strict

3. The ticket concourse soon became a burning inferno.

_______ a. raging blaze

_______ b. internal area

_______ c. tiny spark

4. The scene in the subway was utter bedlam.

_______ a. beauty

_______ b. tranquility

_______ c. confusion

5. It took firefighters several hours to douse the blaze.

_______ a. ignite

_______ b. put out

_______ c. reach

_______ Score 3 points for each correct C answer.

_______ Score 2 points for each correct O answer.

_______ **Total Score:** Using Words Precisely

Enter the four total scores in the spaces below, and add them together to find your Reading Comprehension Score. Then record your score on the graph on page 135.

Score	Question Type	Lesson 10
_______	Finding the Main Idea	
_______	Recalling Facts	
_______	Making Inferences	
_______	Using Words Precisely	
_______	**Reading Comprehension Score**	

Author's Approach

Put an X in the box next to the correct answer.

1. The main purpose of the first paragraph is to

☐ a. explain that London's subway system was unsafe.

☐ b. inform the reader that the London subway is known as the Tube.

☐ c. describe Passenger Transport Review Group.

2. From the statements below, choose those that you believe the author would agree with.

☐ a. London subway officials don't care about the people who use the Tube.

☐ b. The subway fire might have been prevented if the safety suggestions from the 1985 report had been adopted.

☐ c. The people trapped in the subway didn't receive any help from subway attendants.

3. From the statement "On November 17, 1987, Cope's words came back to haunt him," you can conclude that the author wants the reader to think that Cope

☐ a. believed in ghosts.

☐ b. came to regret what he had said.

☐ c. purposefully told a lie.

4. The author probably wrote this article in order to

☐ a. warn the reader about the London subway system.

☐ b. compare the London subway system with that in American cities.

☐ c. tell the reader about the terrible fire in a London subway station.

_______ Number of correct answers

Record your personal assessment of your work on the Critical Thinking Chart on page 136.

Summarizing and Paraphrasing

Put an X in the box next to the correct answer.

1. Below are summaries of the article. Choose the summary that says all the most important things about the article but in the fewest words.

☐ a. A fire in London's King's Cross station killed and badly burned many people. The fire might have been far less tragic if some of the safety standards suggested by a report made in 1985 had been adopted.

☐ b. A fire in the King's Cross subway station killed and injured more than one hundred people.

☐ c. By the time people became aware of the fire in the King's Cross subway station, it was too late. Commuters walked right into the blaze, and many were unable to escape. More than a hundred people died or were injured in the fire.

2. Choose the sentence that correctly restates the following sentence from the article:

"Panic-stricken, people trapped in the concourse tried either to race through the flames toward the exit doors or to go back down the escalator."

☐ a. People held races to see who could reach the exit doors or escalator first.

☐ b. People became panic-stricken when they saw the flames coming from the escalator.

☐ c. Some frightened people ran through the flames to get to the exit doors, while others tried to go back down the escalator.

________ Number of correct answers

Record your personal assessment of your work on the Critical Thinking Chart on page 136.

Critical Thinking

Put an X in the box next to the correct answer for questions 1, 2, and 4. Follow the directions provided for question 3.

1. Which of the following statements from the article is an opinion rather than a fact?

☐ a. "At 7:29 P.M., as the evening rush hour slowed down, a fire broke out at King's Cross subway stop."

☐ b. "'There is more of a danger crossing the road outside the station than there is down here [in the subway].'"

☐ c. "The fire was by far the worst disaster in the history of the London subway."

2. From the information in paragraph 14, you can predict that

☐ a. no one uses the London Tube anymore.

☐ b. London subway directors continued to ignore the suggestions put forth in the 1985 report.

☐ c. many of the suggestions made in the 1985 report were soon put into practice.

3. Choose from the letters below to correctly complete the following statement. Write the letters on the lines.

On the positive side, ________, but on the negative side ________.

a. the fire's death toll was higher than it should have been

b. the fire surprised everyone at the King's Cross subway station

c. the fire didn't break out at the peak of the rush hour

4. What was the effect of the tremendous heat in the ticket concourse?

☐ a. It melted the ticket-vending machines.

☐ b. It created thick, black, choking smoke everywhere.

☐ c. It resulted in an electrical blackout.

_______ Number of correct answers

Record your personal assessment of your work on the Critical Thinking Chart on page 136.

Personal Response

I can't believe

____

____

____

____

Self-Assessment

The part I found most difficult about the article was

____

____

____

____

I found this difficult because

____

____

____

____

THE WORLD SERIES EARTHQUAKE

Candlestick Park was packed with 60,000 noisy and excited baseball fans. They were pumped up for game three of the 1989 World Series. The World Series is always a big event, but fans in the San Francisco Bay Area were more excited than usual. Two local teams—the Giants and the Athletics—were battling for the championship.

2 About a half hour before game time, most of the players and coaches were on the field. The fans were cheering, waiting for the introductions. But within moments, baseball was wiped from their minds when Candlestick Park swayed in a massive earthquake. Millions of television viewers across the country heard the news just before their screens went dark.

3 Although it lasted for only 20 seconds, the quake was the strongest to hit the region since 1906, measuring 6.9 on the Richter scale. It was exactly 5:04 on October 17, 1989, when buildings in downtown San Francisco began to vibrate. The Nimitz Freeway and the Bay Bridge began to shudder. And people all over the Bay Area began to panic.

4 At Candlestick Park, sportswriter Ron Fimrite was chatting with other reporters

Cars teeter on the brink of the collapsed roadway of San Francisco's Bay Bridge.

in the press box. He suddenly felt the stadium begin to move. Above him, the mounted television sets swayed on their stands, and Fimrite heard a low rumbling. But the creaky old stadium did not seem damaged, so he assumed that the quake had not been serious.

5 The fans in the stadium's upper decks, however, knew better. They saw spaces in the concrete open up. They saw people bouncing all over and the foul line poles in right field whip back and forth. And they heard the scoreboard rattle and watched as it went blank.

6 One fan had decided to get a hot dog moments before the quake hit. His hunger saved him from the dangerous chunk of concrete that crashed into his seat.

7 Pitcher Bob Welch was in the trainer's room getting liniment rubbed into his shoulder. He was the starting pitcher for the Oakland A's, and in minutes he would walk out to the bullpen. The rumbling caught his attention. "I thought they were rolling barrels on the ramps above the clubhouse," Welch said. Then he realized it was an earthquake. After the tremors stopped, the pitcher dove into the stands to hug his wife.

8 Amazingly, no one in the baseball park seemed to be seriously hurt. Some shaken fans quickly headed for the exits. Others waited in their seats, and a few even yelled, "Play ball!" But police cars were circling the stadium. And soon officials announced that the game had been canceled.

9 Fans filed out of Candlestick Park slowly and calmly. Some stopped along the way to gather around portable radios. They listened to reports of bridges down and freeways collapsing. And they began to fear what awaited them outside the stadium.

10 On their tense drive home, fans saw plumes of black smoke rising into the sky. Everything was strangely dark. Electricity and telephone lines were dead. Traffic lights weren't working, so residents directed cars with flashlights. Broken glass glinted on sidewalks, and fallen bricks and concrete had tumbled into streets. People were seen huddled on street corners, afraid to go inside crumpled buildings.

11 The Marina district, one of San Francisco's historic neighborhoods, was hardest hit by the tremors. Foundations cracked and crumbled, and 60 homes fell apart. Firefighters found an entire block engulfed in flames after a gas main burst. Police had to evacuate thousands of people, and many had nowhere to go.

12 The most serious destruction occurred on the double-decker Nimitz Freeway in Oakland. During rush hour, a mile-long stretch of the upper deck collapsed onto the lower level. Dozens of motorists had concrete and cars suddenly fall on top of them. Cars on the streets below were also hit with debris. Rescue teams and Oakland

A rescue worker tends to a victim of the Nimitz Freeway collapse.

residents raced to the scene. By then motorists stuck in the concrete sandwich were honking their horns for help.

13 Dorothy Otto was trapped on the lower level. She had been driving along when a car from above slammed down on her hood and another landed on the roof. She knew she was injured. A metal bolt from the emergency hand brake had lodged in her left foot, and her toes were smashed. When Otto's screams for help went unheard, she wrote a good-bye note to her husband. She did not know if she would get out alive. Finally, a woman from the top deck heard Otto's cries and climbed down. It took rescuers four hours to free Otto. "I was in a little coffin," she said later. "I thought I would suffocate."

14 It was difficult for rescuers to reach the stranded motorists. They had only two to four feet of crawl space between the freeway layers. And because the concrete slabs were so heavy, it took hours to break the pieces and move them. They worked frantically despite the danger of more aftershocks. More jolts could have caused the rest of the freeway to collapse. Throughout the night and for several days, rescuers pulled bodies from the freeway.

15 Just as they began to lose hope of finding survivors, workers saw a man clenching his fist in the window of his crushed car. He had been buried alive in the debris for 90 hours! After five hours of digging, rescuers pulled Buck Helm, age 57, from the wreckage. Although he was badly injured and barely conscious, he waved his arms at the workers as he was carried to the ambulance.

16 Helm's family and friends were overjoyed with his rescue. It was a miracle that he survived; 35 other motorists didn't.

17 About a mile away from the Nimitz Freeway, there was more destruction. A 50-foot section of the Bay Bridge, which connects San Francisco with Oakland, buckled and broke in the quake. One driver was killed as the section landed on the lower deck. Some cars were left teetering on the brink. Bruce Stephan thought he and his passenger were going to die as the roadway dropped. But something caught the car, and they were able to crawl out the windows.

18 The massive quake killed 55 people and caused billions of dollars worth of damage. As many as 1,000 buildings were destroyed or declared unsafe. Many residents learned that their homes would have to be torn down. Some 13,000 of them turned to emergency shelters. Still, people in the Bay Area were lucky. The death toll in 1989 could have been much greater. In the 1906 quake, more than 700 people were killed.

19 Scientists who study earthquakes predict an even bigger quake, probably within the next 30 years. And like every earthquake, it will strike when people least expect it. After the 1906 disaster when much of the city was destroyed, the Bay Area began to take earthquake awareness seriously. Cities and towns built new structures designed to withstand earthquakes. They also reinforced older buildings. These changes have been expensive, but the Bay Area's hard work has paid off. In the 1989 quake, not one high-rise building in San Francisco suffered major damage.

20 Candlestick Park also benefited from those new ideas. When Dianne Feinstein was mayor of San Francisco, she decided to reinforce the stadium because an aide had told her it could collapse in an earthquake. That decision saved countless lives. For 60,000 baseball fans, the World Series earthquake was nothing more than an adventure. That afternoon, after the tremor had died away, the elated crowd let out a huge cheer—showing how thankful they were that Candlestick Park had survived.

If you have been timed while reading this article, enter your reading time below. Then turn to the Words-per-Minute Table on page 133 and look up your reading speed (words per minute). Enter your reading speed on the graph on page 134.

Reading Time: Lesson 11

________ : ________

Minutes *Seconds*

A Finding the Main Idea

One statement below expresses the main idea of the article. One statement is too general, or too broad. The other statement explains only part of the article; it is too narrow. Label the statements using the following key:

M—Main Idea **B—Too Broad** **N—Too Narrow**

_______ 1. Earthquakes cause millions of dollars worth of damage.

_______ 2. The 1989 San Francisco earthquake affected many people, including a crowd of baseball fans.

_______ 3. At 5:04 P.M. on October 17, buildings in downtown San Francisco began to vibrate.

_______ Score 15 points for a correct M answer.

_______ Score 5 points for each correct B or N answer.

_______ **Total Score:** Finding the Main Idea

B Recalling Facts

How well do you remember the facts in the article? Put an X in the box next to the answer that correctly completes each statement about the article.

1. Fans were assembled in Candlestick Park to watch

☐ a. an All-Star game.
☐ b. the National League playoffs.
☐ c. a World Series game.

2. The 1989 earthquake was the largest to hit the Bay Area since

☐ a. 1906.
☐ b. 1806.
☐ c. 1986.

3. Buck Helm was injured when

☐ a. his house collapsed in the Marina district.
☐ b. his car was crushed on the Nimitz Freeway.
☐ c. the upper deck swayed at Candlestick Park.

4. Dianne Feinstein was

☐ a. the mayor of San Francisco.
☐ b. the public works director in Oakland.
☐ c. a scientist studying earthquakes.

5. When Bob Welch first heard the earthquake, he thought

☐ a. a volcano was erupting.
☐ b. someone was rolling barrels.
☐ c. the crowd had mobbed the stadium.

Score 5 points for each correct answer.

_______ **Total Score:** Recalling Facts

C Making Inferences

When you combine your own experience and information from a text to draw a conclusion that is not directly stated in that text, you are making an inference. Below are five statements that may or may not be inferences based on information in the article. Label the statements using the following key:

C—Correct Inference **F—Faulty Inference**

______ 1. Baseball fans were expecting an earthquake during the game.

______ 2. California may always have problems with earthquakes.

______ 3. Cities and towns in the Bay Area are not concerned about future quakes.

______ 4. Dianne Feinstein made a good decision about Candlestick Park.

______ 5. Pitcher Bob Welch was worried about his wife.

Score 5 points for each correct answer.

______ **Total Score:** Making Inferences

D Using Words Precisely

Each numbered sentence below contains an underlined word or phrase from the article. Following the sentence are three definitions. One definition is closest to the meaning of the underlined word. One definition is opposite or nearly opposite. Label those two definitions using the following key. Do not label the remaining definition.

C—Closest **O—Opposite or Nearly Opposite**

1. After the <u>tremors</u> stopped, the pitcher dove into the stands to hug his wife.

______ a. vibrations

______ b. fans

______ c. stillness

2. Broken glass <u>glinted</u> on sidewalks, and fallen bricks and concrete had tumbled into streets.

______ a. gleamed

______ b. darkened

______ c. fell

3. People were seen huddled on street corners, afraid to go inside <u>crumpled</u> buildings.

______ a. collapsed

______ b. older

______ c. raised

4. Some cars were left teetering on the <u>brink</u>.

______ a. center

______ b. freeway

______ c. edge

5. That afternoon, after the tremor had died away, the elated crowd let out a huge cheer—showing how thankful they were that Candlestick Park had survived..

_______ a. frightened

_______ b. joyous

_______ c. sorrowful

_______ Score 3 points for each correct C answer.

_______ Score 2 points for each correct O answer.

_______ **Total Score:** Using Words Precisely

Enter the four total scores in the spaces below, and add them together to find your Reading Comprehension Score. Then record your score on the graph on page 135.

Score	Question Type	Lesson 11
_______	Finding the Main Idea	
_______	Recalling Facts	
_______	Making Inferences	
_______	Using Words Precisely	
_______	**Reading Comprehension Score**	

Author's Approach

Put an X in the box next to the correct answer.

1. The main purpose of the first paragraph is to

☐ a. compare the Giants to the Athletics.

☐ b. tell the reader which teams took part in the 1989 World Series.

☐ c. explain why Candlestick Park was full of fans.

2. From the statements below, choose those that you believe the author would agree with.

☐ a. The people who live in the Bay Area aren't prepared to deal with earthquakes.

☐ b. During the earthquake, people in Candlestick Park were safer than those on the Nimitz Freeway.

☐ c. The steps taken to make the Bay Area safer during earthquakes helped save lives.

3. From the statement "[Other fans] waited in their seats, and a few even yelled, 'Play ball!'," you can conclude that the author wants the reader to think that

☐ a. some fans thought that the game would be played.

☐ b. many fans thought that the game should be canceled.

☐ c. some fans were afraid to go home.

4. What does the author imply by saying "After the tremors stopped, the pitcher dove into the stands to hug his wife"?

☐ a. The pitcher and his wife were newlyweds.

☐ b. The pitcher was thankful that both he and his wife were alive.

☐ c. The pitcher wanted to kiss his wife for good luck before the game.

_______ Number of correct answers

Record your personal assessment of your work on the Critical Thinking Chart on page 136.

Summarizing and Paraphrasing

Put an X in the box next to the correct answer.

1. Below are summaries of the article. Choose the summary that says all the most important things about the article but in the fewest words.

- ☐ a. An earthquake struck San Francisco just before game three of the 1989 World Series. Although Candlestick Park was not badly damaged, some parts of the Bay Area were hit hard, including the Nimitz Freeway in Oakland. Fortunately, measures taken to help buildings in the area withstand earthquakes paid off, saving lives.
- ☐ b. Although Candlestick Park withstood the 1989 World Series earthquake, some parts of the Bay Area suffered greater damage. The most serious destruction occurred on the Nimitz Freeway in Oakland. Measures taken to help buildings in the area withstand earthquakes saved lives.
- ☐ c. An earthquake struck the Bay Area on October 17, 1989, just before game three of the World Series got under way at Candlestick Park. Although no one was seriously hurt at the baseball park, the quake killed 55 people, most of them motorists on the area's freeways.

2. Read the statement about the article below. Then read the paraphrase of that statement. Choose the reason that best tells why the paraphrase does not say the same thing as the statement.

Statement: After Dorothy Otto became trapped in her car and her screams for help went unnoticed, she thought that she was going to die and so wrote a good-bye note to her husband.

Paraphrase: Dorothy Otto thought that she was going to die because no one answered her calls for help.

- ☐ a. Paraphrase says too much.
- ☐ b. Paraphrase doesn't say enough.
- ☐ c. Paraphrase doesn't agree with the statement about the article.

3. Choose the sentence that correctly restates the following sentence from the article:

"Although he [Buck Helm] was badly injured and barely conscious, he waved his arms at the workers as he was carried to the ambulance."

- ☐ a. As Helm was carried away, he showed the workers his injuries.
- ☐ b. Even though Helm was hurt and barely conscious, workers waved to him as he was taken to the ambulance.
- ☐ c. Even though Helm was hurt and barely conscious, he waved to the workers who had helped rescue him.

_________ Number of correct answers

Record your personal assessment of your work on the Critical Thinking Chart on page 136.

Critical Thinking

Put an X in the box next to the correct answer for questions 1 and 4. Follow the directions provided for the other questions.

1. From the information in paragraph 19, you can predict that

- ☐ a. the Bay Area will continue to construct buildings that can withstand earthquakes.
- ☐ b. cities and towns all over the country will prepare for possible earthquakes.
- ☐ c. San Francisco will relax its building codes.

2. Using what is told in the article about the 1906 and 1989 earthquakes in the Bay Area, name three ways the 1906 earthquake is similar to and three ways it is different from the 1989 earthquake. Cite the paragraph number(s) where you found details in the article to support your conclusions.

   Similarities

   ____

   ____

   ____

   Differences

   ____

   ____

   ____

3. Read paragraph 17. Then choose from the letters below to correctly complete the following statement. Write the letters on the lines.

   According to paragraph 17, _________ because _________.

   a. the roadway dropped

   b. something caught the car

   c. Bruce Stephan and his passenger were able to crawl out of their car

4. Of the following theme categories, which would this story fit into?

- ☐ a. People are helpless in the face of nature's fury.
- ☐ b. It's better to be safe than sorry.
- ☐ c. There is safety in numbers.

_________ Number of correct answers

Record your personal assessment of your work on the Critical Thinking Chart on page 136.

Personal Response

What would you have done if you had been at Candlestick Park when the earthquake struck?

____

____

____

Self-Assessment

One of the things I did best when reading this article was

____

____

____

I believe I did this well because

____

____

____

A DEADLY MISTAKE

Iran Air Captain Mohsen Rezaian sat calmly in the cockpit of his giant Airbus, checking his instrument panel. Flight 655 was scheduled to fly from Iran south over the Persian Gulf to the United Arab Emirates. The flight was, in the jargon of airline pilots, a "milk run." In other words, it would be a short, easy hop. There would be 290 people aboard, including Rezaian and his crew. At 9:47 A.M. on July 3, 1988, the Airbus took off from Bandar Abbas Airport.

2 Seven minutes later, Rezaian reached his first checkpoint over the Persian Gulf. He radioed his position back to the control tower in Iran. Everything looked smooth and calm. "Have a nice day," the control tower radioed back. "Thank you, good day," answered Rezaian. The captain had no idea that he and everyone else on the plane would be dead in just a few seconds.

3 The Persian Gulf region had been in turmoil for years. In 1988, Iran and Iraq were in the eighth and final year of a bloody war. At stake in the conflict was control of shipping lanes through which half the world's imported oil passed every day. Massive oil tankers streamed through the narrow Strait of Hormuz at the tip of

A rocket is launched from the deck of the U.S.S. Vincennes.

the Persian Gulf. Iranian gunboats often fired on tankers going to and from Kuwait, Iraq's closest ally.

4 The United States did not take sides in this war. Still, several U.S. Navy warships patrolled the Persian Gulf. Their job was to ensure that the vital sea lanes stayed open to peaceful traffic. The United States also wanted to protect its Arab friends in the region from any hostile moves by either Iran or Iraq.

5 Early on July 3, however, trouble began brewing. The warship U.S.S. *Vincennes*, under the command of Captain Will Rogers III, was chasing some Iranian gunboats. These boats posed no threat to the ship. The *Vincennes* was a state-of-the-art cruiser. Still, Rogers felt that other dangers might be lurking, and tensions ran high on the *Vincennes*. The crew knew that a year earlier an Iraqi missile had slammed into the U.S.S. *Stark*, killing 37 sailors. The attack had been a mistake. A lone Iraqi pilot had accidentally launched a missile that hit the ship.

6 Captain Rogers was not about to let something like that happen to his ship. The billion-dollar *Vincennes* was equipped with an Aegis weapons system. This system was a complex network of radar and computers. It was built to fight the Soviet Union's warships, not dinky gunboats. The system could track up to 200 incoming planes and missiles at one time. Earlier, in training drills, Rogers often went beyond the rules of the drill to show off the ship's high-tech equipment. One officer jokingly called the *Vincennes* "Robocruiser." The name stuck. Privately, some officers thought Rogers was a bit "trigger happy." They felt he was too anxious to show his skill in a real battle, something he had never taken part in.

7 At 9:41 A.M., six minutes before Flight 655 took off, Rogers saw high-speed Iranian gunboats headed his way. He felt sure they were up to no good. Earlier that day, higher officials had told Rogers to avoid contact with the gunboats. But now there seemed to be a clear emergency, and so officials let Rogers make decisions on the spot. Rogers went after the gunboats and opened fire on them.

8 Meanwhile, in the *Vincennes* war room, the Aegis computer screens flashed out signals. The computers could track all planes within a 300-mile radius. They tagged each plane with a symbol that indicated whether it was "friendly," "hostile," or "unidentified." The Aegis spewed out so much data that it was hard for the crew to make sense of it. For the moment, though, Rogers wasn't looking for planes; he was concentrating on the gunboats.

9 Then, at 9:47, the Aegis picked up a blip showing something taking off from Iran. It was, as would be discovered later, Iran Air Flight 655. But in the confusion of the war room, the men weren't sure what it was. One officer checked his schedule of all commercial flights over the Gulf. Somehow in the darkness of the war room and with four different time zones to check, he missed the listing for Flight

Captain Will Rogers III, commander of the U.S.S. Vincennes*, ordered the attack on an Iranian passenger jet.*

655. A chilling question arose: Could the blip be a combat jet or perhaps a patrol plane that would coordinate an attack on the *Vincennes?*

10 The Aegis sent radio messages to the Airbus, asking it to identify itself. Was it friend or foe? The first signal the Aegis got back showed that the plane was a commercial airliner. (These signals are sent automatically and don't require any response from the pilot.) Later a second signal came in. This one most likely came from a military plane still on the runway back in Iran. The crew of the *Vincennes* misread the new signal, however. They concluded that the Airbus was in fact a military plane.

11 Rogers and his men now viewed Flight 655 with suspicion. Was it a hostile aircraft? At 9:51 A.M. the Airbus, climbing peacefully to its cruising altitude, was 32 miles away. Perhaps, Rogers thought, it was a jet fighter. Three times the Aegis sent warnings to the plane. The warnings declared, "You are steering into danger and are subject to United States naval defensive measures." Apparently, Captain Rezaian heard none of these warnings.

12 The men in the *Vincennes* war room believed that the danger was real. And somehow, in the panic of the moment, they saw things that weren't there. They reported a jet fighter at 7,800 feet, going 455 knots, and descending. In fact, the data later showed they saw a commercial airliner at 12,000 feet, going 380 knots, and climbing. But working with the wrong numbers, Rogers made his tragic decision. At 9:54 A.M. he gave the green light to fire on the plane. Two SM-2 missiles flashed into the sky. A few moments later, at least one of them hit Iran Air Flight 655. The Airbus was blown out of the sky, killing 290 people.

13 There was a moment of excitement on the *Vincennes* when the plane exploded. It was a direct hit. Then word came from a lookout on the bridge. He saw pieces of the Airbus falling into the water. It wasn't a fighter jet after all. The lookout murmured that it was "bigger than that." An eerie silence descended over the *Vincennes* as Captain Rogers ordered the ship to leave Iranian waters and head south again.

14 Commander David Carlson, the commanding officer of the U.S.S. *Sides*, was aware of the unfolding drama. Carlson's ship was 19 miles away. His radar officer had also picked up the Airbus. He had noted that it was climbing and not a threat. So even if the aircraft had been a jet fighter, there was no reason to fire on it. Carlson said that when he learned missiles had been fired, he nearly vomited.

15 Carlson assumed some of the blame for the tragedy himself. Maybe he could have done something when he discovered that Rogers saw the plane as a threat. "I wondered aloud in disbelief," Carlson wrote, "but did not do the one thing that might have helped. I did not think to ask the *Vincennes* for a reevaluation of...data."

16 In its early statements, the Navy Department tried to defend Rogers. Yes, it was an awful mistake, said department officials, but it was an honest mistake. In some ways, the Navy tried to pin the blame on the victims. They claimed that the Airbus was descending and that it was flying outside the commercial air corridor. These claims were later proved to be false. Commander Carlson would later admit, "View it as you will, Iran Air Flight 655 was shot down for no good reason."

If you have been timed while reading this article, enter your reading time below. Then turn to the Words-per-Minute Table on page 133 and look up your reading speed (words per minute). Enter your reading speed on the graph on page 134.

Reading Time: Lesson 12

________ : ________

Minutes *Seconds*

A Finding the Main Idea

One statement below expresses the main idea of the article. One statement is too general, or too broad. The other statement explains only part of the article; it is too narrow. Label the statements using the following key:

M—Main Idea **B—Too Broad** **N—Too Narrow**

_____ 1. U.S. Navy warships patrolled the Persian Gulf in 1988 to make sure that sea lanes stayed open to peaceful traffic.

_____ 2. The *Vincennes* sent three warnings to the Iranian Airbus.

_____ 3. Believing Iran Air Flight 655 was a hostile aircraft, the U.S.S. *Vincennes* shot the plane down, killing everyone on board.

_____ Score 15 points for a correct M answer.

_____ Score 5 points for each correct B or N answer.

_____ **Total Score:** Finding the Main Idea

B Recalling Facts

How well do you remember the facts in the article? Put an X in the box next to the answer that correctly completes each statement about the article.

1. In 1988, Iran ended its bloody war with
- ☐ a. the United States.
- ☐ b. Kuwait.
- ☐ c. Iraq.

2. The U.S.S. *Vincennes* was under the command of
- ☐ a. Captain Mohsen Rezaian.
- ☐ b. Commander David Carlson.
- ☐ c. Captain Will Rogers III.

3. The Aegis weapons system on the *Vincennes* was built to
- ☐ a. fight Soviet Union warships.
- ☐ b. torpedo Iranian gunboats.
- ☐ c. shoot down Iranian airplanes.

4. The first signal the Aegis received indicated that the Airbus was
- ☐ a. a commercial airliner.
- ☐ b. a military plane.
- ☐ c. an SM-2 missile.

5. After the incident, the U.S. Navy
- ☐ a. accepted full blame for the mistake.
- ☐ b. tried to blame the victims.
- ☐ c. denied that the *Vincennes* had made a mistake.

Score 5 points for each correct answer.

_____ **Total Score:** Recalling Facts

C Making Inferences

When you combine your own experience and information from a text to draw a conclusion that is not directly stated in that text, you are making an inference. Below are five statements that may or may not be inferences based on information in the article. Label the statements using the following key:

C—Correct Inference **F—Faulty Inference**

_______ 1. The men in the *Vincennes* war room were tense and nervous.

_______ 2. Captain Rogers acted hastily when he ordered his men to fire on the Airbus.

_______ 3. The Aegis weapons system is simple to use and foolproof.

_______ 4. The captain of the Iranian Airbus was aware that his plane was being tracked by the *Vincennes*.

_______ 5. The U.S. Navy always tries to cover up its responsibility for mistakes.

Score 5 points for each correct answer.

_______ **Total Score:** Making Inferences

D Using Words Precisely

Each numbered sentence below contains an underlined word or phrase from the article. Following the sentence are three definitions. One definition is closest to the meaning of the underlined word. One definition is opposite or nearly opposite. Label those two definitions using the following key. Do not label the remaining definition.

C—Closest **O—Opposite or Nearly Opposite**

1. The flight was, in the jargon of airline pilots, a "milk run."

_______ a. slang

_______ b. standard speech

_______ c. job

2. The Persian Gulf region had been in turmoil for years.

_______ a. debt

_______ b. order

_______ c. upheaval

3. Their job was to ensure that the vital sea lanes stayed open to peaceful traffic.

_______ a. unnecessary

_______ b. essential

_______ c. commercial

4. An eerie silence descended over the *Vincennes* as Captain Rogers ordered the ship to leave Iranian waters and head south again.

_______ a. strange

_______ b. grateful

_______ c. ordinary

5. Carlson <u>assumed</u> some of the blame for the tragedy himself.

_______ a. questioned

_______ b. took on

_______ c. denied

_______ Score 3 points for each correct C answer.

_______ Score 2 points for each correct O answer.

_______ **Total Score:** Using Words Precisely

Enter the four total scores in the spaces below, and add them together to find your Reading Comprehension Score. Then record your score on the graph on page 135.

Score	Question Type	Lesson 12
_______	Finding the Main Idea	
_______	Recalling Facts	
_______	Making Inferences	
_______	Using Words Precisely	
_______	**Reading Comprehension Score**	

Author's Approach

Put an X in the box next to the correct answer.

1. The author uses the first sentence of the article to

☐ a. describe Captain Rezaian's state of mind.

☐ b. inform the reader about a flight captain's duties.

☐ c. compare an Iranian Airbus to an American plane.

2. What does the author mean by the statement "Privately, some officers thought Rogers was a bit 'trigger happy'"?

☐ a. Rogers was eager to shoot at something.

☐ b. The officers liked to talk about Rogers behind his back.

☐ c. Some officers thought that Rogers was contented with his job.

3. Choose the statement below that is the weakest argument for justifying the attack on Iran Air Flight 655.

☐ a. The officer in the *Vincennes* war room couldn't find the airliner on his schedule of commercial flights.

☐ b. The Airbus didn't respond to the warnings sent to it by the Aegis system.

☐ c. Even if the Airbus had been a jet fighter, it was climbing away from the *Vincennes* and, therefore, was not a threat.

4. Choose the statement below that best describes the author's position in paragraph 16.

☐ a. The Airbus was responsible for the accident because it was flying outside the commercial air corridor.

☐ b. The U.S. Navy and Captain Rogers were responsible for the mistake.

☐ c. Commander Carlson was responsible for shooting down Flight 655.

_______ Number of correct answers

Record your personal assessment of your work on the Critical Thinking Chart on page 136

Summarizing and Paraphrasing

Put an X in the box next to the correct answer for question 3. Follow the directions provided for the other questions.

1. Complete the following one-sentence summary of the article using the lettered phrases from the phrase bank below. Write the letters on the lines.

Phrase Bank:

a. a description of the tense situation in the Persian Gulf in 1988
b. different reactions to the incident
c. the events that led to Rogers's decision to shoot down the Airbus

After a short introduction, the article about the Iranian Airbus begins with _________, goes on to explain _________, and ends with _________.

2. Reread paragraph 9 in the article. Below, write a summary of the paragraph in no more than 25 words.

____

____

____

____

Reread your summary and decide whether it covers the important ideas in the paragraph. Next, decide how to shorten the summary to 15 words or less without leaving out any essential information. Write this summary below.

____

____

____

3. Choose the best one-sentence paraphrase for the following sentence from the article:

"An eerie silence descended over the *Vincennes* as Captain Rogers ordered the ship to leave Iranian waters and head south again."

☐ a. The *Vincennes* quietly left Iranian waters and headed south.
☐ b. The crew of the *Vincennes* was oddly quiet as the ship turned south and left Iranian waters.
☐ c. The waters around the *Vincennes* were strangely calm and quiet as the ship headed south.

_________ Number of correct answers

Record your personal assessment of your work on the Critical Thinking Chart on page 136.

Critical Thinking

Follow the directions provided for questions 1 and 4. Put an X in the box next to the correct answer for the other questions.

1. For each statement below, write O if it expresses an opinion and write F if it expresses a fact.

_______ a. In 1987, an Iraqi pilot launched a missile at an American ship, killing 37 sailors.

_______ b. Captain Rogers should have been court-martialed for his actions on July 3, 1988.

_______ c. All of the people on board the Iranian Airbus died after the *Vincennes* fired on the plane.

2. Judging from Captain Rogers's actions as told in this article, you can conclude that he

☐ a. was anxious to find a target to fire at.

☐ b. thought long and hard before ordering his men to shoot down the Airbus.

☐ c. wanted to avoid any kind of military confrontation.

3. What was the cause of Rogers's decision to send warnings to the Airbus?

☐ a. Captain Rezaian didn't hear the warnings.

☐ b. Rogers shot the plane out of the sky.

☐ c. He thought the plane was a jet fighter.

4. In which paragraph did you find the information or details to answer question 3?

____

_______ Number of correct answers

Record your personal assessment of your work on the Critical Thinking Chart on page 136.

Personal Response

How do you think Captain Rogers felt when he learned that he had shot down a commercial airliner?

____

____

____

____

Self-Assessment

When reading the article, I was having trouble with

____

____

____

____

LESSON 13

THE NORTH SEA OIL RIG EXPLOSION

The North Sea waters were unusually calm around the Piper Alpha oil platform that July evening. Most of the 227 workers were off duty in their cabins, but several dozen men were still outside. They were monitoring the rig, which continued to pump oil from the sea floor. As far as the men knew, everything was operating normally. But deep beneath the sea, a terrible tragedy was building.

2 Every worker on an offshore oil platform knows how dangerous the job can be. In case of an emergency, the sea is the only escape.

3 The Piper Alpha platform was a huge oil rig located in the North Sea 120 miles off the Scottish coast. It began operating in 1976, and by 1988 it was one of the oldest oil platforms in the North Sea. Every day it produced 140,000 barrels of crude oil as well as some natural gas. The Piper Alpha and other platforms like it were an important part of Great Britain's oil industry.

4 The North Sea is rich in oil, but it is also cold and dangerous. It is famous for its violent storms, so oil platforms must be strong enough to stand the weather. And despite a fire in 1984, the Piper Alpha had the reputation of being strong and safe. The massive steel structure loomed 200 feet above the rough water. And it was attached to the sea floor 500 feet below the surface. The entire rig weighed 34,000 tons.

5 From the Piper Alpha, workers could see the *Tharos* anchored nearby. That ship was permanently assigned to the oil platform. On board was emergency fire and rescue equipment, just in case the Piper Alpha ever needed help. But the people on the rig were also prepared. With their lifeboats and firefighting equipment, workers felt confident about handling any problems.

The Piper Alpha oil platform burns in the North Sea after an explosion killed 166 people.

Rescues and attempts to extinguish the fire proved difficult in the rough waters of the North Sea.

6 At 9:30 P.M. on July 6, 1988, everything on the rig seemed normal. But at 9:31, a piercing shriek rose from the sea beneath the platform and squealed through the entire length of the rig. Seconds later a tremendous explosion tore the giant rig into two pieces.

7 For the men off duty in their cabins, there was almost no chance of survival. The explosion had destroyed the crew's quarters, killing more than 100 men instantly. Workers outside on the deck watched in horror as a ball of fire rolled over the rig. Derek Ellington, a survivor, later recalled, "Two-thirds of that platform melted with the heat and disappeared."

8 There was no time to find emergency equipment or lifeboats. The men still alive after the explosion had one chance at survival. They had to jump 200 feet into the icy North Sea. "It was fry or die," said superintendent Andy Mochan. "So I jumped."

9 Even the emergency ship *Tharos* could not put out the raging fire. The continuing explosions forced the ship to turn away from the rig to keep from catching fire. But rescuers did try to save the men floundering in the cold sea. Twenty-eight ships arrived at the disaster, including an international naval force. Air force planes and helicopters also joined the mission.

10 Rescue pilot Patrick Thirkell later described the scene on the oil platform. "People were just running out onto the deck and leaping for their lives into the water." Tony Sinnett was one of the men pulled from the water. When he was safely on a rescue boat, he looked back at the burning rig. "It was as if the platform had been hit by an atom bomb," he said. Sinnett thought he saw a few men standing on the platform's helicopter deck. "They seemed to be waving," he said. "But then the deck keeled over, and the men disappeared."

11 Rescue workers had a deadly task, and some gave up their lives in the effort. The tugboat *Sandhaven* sent out a small rowboat to pick up survivors in the water. Four brave crew members went directly under the burning rig to rescue six men. But the boat suddenly caught fire. It exploded moments later, killing nine men.

12 One hundred sixty-six people were killed in the disaster, making it the worst offshore oil accident in history. But rescuers did manage to save 64 men. Although most survivors had jumped into the sea, many suffered only minor injuries. The cold waters of the North Sea turned out to be the best defense against the flames.

13 Oil experts believe that the explosion was probably caused by a natural-gas leak. Gas pressure may have created the shriek that squealed through the rig. And gas explosions can be sudden and unpredictable.

14 As people in Great Britain mourned the tragedy, researchers began to study ways to avoid future problems. Roger Lyons, a union official, represented the oil workers. He believed that worker safety had not been taken seriously. Lyons asked the government and the oil industry to make worker safety their first priority in the future.

15 Workers on other offshore oil platforms also believed that their lives were in danger. After the Piper Alpha explosion, more than 100 British workers left their jobs on oil rigs. All these workers had been trained to handle disasters. But they knew that training had not saved the lives of the men on the Piper Alpha.

16 Danger is a way of life in the oil business. There have been accidents on platforms and in refineries. Tankers have run aground and spilled oil into the sea. And some people think it may never be possible to avoid accidents. In the words of political leader Neil Kinnock, the disaster on the Piper Alpha is "an awful reminder of the human price of oil."

If you have been timed while reading this article, enter your reading time below. Then turn to the Words-per-Minute Table on page 133 and look up your reading speed (words per minute). Enter your reading speed on the graph on page 134.

Reading Time: Lesson 13

_______ : _______

Minutes *Seconds*

A Finding the Main Idea

One statement below expresses the main idea of the article. One statement is too general, or too broad. The other statement explains only part of the article; it is too narrow. Label the statements using the following key:

M—Main Idea **B—Too Broad** **N—Too Narrow**

_______ 1. In 1988 the Piper Alpha oil rig exploded, killing 166 people; this incident was the worst offshore oil accident in history.

_______ 2. Danger is a way of life in the oil business.

_______ 3. Workers on the deck of the Piper Alpha watched in horror as a ball of fire rolled over the rig.

_______ Score 15 points for a correct M answer.

_______ Score 5 points for each correct B or N answer.

_______ **Total Score:** Finding the Main Idea

B Recalling Facts

How well do you remember the facts in the article? Put an X in the box next to the answer that correctly completes each statement about the article.

1. The Piper Alpha platform was located off the
   - ☐ a. Irish coast.
   - ☐ b. Scottish coast.
   - ☐ c. Kuwaiti coast.
2. The *Tharos* was anchored near the platform to provide
   - ☐ a. entertainment.
   - ☐ b. military protection.
   - ☐ c. emergency support.
3. Before the explosion, workers heard a
   - ☐ a. rumble of thunder.
   - ☐ b. piercing shriek.
   - ☐ c. low hiss.
4. Most of the people killed were
   - ☐ a. in their cabins.
   - ☐ b. outside on the deck.
   - ☐ c. in the rescue boats.
5. The explosion was probably caused by
   - ☐ a. arson.
   - ☐ b. a natural-gas leak.
   - ☐ c. bad weather.

Score 5 points for each correct answer.

_______ **Total Score:** Recalling Facts

C Making Inferences

When you combine your own experience and information from a text to draw a conclusion that is not directly stated in that text, you are making an inference. Below are five statements that may or may not be inferences based on information in the article. Label the statements using the following key:

C—Correct Inference **F—Faulty Inference**

_______ 1. The oil rig was not strong enough to withstand North Sea weather.

_______ 2. Workers made a bad decision when they jumped into the sea.

_______ 3. Rescue workers were in a dangerous situation.

_______ 4. Most offshore oil workers are not worried about safety.

_______ 5. Neil Kinnock worries about the dangers faced by oil workers.

Score 5 points for each correct answer.

_______ **Total Score:** Making Inferences

D Using Words Precisely

Each numbered sentence below contains an underlined word or phrase from the article. Following the sentence are three definitions. One definition is closest to the meaning of the underlined word. One definition is opposite or nearly opposite. Label those two definitions using the following key. Do not label the remaining definition.

C—Closest **O—Opposite or Nearly Opposite**

1. Every day it produced 140,000 barrels of crude oil as well as some natural gas.

_______ a. unprocessed

_______ b. expensive

_______ c. refined

2. The massive steel structure loomed 200 feet above the rough water.

_______ a. exploded

_______ b. shrank

_______ c. towered

3. But rescuers did try to save the men floundering in the cold sea.

_______ a. shouting

_______ b. struggling awkwardly

_______ c. proceeding easily

4. "They seemed to be waving," he said. "But then the deck keeled over, and the men disappeared.

_______ a. returned to the correct position

_______ b. caught on fire

_______ c. turned or fell over

5. Lyons asked the government and the oil industry to make worker safety their first priority in the future.

_______ a. trivial concern

_______ b. unanswered question

_______ c. most important issue

_______ Score 3 points for each correct C answer.

_______ Score 2 points for each correct O answer.

_______ **Total Score:** Using Words Precisely

Enter the four total scores in the spaces below, and add them together to find your Reading Comprehension Score. Then record your score on the graph on page 135.

Score	Question Type	Lesson 13
_______	Finding the Main Idea	
_______	Recalling Facts	
_______	Making Inferences	
_______	Using Words Precisely	
_______	**Reading Comprehension Score**	

Author's Approach

Put an X in the box next to the correct answer.

1. The author uses the first sentence of the article to
   - ☐ a. inform the reader about the article's setting.
   - ☐ b. describe the Piper Alpha oil platform.
   - ☐ c. compare the North Sea to other large bodies of water.

2. Choose the statement below that is the weakest argument for claiming that working on an offshore oil platform is safe.
   - ☐ a. Every worker has been trained to handle disasters.
   - ☐ b. The oil rigs are equipped with lifeboats and firefighting equipment.
   - ☐ c. Training and equipment did not save the lives of the men on the Piper Alpha.

3. In this article, "the disaster on the Piper Alpha is 'an awful reminder of the human price of oil'" means
   - ☐ a. oil is expensive because so few people are willing to work on oil rigs.
   - ☐ b. the dangerous job of oil extraction can involve the loss of life.
   - ☐ c. people shouldn't use so much oil because it costs too much.

4. Choose the statement below that best describes the author's position in paragraph 16.
   - ☐ a. The oil business is very dangerous.
   - ☐ b. No one should work in the oil business because it is so dangerous.
   - ☐ c. Accidents are very common in the oil business.

_______ Number of correct answers

Record your personal assessment of your work on the Critical Thinking Chart on page 136.

Summarizing and Paraphrasing

Follow the directions provided for questions 1 and 2. Put an X in the box next to the correct answer for question 3.

1. Complete the following one-sentence summary of the article using the lettered phrases from the phrase bank below. Write the letters on the lines.

Phrase Bank:
a. survival and rescue efforts
b. the dangers involved in the oil business
c. the explosion on the rig

The article about the Piper Alpha oil platform begins with ________, goes on to explain ________, and ends with ________.

2. Reread paragraph 11 in the article. Below, write a summary of the paragraph in no more than 25 words.

____

____

____

____

Reread your summary and decide whether it covers the important ideas in the paragraph. Next, decide how to shorten the summary to 15 words or less without leaving out any essential information. Write this summary below.

____

____

____

3. Choose the best one-sentence paraphrase for the following sentence from the article:

"But at 9:31, a piercing shriek rose from the sea beneath the platform and squealed through the entire length of the rig."

☐ a. The screams of the men after the explosion could be heard up and down the entire rig.
☐ b. At 9:31, an emergency alarm sounded beneath the platform and was heard all over the rig.
☐ c. At 9:31, a high-pitched squeal rose from the sea and sounded up and down the rig.

________ Number of correct answers

Record your personal assessment of your work on the Critical Thinking Chart on page 136.

Critical Thinking

Put an X in the box next to the correct answer for questions 1 and 3. Follow the directions provided for the other questions.

1. From the events in the article, you can predict that the following will happen next :

☐ a. Worker safety in the oil industry will be taken more seriously.
☐ b. No more oil will be drilled in the North Sea.
☐ c. All workers will refuse to drill oil in the North Sea.

2. Choose from the letters below to correctly complete the following statement. Write the letters on the lines.

   In the article, _________ and _________ are alike.

   a. Andy Mochan's experience of the disaster
   b. Patrick Thirkell's experience of the disaster
   c. Tony Sinnett's experience of the disaster

3. What was the effect of the Piper Alpha's continuing explosions on the actions of the *Tharos?*

- ☐ a. The emergency ship put out the raging fires.
- ☐ b. The emergency ship turned away to keep from catching fire.
- ☐ c. The emergency ship picked up survivors from the water.

4. In which paragraph did you find the information or details to answer question 3?

____

_________ Number of correct answers

Record your personal assessment of your work on the Critical Thinking Chart on page 136.

Personal Response

What new question do you have about this topic?

____

____

____

____

Self-Assessment

From reading this article, I have learned

____

____

____

____

BABY JESSICA
The Miracle of Midland

Reba and Chip McClure lived every parent's worst nightmare. Their baby daughter, left alone for a brief moment, stumbled into danger. Little Jessica somehow fell 22 feet into an abandoned well. For 58 hours, the small town of Midland, Texas, as well as the entire nation, anxiously followed Jessica's rescue.

2 All was normal that morning in October 1987. Eighteen-month-old Jessica was playing with four young children in her aunt's backyard. Suddenly the screams of Jessica's playmates brought her mom, Reba, running out the house. Jessica had vanished! The children all pointed to the well. Reba frantically peered down the hole, but she was unable to see her daughter. She rushed inside to call the police. "I was scared…I didn't know what to do," Reba McClure said later. "I just ran in and called the police. They were there within three minutes, but it felt like a lifetime."

3 Police and paramedics did not arrive to a hopeful situation. Jessica was not responding to the frantic calls of her mom, and no one could see her. Finally, after a police officer called Jessica's name

Huge drilling and earth-moving equipment were brought in to rescue 18-month-old Jessica McClure after she fell into an abandoned well. Inset: Baby Jessica is brought out from the well where she was trapped for 58 hours.

several times, a tiny cry was heard. A tape measure attached to a flashlight was lowered into the hole to find out how far the child had fallen.

4 Within 15 minutes, rescue operations were under way. Crews tore down fences to make room in the backyard for a backhoe and drilling equipment. Heated air was forced into the well's eight-inch opening to keep Jessica warm, and a microphone was lowered so that rescue workers could hear and monitor her. Since the hole was too small for a rescue attempt, a plan had to be devised—quickly. No one knew how long Jessica could hold on. Even more terrifying for everyone was not knowing her condition.

5 Rescuers decided to drill a three-foot-wide hole beside the well shaft. They needed expert drillers, and in Midland they were easy to find. During the late 1970s, Midland had been a booming oil-drilling town. Later, when the price of oil tumbled, the town's economy suffered. A lot of drillers lost their jobs.

6 When the drillers began digging to save Jessica, the outlook seemed optimistic. The rescue team planned to drill the new shaft parallel to and deeper than the one Jessica was trapped in, and then work their way across to her. That way any loose rock would fall away from the child. Initially, the rescuers thought they would reach Jessica within a few hours. But the drilling equipment did not adequately cut through the layers of rock. Progress was painfully slow.

7 On Thursday morning, about 24 hours after Jessica's fall, David Lilly, a special investigator with the United States Mine Safety and Health Administration, arrived in Midland. He described the rescue scene as total chaos. The local officials "had no experience and didn't know what they were doing," Lilly said.

8 Lilly was made rescue director and quickly set about making changes. He first changed the angle of the tunnel leading to Jessica. Instead of working directly across toward the child, Lilly planned to break through two feet below her. He believed his plan would be safer for Jessica. He wanted to avoid breaking the well in on the child. Lilly also decided to use stronger drill bits to cut through the granite.

9 As the drilling progressed, all attempts were made to keep Jessica calm. Workers were in constant communication with the child and began to understand her moods. Detective Andy Glasscock said, "When we weren't calling words of encouragement, we'd tell her to sing for us. I'll never forget her singing 'Winnie-the-Pooh.' We'd say, 'How does a kitten go?' And she'd respond to us." Her singing and repeating of nursery rhymes kept family and rescuers hopeful. Jessica was alert and responding to voices. Yet any lag in the baby's chatter sent everyone into panic.

10 With every hour, doctors became increasingly concerned about Jessica's general health. She was dehydrating and by losing a little weight, she had slipped lower into the well. Doctors decided, however, not to attempt to give Jessica any food or water. If she had internal injuries, food or water would only make the situation worse, especially if she were in need of immediate surgery.

11 On Friday morning rescuers still had not reached the point where Jessica was trapped. She had been in the well now for over 48 hours. Workers were suffering from exhaustion. They took turns operating a 45-pound jackhammer while lying on their stomachs, 29 feet below the ground. Even though they were able to chip away only one inch of rock per hour, they refused to give up. David Lilly was impressed by the people of Midland. "I've never seen more dedicated people. We actually had to force some of the men to leave because they were about to drop."

No longer a baby, Jessica McClure in 1993, six years after the accident

12 Late Friday morning Lilly finally broke into the shaft of the well directly below Jessica, and she started crying. He was able to reach in and touch her leg. His first concern was to prevent Jessica from slipping any lower than she had already. Therefore, he decided to insert a metal rod and a balloon beneath her to hold her in place. The balloon would also protect Jessica from the dust and noise.

13 For the last stretch, Lilly would not allow rescuers to chip away anymore at the well. He decided to use a high-pressure water drill, which sprays about 30,000 pounds of water, to cut through the rock. The force of the water enlarged the passageway without harming Jessica. Then Lilly broke out an opening the size of the well itself, eight inches by ten inches. At this point, he turned over the operation to the paramedics. It was one o'clock Friday afternoon. Jessica had been in the well for more than 51 hours.

14 Robert O'Donnell, a Midland paramedic, was very concerned that Jessica might have head and spine damage. He insisted that rescue workers leave the maneuvering of the baby to him and fellow paramedic Steve Forbes. "We more or less volunteered ourselves because we both have children, and I've gotten kids unstuck from different situations before," O'Donnell said. Shortly after 1:00 P.M., he was lowered into the shaft. He had to slither like a snake through the tunnel. When he finally saw Jessica's left foot, he asked her to move it, and she did. Then he pushed up on her left leg. Jessica whined a little, but she did not cry out in pain.

15 O'Donnell couldn't tell what position she was in. He tried to move her several times without success. He was forced to leave her and head back to the surface. "That's the hardest thing I ever did, leaving that baby in there...." O'Donnell said.

16 Rescue workers needed to widen the tunnel for the paramedics. When O'Donnell reentered the tunnel at about 6:00 P.M., he had two or three more inches of headroom. Now he was able to tell the child's position. Jessica was sitting upright with her left leg hanging down. Her right leg was straight up against her head. O'Donnell began the slow struggle of pulling the child free. Out of fear Jessica often tensed up, but each time she relaxed, O'Donnell tugged at her even harder. With the help of lubricating jelly, Jessica finally slipped free. Lack of circulation had turned her right leg black, but the child appeared calm.

17 Steve Forbes strapped her to a board to keep her head and neck straight. He held on tightly while they were towed back to the surface. At approximately 8:00 P.M. Friday, all eyes were on Midland and Jessica. She emerged from her 58-hour ordeal bandaged, bruised, and dirty. As millions of Americans and rescuers watched, Jessica blinked her bright, blue eyes. She had survived!

18 A feeling of relief swept across the entire country. Rescue workers wept and celebrated when Jessica reached the surface. The streets of Midland were lined with cheering people. Church bells rang as Jessica was rushed to the hospital with her parents. The entire town had joined together to save the life of one child.

19 To the astonishment of everyone, Jessica had emerged from the well relatively healthy. She had lost a few pounds during the ordeal, but no bones were broken. Doctors later had to remove a small portion of her baby toe on her right foot, due to a lack of blood circulation, and some plastic surgery was required on her forehead as well as on the back of her head.

20 Jessica soon recovered from her minor injuries. By 1997, ten years after the rescue, she was a happy sixth-grader who played the piano and French horn and enjoyed skating. She remembered little of what happened. Andy Glasscock said, "[Jessica] doesn't remember any of it. About the only thing she remembers is what people tell her and what she sees on the news."

If you have been timed while reading this article, enter your reading time below. Then turn to the Words-per-Minute Table on page 133 and look up your reading speed (words per minute). Enter your reading speed on the graph on page 134.

Reading Time: Lesson 14

________ : ________

Minutes *Seconds*

A Finding the Main Idea

One statement below expresses the main idea of the article. One statement is too general, or too broad. The other statement explains only part of the article; it is too narrow. Label the statements using the following key:

M—Main Idea **B—Too Broad** **N—Too Narrow**

_______ 1. Young children often stumble into dangerous situations.

_______ 2. Jessica McClure fell 22 feet into an abandoned well.

_______ 3. As the country watched, rescue workers tried desperately to save little Jessica, who had fallen into a well.

_______ Score 15 points for a correct M answer.

_______ Score 5 points for each correct B or N answer.

_______ **Total Score:** Finding the Main Idea

B Recalling Facts

How well do you remember the facts in the article? Put an X in the box next to the answer that correctly completes each statement about the article.

1. Rescue operations were led by
   - ☐ a. special investigator David Lilly.
   - ☐ b. Detective Andy Glasscock.
   - ☐ c, paramedic Robert O'Donnell.
2. The McClure family lived in a small town in Texas called
   - ☐ a. Middlefield.
   - ☐ b. Middletown.
   - ☐ c. Midland.
3. Jessica remained trapped in the well for more than
   - ☐ a. 48 hours.
   - ☐ b. 24 hours.
   - ☐ c. 58 hours.
4. Jessica was playing with other children
   - ☐ a. at a local playground.
   - ☐ b. in her aunt's backyard.
   - ☐ c. in her backyard.
5. Jessica was eventually pulled free by
   - ☐ a. her father.
   - ☐ b. a local paramedic.
   - ☐ c. rescue leader David Lilly.

Score 5 points for each correct answer.

_______ **Total Score:** Recalling Facts

C Making Inferences

When you combine your own experience and information from a text to draw a conclusion that is not directly stated in that text, you are making an inference. Below are five statements that may or may not be inferences based on information in the article. Label the statements using the following key:

C—Correct Inference **F—Faulty Inference**

_______ 1. An unattended child can easily stumble into a dangerous situation.

_______ 2. The drillers in Midland were not experienced in rescue operations.

_______ 3. Because Jessica was conscious, there was no cause for concern.

_______ 4. Workers volunteered without any thought of reward.

_______ 5. Rescue workers tried to keep Jessica from talking.

Score 5 points for each correct answer.

_______ **Total Score:** Making Inferences

D Using Words Precisely

Each numbered sentence below contains an underlined word or phrase from the article. Following the sentence are three definitions. One definition is closest to the meaning of the underlined word. One definition is opposite or nearly opposite. Label those two definitions using the following key. Do not label the remaining definition.

C—Closest **O—Opposite or Nearly Opposite**

1. Heated air was forced into the well's eight-inch opening…, and a microphone was lowered so that rescue workers could hear and monitor her.

_______ a. feed
_______ b. observe closely
_______ c. ignore

2. When the drillers began digging to save Jessica, the outlook seemed optimistic.

_______ a. hopeless
_______ b. uninteresting
_______ c. promising

3. But the drilling equipment did not adequately cut through the layers of rock.

_______ a. poorly
_______ b. acceptably
_______ c. rapidly

4. She emerged from her 58-hour ordeal bandaged, bruised, and dirty.

_____ a. a very trying situation

_____ b. an easy situation

_____ c. an unusual situation

5. To the astonishment of everyone, Jessica had emerged from the well relatively healthy.

_____ a. come out of

_____ b. plunged into

_____ c. drunk from

_____ Score 3 points for each correct C answer.

_____ Score 2 points for each correct O answer.

_____ **Total Score:** Using Words Precisely

Enter the four total scores in the spaces below, and add them together to find your Reading Comprehension Score. Then record your score on the graph on page 135.

Score	Question Type	Lesson 14
_____	Finding the Main Idea	
_____	Recalling Facts	
_____	Making Inferences	
_____	Using Words Precisely	
_____	**Reading Comprehension Score**	

Author's Approach

Put an X in the box next to the correct answer.

1. The author uses the first sentence of the article to

☐ a. convey a fearful mood.

☐ b. tell the reader that something bad happened to the McClures' child.

☐ c. compare the McClures to other parents.

2. What does the author imply by saying "For the last stretch, Lilly would not allow rescuers to chip away anymore at the well. He decided to use a high-pressure water drill, which sprays about 30,000 pounds of water, to cut through the rock"?

☐ a. Lilly felt that chipping was not the right method to use at this point in the process.

☐ b. Lilly decided that the rescuers were incompetent.

☐ c. Lilly felt the situation was hopeless.

3. The author probably wrote this article in order to

☐ a. tell the reader about the rescue effort that saved Jessica's life.

☐ b. encourage readers to make their yards and homes safe for children.

☐ c. remind the reader that small children should never be left alone.

4. The author tells this story mainly by

☐ a. retelling his or her own personal experiences.

☐ b. using his or her imagination and creativity.

☐ c. describing events in time order.

_____ Number of correct answers

Record your personal assessment of your work on the Critical Thinking Chart on page 136.

Summarizing and Paraphrasing

Follow the directions provided for question 1. Put an X in the box next to the correct answer for question 2.

1. Look for the important ideas and events in paragraphs 18 and 19. Summarize those paragraphs in one or two sentences.

____

____

____

2. Choose the sentence that correctly restates the following sentence from the article:

   "Heated air was forced into the well's eight-inch opening to keep Jessica warm, and a microphone was lowered so that rescue workers could hear and monitor her."

☐ a. Jessica stayed warm while rescue workers listened to the sounds she made.

☐ b. A microphone was forced and lowered into the well so that rescue workers could speak to Jessica.

☐ c. Rescue workers pumped warm air down the well and lowered a microphone into the opening so that they could listen to Jessica.

_________ Number of correct answers

Record your personal assessment of your work on the Critical Thinking Chart on page 136.

Critical Thinking

Put an X in the box next to the correct answer for questions 1, 2, and 5. Follow the directions provided for the other questions.

1. Which of the following statements from the article is an opinion rather than a fact?

☐ a. "During the late 1970s, Midland was a booming oil-drilling town."

☐ b. "The local officials 'had no experience and didn't know what they were doing.'"

☐ c. "On Thursday morning, about 24 hours after Jessica's fall, David Lilly, a special investigator with the United States Mine Safety and Health Administration, arrived in Midland."

2. Judging from the rescue workers' actions as told in this article, you can predict that they would have

☐ a. blamed Jessica's parents if Jessica had not survived the fall.

☐ b. expected to be paid for their efforts.

☐ c. been brokenhearted if they had not been able to save Jessica.

3. Choose from the letters below to correctly complete the following statement. Write the letters on the lines.

   On the positive side, _________, but on the negative side _________.

   a. the McClures were worried and upset for more than 58 hours

   b. Jessica suffered only minor injuries as a result of her fall

   c. Jessica answered the workers' questions and sang "Winnie-the-Pooh"

4. Choose from the letters below to correctly complete the following statement. Write the letters on the lines.

   According to the article, _________ caused Jessica's right leg to _________, and the effect was _________.

   a. lack of circulation

   b. part of her baby toe had to be removed

   c. turn black

5. What did you have to do to answer question 1?

☐ a. find an opinion (what someone thinks about something)

☐ b. find a fact (something that you can prove is true)

☐ c. find a cause (why something happened)

_________ Number of correct answers

Record your personal assessment of your work on the Critical Thinking Chart on page 136.

Personal Response

This article is different from other articles about calamities I've read because

____

____

____

____

and Jessica is unlike other victims of calamities because

____

____

____

____

Self-Assessment

Which concepts or ideas from the article were difficult to understand?

____

____

____

____

Which were easy to understand?

____

____

____

____

Compare and Contrast

Think about the articles you have read in Unit Two. Pick four calamities that brought out the best in people who suffered through them. Write the titles of the articles in the first column of the chart below. Use information you learned from the articles to fill in the empty boxes in the chart.

Title	How did people help one another during this calamity?	How could people have helped each other more?	How could this calamity be avoided in the future?

What emotions do you think rescue workers feel as they do their jobs? What emotions fill the hearts of those they help? ____________________

____

____

Words-per-Minute Table

Unit Two

Directions: If you were timed while reading an article, refer to the Reading Time you recorded in the box at the end of the article. Use this words-per-minute table to determine your reading speed for that article. Then plot your reading speed on the graph on page 134.

Lesson	8	9	10	11	12	13	14	
No. of Words	976	1032	938	1259	1307	938	1487	
Minutes and Seconds								*Seconds*
1:30	651	688	625	839	871	625	991	**90**
1:40	586	619	563	755	784	563	892	**100**
1:50	532	563	512	687	713	512	811	**110**
2:00	488	516	469	630	654	469	744	**120**
2:10	450	476	433	581	603	433	686	**130**
2:20	418	442	402	540	560	402	637	**140**
2:30	390	413	375	504	523	375	595	**150**
2:40	366	387	352	472	490	352	558	**160**
2:50	344	364	331	444	461	331	525	**170**
3:00	325	344	313	420	436	313	496	**180**
3:10	308	326	296	398	413	296	470	**190**
3:20	293	310	281	378	392	281	446	**200**
3:30	279	295	268	360	373	268	425	**210**
3:40	266	281	256	343	356	256	406	**220**
3:50	255	269	245	328	341	245	388	**230**
4:00	244	258	235	315	327	235	372	**240**
4:10	234	248	225	302	314	225	357	**250**
4:20	225	238	216	291	302	216	343	**260**
4:30	217	229	208	280	290	208	330	**270**
4:40	209	221	201	270	280	201	319	**280**
4:50	202	214	194	260	270	194	308	**290**
5:00	195	206	188	252	261	188	297	**300**
5:10	189	200	182	244	253	182	288	**310**
5:20	183	194	176	236	245	176	279	**320**
5:30	177	188	171	229	238	171	270	**330**
5:40	172	182	166	222	231	166	262	**340**
5:50	167	177	161	216	224	161	255	**350**
6:00	163	172	156	210	218	156	248	**360**
6:10	158	167	152	204	212	152	241	**370**
6:20	154	163	148	199	206	148	235	**380**
6:30	150	159	144	194	201	144	229	**390**
6:40	146	155	141	189	196	141	223	**400**
6:50	143	151	137	184	191	137	218	**410**
7:00	139	147	134	180	187	134	212	**420**
7:10	136	144	131	176	182	131	207	**430**
7:20	133	141	128	172	178	128	203	**440**
7:30	130	138	125	168	174	125	198	**450**
7:40	127	135	122	164	170	122	194	**460**
7:50	125	132	120	161	167	120	190	**470**
8:00	122	129	117	157	163	117	186	**480**

Plotting Your Progress: Reading Speed

Unit Two

Directions: If you were timed while reading an article, write your words-per-minute rate for that article in the box under the number of the lesson. Then plot your reading speed on the graph by putting a small X on the line directly above the number of the lesson, across from the number of words per minute you read. As you mark your speed for each lesson, graph your progress by drawing a line to connect the X's.

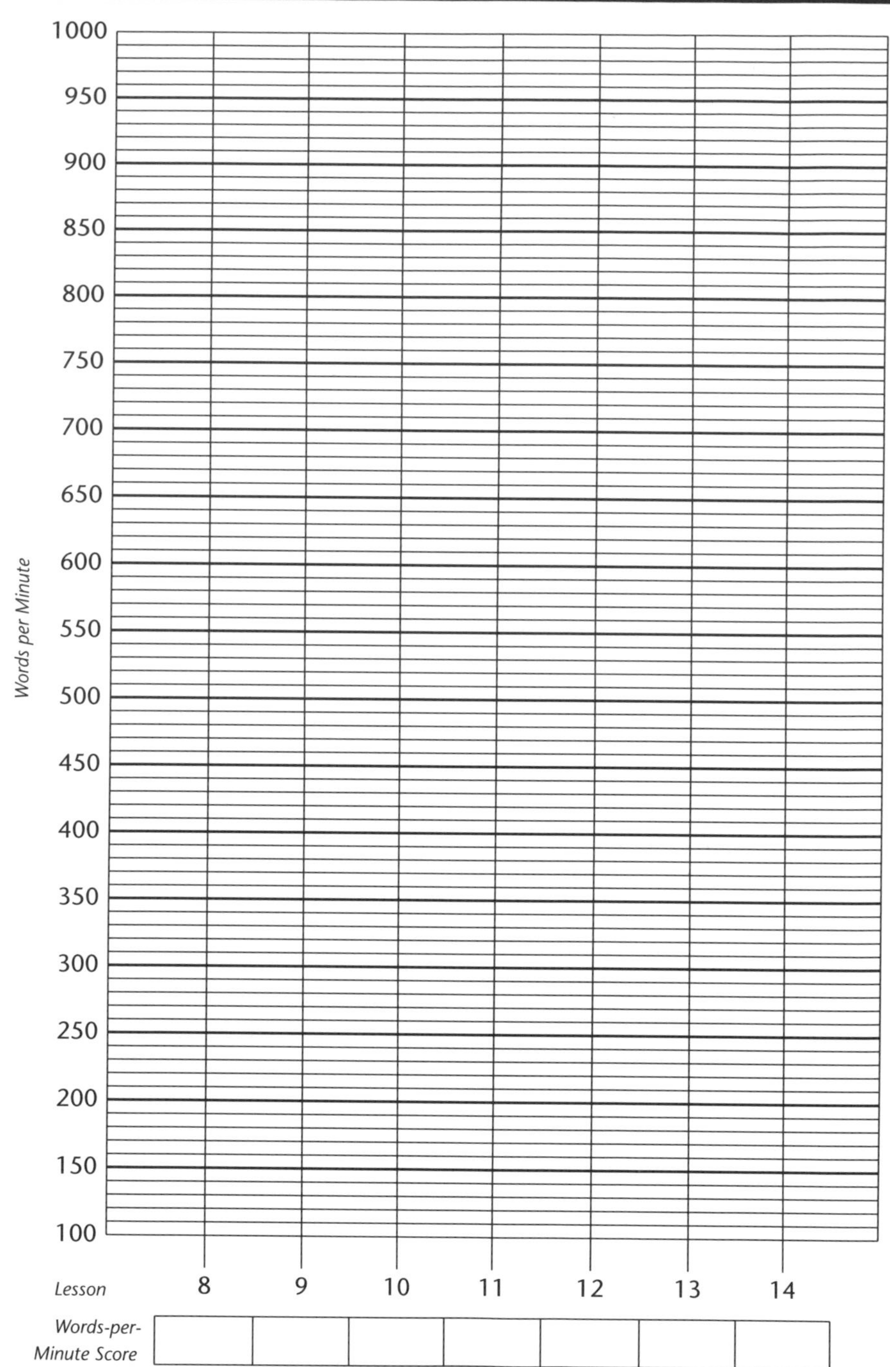

Plotting Your Progress: Reading Comprehension

Unit Two

Directions: Write your Reading Comprehension score for each lesson in the box under the number of the lesson. Then plot your score on the graph by putting a small X on the line directly above the number of the lesson and across from the score you earned. As you mark your score for each lesson, graph your progress by drawing a line to connect the X's.

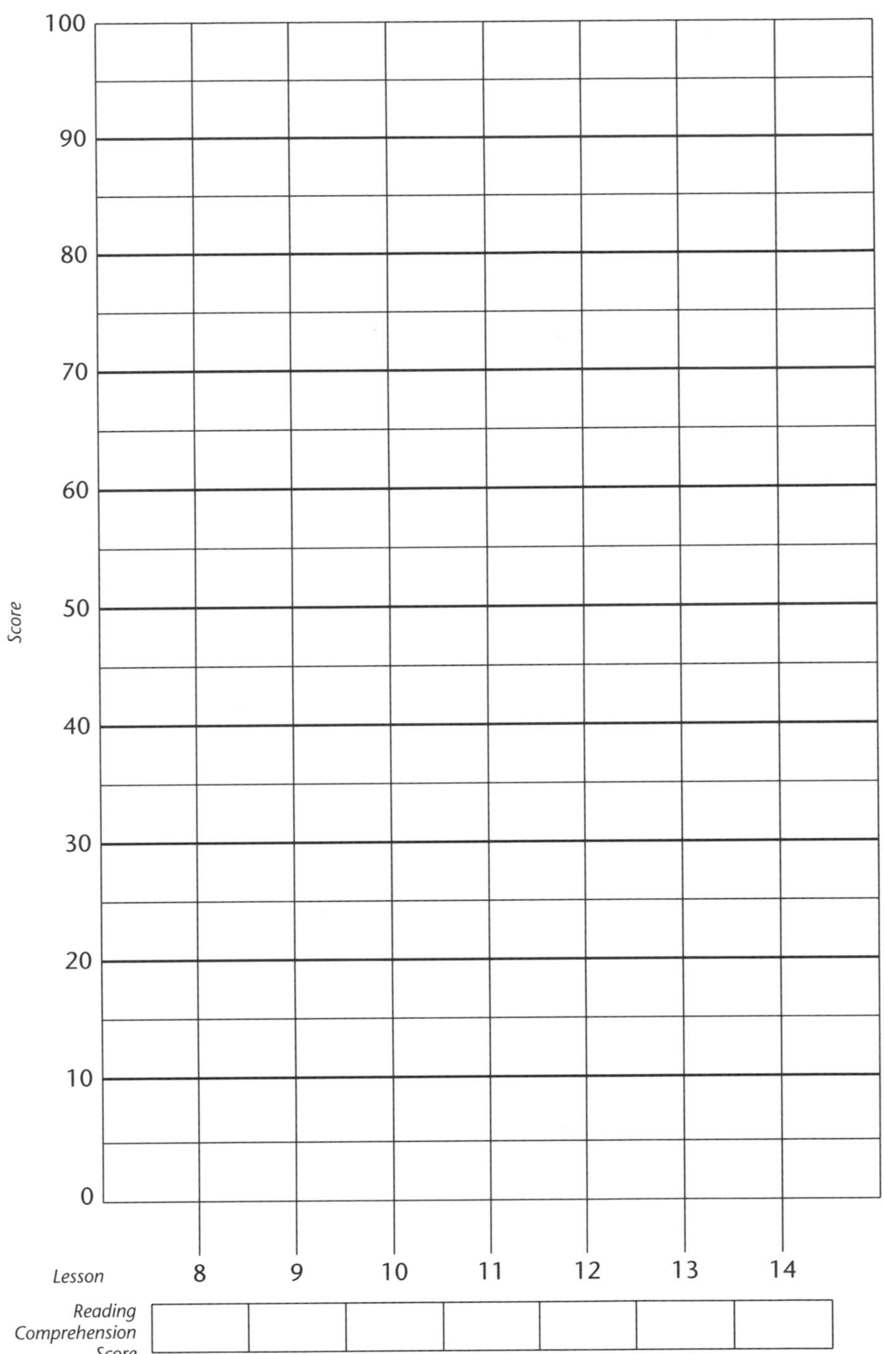

Plotting Your Progress: Critical Thinking

Unit Two

Directions: Work with your teacher to evaluate your responses to the Critical Thinking questions for each lesson. Then fill in the appropriate spaces in the chart below. For each lesson and each type of Critical Thinking question, do the following: Mark a minus sign (–) in the box to indicate areas in which you feel you could improve. Mark a plus sign (+) to indicate areas in which you feel you did well. Mark a minus-slash-plus sign (–/+) to indicate areas in which you had mixed success. Then write any comments you have about your performance, including ideas for improvement.

Lesson	Author's Approach	Summarizing and Paraphrasing	Critical Thinking
8			
9			
10			
11			
12			
13			
14			

UNIT THREE

OIL, OIL EVERYWHERE

Alaska's Prince William Sound: a dazzling jewel in America's last frontier. The jagged coast of the unspoiled sound is dotted with coves and inlets where fish spawn and otters and seals play. Along the shoreline, brown bears catch fish, and deer forage for sea kelp. For years the wildlife and marine life had the beauty of the sound to themselves. Then came the discovery of oil.

2 In the late 1960s huge reserves of oil were found in Prudhoe Bay on Alaska's northern Arctic coast. The state realized that millions could be made by selling oil-drilling leases. It didn't take long for drilling crews to move into the icy, barren territory. In the late 1970s an 800-mile pipeline was built to carry the thick crude from Prudhoe Bay to the southern port of Valdez. When the oil began to flow, huge oceangoing tankers pulled into the Valdez terminal. They loaded their cargo, and then headed out through Prince William Sound.

3 Environmentalists knew there was a potential for a massive oil spill. The state of Alaska and the oil companies who manage the pipeline grudgingly drafted a

A smaller oil tanker tries to remove crude oil from the Exxon Valdez *after 270,000 gallons were spilled in Prince William Sound.*

cleanup plan. They believed that a catastrophic spill in the sound was "highly unlikely." The oil companies said they had complete faith in their tanker pilots.

4 But then the unthinkable happened in March 1989, and no one was prepared. It was a tragic case of Murphy's Law—everything that could go wrong did go wrong.

5 Joseph Hazelwood, captain of the Exxon *Valdez*, had a couple of drinks on shore with shipmates before boarding the tanker that Thursday night. Once inside his cabin, he drank two bottles of low-alcohol beer. He was scheduled to leave the port of Valdez in 45 minutes.

6 Following routine, a harbor pilot came on board to steer the 987-foot tanker out of the port. About two hours later, the harbor pilot departed the ship. Hazelwood radioed the Coast Guard, saying he would move the tanker from the outbound shipping lane to the inbound shipping lane to avoid icebergs. He then gave control of the tanker to Third Mate Gregory Cousins. Hazelwood returned to his cabin to finish some paperwork. For some reason, the Coast Guard no longer monitored the *Valdez*.

7 Hazelwood had ordered Cousins to make a right turn back into the outbound lane when the ship reached a point near Busby Island. Cousins called the captain and told him when he was starting to turn. But it would be seven minutes before the *Valdez* actually changed direction. A lookout spotted something wrong. He raced into the pilothouse and reported that a flashing red buoy near Bligh Reef was on the ship's right side when it should have been on the left side. Cousins tried hard to turn the ship, but it was already too late. He picked up the phone and called Hazelwood. "We are in trouble."

8 Hazelwood felt the jolt when the *Valdez* impaled itself on Bligh Reef. He rushed to the bridge and immediately slowed the engines. He tried to keep the ship from sliding off the rocky reef and capsizing. Hazelwood knew he couldn't prevent the inevitable—an oil spill in the pure waters of Prince William Sound. But he did try to minimize the size of the disaster.

9 With its side split open, the *Valdez* spewed oil at the rate of 20,000 gallons an hour. Eventually, 11 million gallons would foul the sound. According to the cleanup plan, emergency teams were supposed to be on the scene within five hours of the accident. In fact, it took 10 hours before even the first crews arrived. Worse yet, they could do little with their equipment. The oil booms and skimmers were insufficient. The barge that would carry the skimmed oil was damaged and couldn't be used until the next day. The Coast Guard was equally ill-prepared. Its closest cleanup ships were in San Francisco, 2,000 miles south of Alaska. Many marine animals were already in danger. Ducks were drenched in oil, and sea lions, their flippers coated with crude, were clinging to a buoy near the *Valdez*.

10 As the oil slick snaked through the sound, Exxon Corporation took over the cleanup operation. Local residents, angry

An oil-soaked bird is rescued from Prince William Sound.

and heartsick, accused Exxon of not moving fast enough. They didn't believe Exxon's efforts would protect the fisheries and save the rich wildlife. Commercial fishermen feared the upcoming harvest of salmon and herring would be ruined.

11 Animal rescue centers were being flooded with sick, oily animals. Georgia Ruff, a local travel agent, took a leave of absence from her job to volunteer at a center. She learned to wash, dry, feed, and nurse sea otters. The animals' suffering became too much for her to bear. "To hear those animals screaming in pain—it's just awful," Ruff said.

12 The town of Valdez and other nearby villages came close to the breaking point. It was difficult for them to cope with the tragedy and adjust to all the attention from oil company officials, cleanup crews, and the media. In some villages, flags flew at half-staff. Some fishermen wore black armbands; they knew that they would face financial hardships.

13 By mid-May the thick sludge had stained an 1,800-square-mile area. Windy, stormy weather hampered the cleanup operation, which resembled a small army. Crews along the shoreline hosed down the slimy rocks with heated seawater. But progress was very slow. The crews had cleaned only 3,300 feet of beach so far, leaving over 300 miles of oil-covered shoreline to go. On the water the cleanup wasn't any easier. Skimming ships had trouble pumping the oil from the surface because it was so thick.

14 In a small village called Cordova, saddened townspeople stood in the rain near the waterfront one day and held a "requiem" for Prince William Sound. They could think of little besides the spill. They shared their grief, and some wept openly. The oil slick had already killed about 450 otters and almost 3,000 birds.

15 A state environmentalist said, "People are going to have strong feelings about this for a long time. Every time people here go to a favorite fishing hole, they will think of the spill and they will be angry."

16 Exxon fired Captain Hazelwood after receiving the results from his blood-alcohol test. Many felt the company's action came way too late. Exxon knew Hazelwood had a long history of alcohol abuse, and yet it still allowed the captain to command a tanker. Hazelwood went to trial a year after the accident, facing a felony and several misdemeanor counts. He was convicted of one charge: negligent discharge of oil. The jury did not believe that Hazelwood was drunk at the time the *Valdez* ran aground.

17 Who was to blame for the biggest oil spill in the history of the United States? After a long inquiry, it seems to be mostly Hazelwood, but also the Coast Guard and Exxon. Third Mate Cousins was probably not qualified to steer the *Valdez* through the sound. Captain Hazelwood should have been at the helm. And the Coast Guard should have tracked the ship by radar. Exxon shouldn't have ignored Hazelwood's drinking problem. And the *Valdez* crew shouldn't have been short-staffed and fatigued.

18 Exxon spent billions of dollars to clean Prince William Sound, and it compensated the residents who lost income because of the oil spill. The company also vowed to return to Alaska the following summer to pick up where nature's cleaning left off.

* * *

19 Four years after the spill, the blackened shoreline was bright again. But otters, ducks, birds, and shellfish were still being poisoned by oil buried in coves. Some species were failing to breed. Scientists who have researched the spill claim it will take decades for Prince William Sound to recover.

If you have been timed while reading this article, enter your reading time below. Then turn to the Words-per-Minute Table on page 195 and look up your reading speed (words per minute). Enter your reading speed on the graph on page 196.

Reading Time: Lesson 15

_______ : _______

Minutes *Seconds*

A Finding the Main Idea

One statement below expresses the main idea of the article. One statement is too general, or too broad. The other statement explains only part of the article; it is too narrow. Label the statements using the following key:

M—Main Idea **B—Too Broad** **N—Too Narrow**

_______ 1. The worst oil spill in the history of the United States happened in Alaska's Prince William Sound.

_______ 2. Approximately 11 million gallons of oil contaminated the once unspoiled Alaskan coastline.

_______ 3. Although oil companies had drafted cleanup plans, they never thought an oil spill would happen.

_______ Score 15 points for a correct M answer.

_______ Score 5 points for each correct B or N answer.

_______ **Total Score:** Finding the Main Idea

B Recalling Facts

How well do you remember the facts in the article? Put an X in the box next to the answer that correctly completes each statement about the article.

1. In the late 1960s, oil was discovered at
- ☐ a. the port of Valdez.
- ☐ b. Prince William Sound.
- ☐ c. Prudhoe Bay.

2. Georgia Ruff was a(n)
- ☐ a. animal rescue volunteer.
- ☐ b. member of the Coast Guard.
- ☐ c. Exxon official

3. At the time of the accident, the *Valdez* was piloted by
- ☐ a. Joseph Hazelwood.
- ☐ b. a local harbor pilot.
- ☐ c. Gregory Cousins.

4. The side of the *Valdez* was ripped open by
- ☐ a. an iceberg.
- ☐ b. Bligh Reef.
- ☐ c. another tanker.

5. Captain Joseph Hazelwood was eventually convicted of
- ☐ a. all charges.
- ☐ b. negligent discharge of oil.
- ☐ c. alcohol-related charges.

Score 5 points for each correct answer.

_______ **Total Score:** Recalling Facts

C Making Inferences

When you combine your own experience and information from a text to draw a conclusion that is not directly stated in that text, you are making an inference. Below are five statements that may or may not be inferences based on information in the article. Label the statements using the following key:

C—Correct Inference **F—Faulty Inference**

________ 1. Oil companies should have had better emergency plans in case there was a catastrophic spill.

________ 2. Captain Hazelwood is solely responsible for the spill.

________ 3. Cleanup crews immediately responded to the disaster.

________ 4. Countless birds, otters, seals, and sea lions died as a result of the spill.

________ 5. The oil spill had a devastating impact on local residents.

Score 5 points for each correct answer.

________ **Total Score:** Making Inferences

D Using Words Precisely

Each numbered sentence below contains an underlined word or phrase from the article. Following the sentence are three definitions. One definition is closest to the meaning of the underlined word. One definition is opposite or nearly opposite. Label those two definitions using the following key. Do not label the remaining definition.

C—Closest **O—Opposite or Nearly Opposite**

1. It didn't take long for drilling crews to move into the icy, <u>barren</u> territory.

________ a. fertile

________ b. dry and desolate

________ c. distant

2. They believed that a <u>catastrophic</u> spill in the sound was "highly unlikely."

________ a. disastrous

________ b. accidental

________ c. beneficial

3. With its side split open, the *Valdez* <u>spewed</u> oil at the rate of 20,000 gallons an hour.

________ a. heated up

________ b. spit out

________ c. sucked in

4. He [Hazelwood] was convicted of one charge: <u>negligent</u> discharge of oil.

________ a. late

________ b. responsible

________ c. careless

5. ...saddened townspeople stood in the rain one day and held a "requiem" for Prince William Sound.

_______ a. solemn memorial

_______ b. birthday celebration

_______ c. public trial

_______ Score 3 points for each correct C answer.

_______ Score 2 points for each correct O answer.

_______ **Total Score:** Using Words Precisely

Enter the four total scores in the spaces below, and add them together to find your Reading Comprehension Score. Then record your score on the graph on page 197.

Score	Question Type	Lesson 15
_______	Finding the Main Idea	
_______	Recalling Facts	
_______	Making Inferences	
_______	Using Words Precisely	
_______	**Reading Comprehension Score**	

Author's Approach

Put an X in the box next to the correct answer.

1. The main purpose of the first paragraph is to

☐ a. encourage the reader to visit Prince William Sound.

☐ b. inform the reader about the exact location of Prince William Sound.

☐ c. emphasize the beauty and peace of the area near Prince William Sound.

2. From the statements below, choose those that you believe the author would agree with.

☐ a. The people who lived along Prince William Sound were angered by the oil spill only because it would hurt them financially.

☐ b. Captain Hazelwood should have been more severely punished for his part in the spill.

☐ c. It will take many years for Prince William Sound to recover from the oil spill.

3. From the statement "The state of Alaska and the oil companies who manage the pipeline grudgingly drafted a cleanup plan," you can conclude that the author wants the reader to think that

☐ a. those in charge did everything they could to prepare for an oil spill.

☐ b. the cleanup plan hadn't been completed yet.

☐ c. the state and the oil companies did not seem interested in preserving the environment.

4. Choose the statement below that best describes the author's position in paragraph 17.
- ☐ a. Hazelwood, Exxon, and the Coast Guard were responsible for the oil spill.
- ☐ b. No one really knows who was responsible for the oil spill.
- ☐ c. Third Mate Cousins was mostly responsible for the oil spill.

_______ Number of correct answers

Record your personal assessment of your work on the Critical Thinking Chart on page 198.

Summarizing and Paraphrasing

Put an X in the box next to the correct answer.

1. Below are summaries of the article. Choose the summary that says all the most important things about the article but in the fewest words.
- ☐ a. The biggest oil spill in the history of the United States occurred when the Exxon *Valdez* impaled itself on Bligh Reef in Prince William Sound.
- ☐ b. The oil spill from the Exxon *Valdez* dumped millions of gallons of crude oil into Prince William Sound, greatly endangering the area's wildlife. Exxon and the ship's captain, Joseph Hazelwood, were largely to blame for the spill.
- ☐ c. Captain Joseph Hazelwood of the Exxon *Valdez* turned over control of the tanker to Third Mate Gregory Cousins. Thus, Cousins was steering the tanker when it hit Bligh Reef and began spewing oil into Prince William Sound. Cleanup efforts were slow and inefficient; the rich wildlife area in the sound became coated with oil. Although Hazelwood was largely responsible for the spill, he was convicted of only one charge: the negligent discharge of oil.

2. Read the statement about the article below. Then read the paraphrase of that statement. Choose the reason that best tells why the paraphrase does not say the same thing as the statement.

Statement: The people in the town of Valdez and other nearby villages had trouble coping with the tragedy and adjusting to the attention from the oil company officials, cleanup crews, and the media.

Paraphrase: After the tragedy, the people in the area had trouble gaining the attention of oil company officials, cleanup crews, and the media.

- ☐ a. Paraphrase says too much.
- ☐ b. Paraphrase doesn't say enough.
- ☐ c. Paraphrase doesn't agree with the statement about the article.

_______ Number of correct answers

Record your personal assessment of your work on the Critical Thinking Chart on page 198.

Critical Thinking

Put an X in the box next to the correct answer for questions 1, 4, and 5. Follow the directions provided for the other questions.

1. Judging from Joseph Hazelwood's actions as described in this article, you can predict that
- ☐ a. the captain would become a commercial airline pilot.
- ☐ b. Exxon would rehire the captain after a few years' probation.
- ☐ c. he would never again be put in charge of an oil tanker.

2. Choose from the letters below to correctly complete the following statement. Write the letters on the lines.

   In the article, ________ and ________ are different.

   a. the suffering experienced by the people of Valdez
   b. the suffering experienced by the people of Cordova
   c. the suffering experienced by the people of San Francisco

3. Think about cause-effect relationships in the article. Fill in the blanks in the cause-effect chart, drawing from the letters below.

Cause	Effect
The ship did not correctly execute a turn.	____________
____________	Fishermen wore black armbands.
The jury didn't believe that he was drunk.	____________

   a. Captain Hazelwood was convicted of only one minor charge.
   b. The Exxon *Valdez* ran aground on Bligh Reef.
   c. They knew that they would face financial hardships.

4. If you were an oil company official, how could you use the information in the article to draft a cleanup plan in case of an oil spill?

   ☐ a. Make sure that emergency teams understand their job, and insist that the Coast Guard monitor tankers.
   ☐ b. Assure the people living in the area that a catastrophic spill is highly unlikely.
   ☐ c. Allow time and nature to take care of most of the cleanup.

5. What did you have to do to answer question 2?

   ☐ a. find a cause (why something happened)
   ☐ b. find a contrast (how things are different)
   ☐ c. find a purpose (why something is done)

________ Number of correct answers

Record your personal assessment of your work on the Critical Thinking Chart on page 198.

Personal Response

I know how Georgia Ruff feels because

____

____

____

____

Self-Assessment

When reading the article, I was having trouble with

____

____

____

____

SOCCER FANS IN A DEATH TRAP

Chris Parsonage will probably always be a soccer fan. But he may think twice about ever going to another match. For the rest of his life, he will remember April 15, 1989—when an afternoon soccer game turned into a deadly stampede.

2 Chris, a 29-year-old math teacher, was looking forward to Saturday's soccer match at Hillsborough Stadium in Sheffield, England. He lived just outside the city of Liverpool, and he had been excited about the game all week. He was planning to watch Liverpool's team play in the semifinal match for the national cup. Liverpool fans love their soccer team, so Chris knew the stadium would be crowded.

3 Soccer is tremendously popular all over Europe, and English fans are famous for their team loyalty. But that loyalty has sometimes gotten out of hand. Mobs of supporters have damaged property and started deadly brawls with rival fans. In fact, English soccer fans have been so violent that for several years their teams were barred from European competition.

4 But Chris Parsonage didn't expect any trouble at Saturday's playoff game. He and

Soccer fans are crushed against fencing in the Hillsborough Stadium in Liverpool.

two friends arrived at the stadium and began to make their way through the crowded turnstiles. His friends had tickets for seats in the stands, but Chris was headed for the terrace behind the Liverpool goal. It was cheaper than his friends' seats because it had standing room only.

5 Local police and England's soccer association knew that soccer matches had a reputation for violence. And Liverpool fans were especially prone to brawls. So officials had erected security fences at either end of the field, between each terrace and goal. They hoped the steel mesh would keep Liverpool fans from pouring onto the field to attack the fans of the rival team.

6 Outside the turnstiles, the crowd began to thicken as Liverpool fans gathered at their gate. Most people in the crowd did not have tickets. They came to the match planning to buy them at the door. But for some reason, fans of Liverpool's opponent, Nottingham Forest, had been allotted more tickets. So while the rival fans streamed in at their gate, many Liverpool fans were forced to wait outside.

7 Angry and noisy, the fans milled around the gate. The crowd had swollen to 3,000 people by now, and police began to fear a riot. To keep the pressure from building up outside the arena, an officer opened a gate to the stadium.

8 Meanwhile, Chris Parsonage had managed to get through the turnstiles. He walked along the tunnel that led from the gate to the terrace. Nearby he heard someone mention that the police had opened the gates behind him, but he wasn't worried. He said later, "Everyone was pushing forward to get in and see the kickoff, but I had been in crowds like this before." Confident that he would find a place to stand, Chris just wasn't prepared for the chaos that happened next.

9 He made his way to the terrace and tried to move to a place where he could see the game. But then he realized that he was trapped. The crowd was so tight that he could not move to either side, and the situation was getting worse. He felt the pressure building up behind him like the swell of a giant wave. Thousands of fans had now surged through the tunnel.

10 Chris and the people around him were lifted off their feet from the extreme pressure. One of Chris's legs was pulled forward while the other was trapped against a barrier. He began to scream. "I honestly thought my leg would snap," he remembered, "and I was panicking."

11 All around him people were screaming and fainting. He watched in horror as a man in front of him turned blue. But there was nothing Chris could do to help. His arms and legs were pinned by the crowd around him.

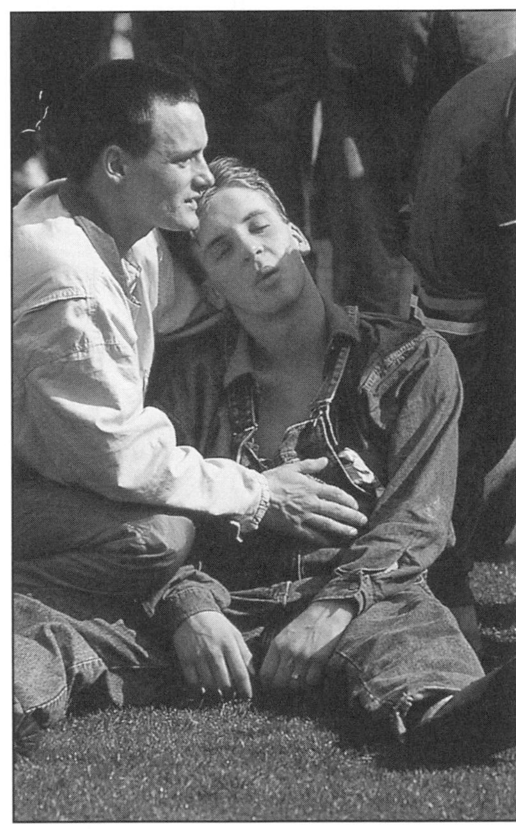

An injured soccer fan is comforted by a friend after the tragedy at the Hillsborough Stadium.

12 The fans tried yelling for the police to stop the game. But they couldn't scream for long because they had to save their breath. Chris said he struggled to keep his mouth up high so that he could keep breathing.

13 At the front of the terrace, hundreds of fans were pressed against the steel-mesh security fence, as the crowd continued to squeeze forward. Some people fell and were trampled, while others were crushed to death against the 10-foot-high immovable fence. Bill Eastwood, a safety expert who was present at the disaster, said, "There must have been a half ton of pressure across each person's midriff."

14 Chris Parsonage was lucky. Somehow the surge of the crowd pushed him into an empty seat. He sat there for an hour and a half, unable to walk on his injured leg. He recalled, "I started shaking and crying because I knew very well I could have been dead. I could see all those people being carried away like dolls in a toy shop, with arms hanging all over the place."

15 Ninety-four fans were killed in the stampede, and nearly 200 more were injured. Many of the dead were children and teenagers, who had been crushed and suffocated by a crowd of taller adults. Chris Parsonage, who is more than six feet tall, believes that his height saved his life.

16 Amazingly, many people at the soccer match had no idea that fellow fans were being pressed to death. Because the people on the terrace couldn't breathe, they also couldn't scream. So the danger wasn't realized until it was too late. Soccer officials, unaware of the tragedy, did not call off the match immediately. The players on the field continued the game for six minutes while their fans were being killed in front of them.

17 The tragedy at Sheffield is just one example of the ongoing problem with English soccer crowds. And some researchers believe that the stadiums themselves are the cause of many incidents. A number of popular stadiums are small and outdated. Others are built in cramped city neighborhoods, where there is no room to organize a crowd. Some people believe that if England wants to avoid crowd disasters in the future, the country must invest in larger, more modern stadiums. They will make police security easier and safer. And they will also attract families who are now afraid to attend soccer matches.

18 But a new stadium won't make Chris Parsonage forget Sheffield. "I still wake up crying in the middle of the night and see that guy's face in front of me. At the stadium I think I was crying because I was alive. Now I don't know. I think I am crying for the dead."

If you have been timed while reading this article, enter your reading time below. Then turn to the Words-per-Minute Table on page 195 and look up your reading speed (words per minute). Enter your reading speed on the graph on page 196.

Reading Time: Lesson 16

________ : ________

Minutes *Seconds*

A Finding the Main Idea

One statement below expresses the main idea of the article. One statement is too general, or too broad. The other statement explains only part of the article; it is too narrow. Label the statements using the following key:

M—Main Idea **B—Too Broad** **N—Too Narrow**

_____ 1. English soccer stadiums cause many crowd problems.

_____ 2. The Sheffield tragedy was caused by a crowd that surged against a security fence.

_____ 3. Chris Parsonage had been looking forward to watching the Liverpool team.

_____ Score 15 points for a correct M answer.

_____ Score 5 points for each correct B or N answer.

_____ **Total Score:** Finding the Main Idea

B Recalling Facts

How well do you remember the facts in the article? Put an X in the box next to the answer that correctly completes each statement about the article.

1. Chris Parsonage worked as a
   - ☐ a. social studies teacher.
   - ☐ b. police officer.
   - ☐ c. math teacher.
2. The Nottingham Forest fans had
   - ☐ a. received more tickets.
   - ☐ b. been crushed against a fence.
   - ☐ c. started a riot at the gate.
3. When the crowd began pushing, Chris was
   - ☐ a. lifted off his feet.
   - ☐ b. squeezed against the fence.
   - ☐ c. able to leave by an exit.
4. Most of the people killed were
   - ☐ a. elderly people.
   - ☐ b. players and officials.
   - ☐ c. children and teenagers.
5. Some researchers believe that crowd problems are caused by
   - ☐ a. political disagreements.
   - ☐ b. the stadiums themselves.
   - ☐ c. difficulties with the players.

Score 5 points for each correct answer.

_____ **Total Score:** Recalling Facts

C Making Inferences

When you combine your own experience and information from a text to draw a conclusion that is not directly stated in that text, you are making an inference. Below are five statements that may or may not be inferences based on information in the article. Label the statements using the following key:

C—Correct Inference **F—Faulty Inference**

_______ 1. Chris Parsonage had never been very interested in soccer.

_______ 2. English fans have caused trouble at European matches.

_______ 3. Chris didn't want to spend very much money to see the game.

_______ 4. A police officer solved the problem by opening the gate.

_______ 5. Sometimes it can be difficult to control a crowd.

Score 5 points for each correct answer.

_______ **Total Score:** Making Inferences

D Using Words Precisely

Each numbered sentence below contains an underlined word or phrase from the article. Following the sentence are three definitions. One definition is closest to the meaning of the underlined word. One definition is opposite or nearly opposite. Label those two definitions using the following key. Do not label the remaining definition.

C—Closest **O—Opposite or Nearly Opposite**

1. In fact, English soccer fans have been so violent that for several years their teams were <u>barred from</u> European competition.

_______ a. necessary for

_______ b. invited to take part in

_______ c. excluded from

2. And Liverpool fans were especially <u>prone to</u> brawls.

_______ a. ready to participate in

_______ b. fearful of

_______ c. unwilling to participate in

3. But for some reason, fans of Liverpool's opponent, Nottingham Forest, had been <u>allotted</u> more tickets.

_______ a. overcharged for

_______ b. refused

_______ c. given

4. Angry and noisy, the fans <u>milled</u> around the gate.

_______ a. moved about in an aimless way

_______ b. marched with a clear purpose

_______ c. set small fires

5. The tragedy at Sheffield is just one example of the ongoing problem with English soccer crowds.

_______ a. one time only

_______ b. terrible

_______ c. continuous

_______ Score 3 points for each correct C answer.

_______ Score 2 points for each correct O answer.

_______ **Total Score:** Using Words Precisely

Enter the four total scores in the spaces below, and add them together to find your Reading Comprehension Score. Then record your score on the graph on page 197.

Score	Question Type	Lesson 16
_______	Finding the Main Idea	
_______	Recalling Facts	
_______	Making Inferences	
_______	Using Words Precisely	
_______	**Reading Comprehension Score**	

Author's Approach

Put an X in the box next to the correct answer.

1. What does the author mean by the statement "[Chris] watched in horror as a man in front of him turned blue"?

☐ a. Rival fans painted the man blue.

☐ b. The man turned blue because he couldn't breathe.

☐ c. The man turned blue because he was angry at the crowd surging around him.

2. What is the author's purpose in writing "Soccer Fans in a Death Trap"?

☐ a. To express an opinion about the rowdiness of English soccer fans

☐ b. To inform the reader about the outdated soccer stadiums in England

☐ c. To describe a situation in which fans at a soccer stadium were caught in a stampede

3. How is the author's purpose for writing the article expressed in paragraph 17?

☐ a. The author explains some of the reasons for the stampede.

☐ b. The author tells the reader that families are afraid to attend soccer matches.

☐ c. The author tells the reader that the stadium was too small for the crush of fans anxious to see the game.

4. The author tells this story mainly by

☐ a. retelling Chris Parsonage's experience at the stadium.

☐ b. comparing English soccer fans with other European fans.

☐ c. retelling several people's experiences at the stadium.

_______ Number of correct answers

Record your personal assessment of your work on the Critical Thinking Chart on page 198.

Summarizing and Paraphrasing

Follow the directions provided for questions 1 and 2. Put an X in the box next to the correct answer for question 3.

1. Look for the important ideas and events in paragraphs 9 and 10. Summarize those paragraphs in one or two sentences.

____

____

____

2. Reread paragraph 14 in the article. Below, write a summary of the paragraph in no more than 25 words.

____

____

____

____

Reread your summary and decide whether it covers the important ideas in the paragraph. Next, decide how to shorten the summary to 15 words or less without leaving out any essential information. Write this summary below.

____

____

____

3. Read the statement about the article below. Then read the paraphrase of that statement. Choose the reason that best tells why the paraphrase does not say the same thing as the statement.

Statement: Although English soccer fans are famous for their loyalty, they are also known for their violent behavior, which has sometimes led to deadly fights with rival fans.

Paraphrase: English soccer fans are loyal, but they are also so violent that, for several years, their teams were not allowed to take part in European competitions.

- ☐ a. Paraphrase says too much.
- ☐ b. Paraphrase doesn't say enough.
- ☐ c. Paraphrase doesn't agree with the statement about the article.

________ Number of correct answers

Record your personal assessment of your work on the Critical Thinking Chart on page 198.

Critical Thinking

Put an X in the box next to the correct answer for questions 1 and 3. Follow the directions provided for the other questions.

1. Judging by the events in the article, you can predict that the following will happen next:

- ☐ a. the English people will no longer care about soccer.
- ☐ b. English soccer stadiums will be made differently in the future.
- ☐ c. English soccer teams will play all their games in other countries.

2. Choose from the letters below to correctly complete the following statement. Write the letters on the lines.

   On the positive side, _________, but on the negative side _________.

   a. English fans are famous for their loyalty to their teams
   b. 94 people were crushed or suffocated in the stampede
   c. Chris Parsonage managed to break free from the crowd

3. What was the cause of the officer's decision to open a gate into the stadium?

   ☐ a. Chris Parsonage walked through the turnstiles.
   ☐ b. People pushed forward to see the kickoff.
   ☐ c. He was afraid that the fans would start a riot.

4. In which paragraph did you find the information or details to answer question 3?

   ____

_________ Number of correct answers

Record your personal assessment of your work on the Critical Thinking Chart on page 198.

Personal Response

I know the feeling

____

____

____

____

Self-Assessment

I can't really understand how

____

____

____

____

CHALLENGER
The Final Countdown

Christa McAuliffe. Francis Scobee. Ellison Onizuka. Judith Resnik. Michael Smith. Ronald McNair. Gregory Jarvis.

2 These were the crew members of the space shuttle *Challenger*. What happened to them on January 28, 1986, shocked millions of people and left a nation in mourning.

* * *

3 For Christa McAuliffe, the journey began in 1984. That was the year President Ronald Reagan announced that a teacher would be the first civilian to travel in space. McAuliffe, a social studies teacher from New Hampshire, eagerly applied for the job. She was among 11,000 teachers who sent applications to the National Aeronautics and Space Administration (NASA). Ever since childhood, McAuliffe had been fascinated with space. She told NASA how excited she was when she watched the first satellites being launched. And when Alan Shepard became the first American in space in 1961, McAuliffe was thrilled. She was always envious of astronauts and hoped

The Challenger *lifts off at the Kennedy Space Center. Seventy-three seconds later the spacecraft exploded.*

that some day women would have careers in space, too.

4 NASA chose McAuliffe for the teacher-in-space program in 1985. As part of her historic mission, she planned to teach two science classes in space. The lessons would be beamed live via satellite to classrooms across the country. McAuliffe, age 37, also planned to keep journals as a "pioneer space traveler."

5 Beginning in September of 1985, McAuliffe went through 114 hours of space flight training at the Johnson Space Center in Houston, Texas. There she trained with the other *Challenger* astronauts. All but Jarvis, a civilian engineer, had previously flown on shuttle missions. In 1984 Resnik became the second woman in space (Sally Ride was the first). That same year McNair became the second African American to travel in space. Onizuka flew on a secret Defense Department shuttle flight in 1985. Smith, the *Challenger*'s pilot, was one of NASA's most experienced pilots. And Scobee, who had piloted *Challenger* before, was the flight's mission commander.

6 *Challenger's* celebrated launch from Cape Canaveral, Florida, originally was scheduled for January 23, 1986. But bad weather postponed the flight several times. The astronauts remained in quarantine and in good spirits. They relaxed and studied flight plans while they waited in their quarters.

7 January 28 was a clear but unusually cold, windy day. In the VIP stands on the roof of Mission Control, the families of the *Challenger* crew shook with anticipation and huddled as the winds blew. The official countdown had begun. Across the nation, people were turning on their televisions. Students were gathered in auditoriums and classrooms to view the launch. At McAuliffe's school in Concord, New Hampshire, students and faculty were cheering loudly. Some wore party hats and waved noisemakers. In unison they chanted the countdown: "5! 4! 3! 2! 1!"

8 The 11:38 A.M. liftoff was spectacular. Christa McAuliffe's proud parents smiled and hugged each other as *Challenger* cleared the tower. McAuliffe's husband, Steve, and their children, Scott and Caroline, were jubilant. It was a great day. Then something went terribly wrong.

9 Seventy-five seconds into the flight, Mission Control told the shuttle crew: "*Challenger*, go at throttle up." *Challenger*'s pilot followed the order. At that point, the shuttle's engines were thrust into full power. Suddenly the spacecraft erupted into a giant fireball. At first, spectators thought the brilliant burst of fire was the separation of the shuttle from its rocket boosters. But seconds later, trails of white and orange smoke streaked across the sky. There was silence for about 30 seconds. Then Mission Control announced that the shuttle had exploded.

10 The families of the crew members stood still in disbelief. McAuliffe's parents hugged but did not move. Jo Ann Jordan, McAuliffe's best friend, cried, "It didn't

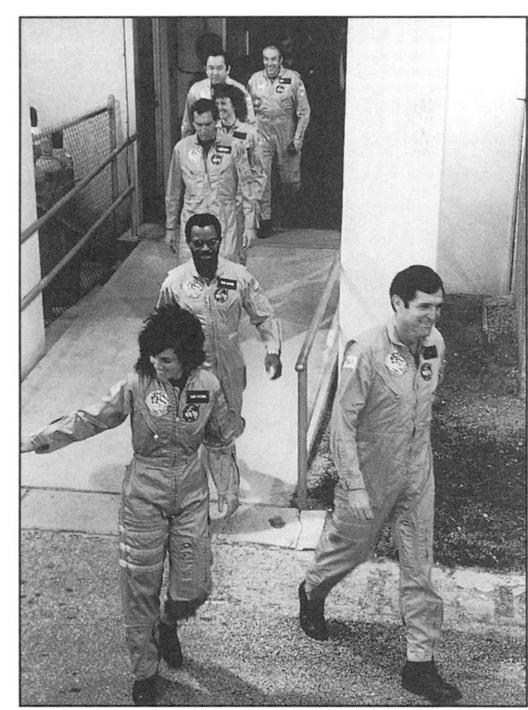

Crew members walk to the launch pad to board the Challenger.

explode, it didn't explode." Everywhere people started to cry. At Concord High School, students stared blankly at the television screen. Many did not understand what had happened. Bonnie Wakeley, a sophomore, said later, "We were watching and then they [the crew] were gone. We couldn't believe it."

11 NASA immediately sent rescue crews to the crash site about 18 miles offshore. There was a slim chance that the astronauts might be found at sea. Ships and helicopters desperately searched the area. But later that afternoon, NASA gave the world the horrible news. *Challenger*'s crew members died in the explosion. Rescuers had found only chunks of debris in the Atlantic Ocean. However, their search would continue and cover many miles. Later, in a huge warehouse, NASA investigators sifted through what was left of the 110-ton, $1.2 billion shuttle, looking for clues.

12 The *Challenger* disaster was a devastating setback for NASA and its shuttle program. Thirteen more flights had been scheduled for 1986, but those missions were canceled. McAuliffe's flight would have been the 25th for the shuttle program. In one of her last public statements, she said, "I realize there is a risk outside your everyday life, but it doesn't frighten me."

13 About a month after the tragic explosion, rescuers found *Challenger*'s cabin and the crew's remains deep in the ocean. NASA was able to determine that the astronauts survived at least several seconds after the explosion. They may have even been alive but unconscious until they struck the ocean surface.

14 A presidential commission investigated the shuttle disaster for six months. It blamed NASA for allowing the spacecraft to take off in such cold weather. The 30-degree weather caused a rubber seal between segments of the right rocket booster to fail. Fiery gases then escaped through the defective seal. Like a blowtorch, the hot gases burned through the rocket and ignited the fuel in the shuttle's huge external tank. This created the catastrophic fireball that destroyed the shuttle. A film of the flight showed that *Challenger* was in trouble at least 14 seconds before the fatal blast. The crew may have sensed the impending danger. A split second before the spaceship blew apart, pilot Mike Smith said, "Uh-oh."

15 It would be two and a half years before the United States launched another shuttle. And there were no immediate plans for another civilian to travel in space.

16 The families of the *Challenger* crew still grieve for their loved ones. But in their grief, they carry on *Challenger*'s mission—to educate. The families have praised various projects promoting space exploration and education. And together they founded the Challenger Center for Space Science Education in Virginia. They wanted to have something "dynamic" for children and teachers. "The eyes of those little children who were glued to television—you couldn't just let it end that way, with that terrible loss," said June Scobee, widow of Francis Scobee. "The Challenger center is a way to talk about how the mission continues...." And not how the mission ended.

If you have been timed while reading this article, enter your reading time below. Then turn to the Words-per-Minute Table on page 195 and look up your reading speed (words per minute). Enter your reading speed on the graph on page 196.

Reading Time: Lesson 17

________ : ________

Minutes *Seconds*

A Finding the Main Idea

One statement below expresses the main idea of the article. One statement is too general, or too broad. The other statement explains only part of the article; it is too narrow. Label the statements using the following key:

M—Main Idea **B—Too Broad** **N—Too Narrow**

_______ 1. The launch date for the *Challenger* had been postponed several times because of bad weather.

_______ 2. The space program in the United States slowed down because of the *Challenger* explosion.

_______ 3. The United States was stunned when the first shuttle launch to include a private citizen, Christa McAuliffe, exploded.

_______ Score 15 points for a correct M answer.

_______ Score 5 points for each correct B or N answer.

_______ **Total Score:** Finding the Main Idea

B Recalling Facts

How well do you remember the facts in the article? Put an X in the box next to the answer that correctly completes each statement about the article.

1. The decision that the first civilian on the space shuttle would be a teacher was announced by

☐ a. astronaut Sally Ride.
☐ b. President Ronald Reagan.
☐ c. NASA officials.

2. The first woman astronaut to travel in space was

☐ a. Judith Resnik.
☐ b. Sally Ride.
☐ c. Christa McAuliffe.

3. The space shuttle exploded because

☐ a. a rubber seal was defective.
☐ b. there was too much fuel in the tank.
☐ c. the computer system on board failed.

4. The *Challenger* was launched from

☐ a. Houston, Texas.
☐ b. Washington, D.C.
☐ c. Cape Canaveral, Florida.

5. During her flight aboard the *Challenger*, McAuliffe planned to

☐ a. keep a journal and teach two science classes.
☐ b. observe the other astronauts.
☐ c. record the technical aspects of spaceflight.

Score 5 points for each correct answer.

_______ **Total Score:** Recalling Facts

C Making Inferences

When you combine your own experience and information from a text to draw a conclusion that is not directly stated in that text, you are making an inference. Below are five statements that may or may not be inferences based on information in the article. Label the statements using the following key:

C—Correct Inference **F—Faulty Inference**

_______ 1. Christa McAuliffe felt lucky to be chosen as the first teacher in space.

_______ 2. President Ronald Reagan believed that the space shuttle program was not worth the risks.

_______ 3. Despite the disaster, the families of the *Challenger* crew still believe in and support the space program.

_______ 4. Everyone felt that the astronauts would be found alive at sea.

_______ 5. Because of the *Challenger* disaster, there will never be another chance for a civilian to travel in space.

Score 5 points for each correct answer.

_______ **Total Score:** Making Inferences

D Using Words Precisely

Each numbered sentence below contains an underlined word or phrase from the article. Following the sentence are three definitions. One definition is closest to the meaning of the underlined word. One definition is opposite or nearly opposite. Label those two definitions using the following key. Do not label the remaining definition.

C—Closest **O—Opposite or Nearly Opposite**

1. *Challenger*'s celebrated launch from Cape Canaveral, Florida, originally was scheduled for January 23, 1986.

_______ a. happy

_______ b. famous

_______ c. little known

2. In the VIP stands…the families of the *Challenger* crew shook with anticipation and huddled as the winds blew.

_______ a. boredom

_______ b. expectation

_______ c. cold

3. In unison they chanted the countdown: "5! 4! 3! 2! 1!"

_______ a. together

_______ b. separately

_______ c. loudly

4. McAuliffe's husband, Steve, and their children, Scott and Caroline, were jubilant.

_______ a. depressed and unhappy

_______ b. tired and sleepy

_______ c. very joyous and excited

5. They [the families of the crew] wanted to have something "dynamic" for children and teachers.

_______ a. new

_______ b. inactive

_______ c. energetic

_______ Score 3 points for each correct C answer.

_______ Score 2 points for each correct O answer.

_______ **Total Score:** Using Words Precisely

Enter the four total scores in the spaces below, and add them together to find your Reading Comprehension Score. Then record your score on the graph on page 197.

Score	Question Type	Lesson 17
_______	Finding the Main Idea	
_______	Recalling Facts	
_______	Making Inferences	
_______	Using Words Precisely	
_______	**Reading Comprehension Score**	

Author's Approach

Put an X in the box next to the correct answer.

1. The main purpose of the first paragraph is to tell the reader the

☐ a. names of the crew members who died on *Challenger*.

☐ b. names of crew members of successful space shuttle flights.

☐ c. name of the teacher who died on *Challenger*.

2. Which of the following statements from the article best describes Christa McAuliffe's feelings about space exploration?

☐ a. "She was among 11,000 teachers who sent applications to the National Aeronautics and Space Administration (NASA)."

☐ b. "Beginning in September of 1985, McAuliffe went through 114 hours of space flight training at the Johnson Space Center in Houston, Texas."

☐ c. "Ever since childhood McAuliffe had been fascinated with space."

3. From the statements below, choose those that you believe the author would agree with.

☐ a. Christa McAuliffe did not realize that her mission on the *Challenger* space shuttle could be dangerous.

☐ b. NASA officials acted irresponsibly when they insisted on launching *Challenger* on such an unusually cold day.

☐ c. After the *Challenger* disaster, many people lost faith in NASA and its shuttle program.

4. From the statement "Jo Ann Jordan, McAuliffe's best friend, cried, 'It didn't explode, it didn't explode,'" you can conclude that the author wants the reader to think that Jordan

☐ a. didn't want to believe what had happened.

☐ b. had inside information about the explosion.

☐ c. was trying to cheer up the other spectators.

_________ Number of correct answers

Record your personal assessment of your work on the Critical Thinking Chart on page 198.

Summarizing and Paraphrasing

Follow the directions provided for question 1. Put an X in the box next to the correct answer for question 2.

1. Complete the following one-sentence summary of the article using the lettered phrases from the phrase bank below. Write the letters on the lines.

Phrase Bank:

a. a description of Christa McAuliffe's selection and training for the teacher-in-space program

b. the causes and effects of the explosion

c. the space shuttle's explosion seconds after liftoff

After a short introduction, the article about the *Challenger* disaster begins with _________, goes on to describe _________, and ends with _________.

2. Choose the best one-sentence paraphrase for the following sentence from the article:

"In the VIP stands on the roof of Mission Control, the families of the *Challenger* crew shook with anticipation and huddled as the winds blew."

☐ a. The families of the crew members shook with fear as they waited for the *Challenger* launch.

☐ b. The families of the crew members clung to each other to keep from being blown off the roof of Mission Control.

☐ c. The families of the crew members trembled with excitement and pressed close together against the wind as they waited for the *Challenger* launch.

_________ Number of correct answers

Record your personal assessment of your work on the Critical Thinking Chart on page 198.

Critical Thinking

Put an X in the box next to the correct answer for questions 1, 3, and 4. Follow the directions provided for the other questions.

1. From the information in paragraph 14, you can predict that *Challenger* might not have exploded if

☐ a. the launch had taken place on a warm day.

☐ b. Mike Smith had been a more experienced pilot.

☐ c. the crew had carried fire extinguishers on board.

2. Choose from the letters below to correctly complete the following statement. Write the letters on the lines.

   In the article, _________ and _________ are different.

   a. Judith Resnik's previous experience on shuttle missions
   b. Gregory Jarvis's previous experience on shuttle missions
   c. Ronald McNair's previous experience on shuttle missions

3. What was the effect of the *Challenger* disaster on NASA's shuttle program?

☐ a. NASA founded the Challenger Center for Space Science Education.
☐ b. Thirteen flights scheduled in 1986 were canceled.
☐ c. NASA continued to launch shuttle missions in 1986.

4. How is the *Challenger* explosion an example of a calamity?

☐ a. The explosion was a devastating setback for NASA.
☐ b. The explosion destroyed a $1.2 billion shuttle.
☐ c. The explosion killed everyone on board and shocked millions of American viewers.

5. In which paragraph did you find the information or details to answer question 3?

____

_________ Number of correct answers

Record your personal assessment of your work on the Critical Thinking Chart on page 198.

Personal Response

Would you recommend this article to other students? Explain.

____

____

____

____

Self-Assessment

The part I found most difficult about the article was

____

____

____

____

I found this difficult because

____

____

____

____

THE GREAT MISSISSIPPI FLOOD OF 1993

Most calamities are fast-striking affairs—they kill quickly and then they are done. Tornadoes, explosions, fires, and plane crashes are usually over in a matter of minutes, if not seconds. But the Great Flood of 1993 was different. It began slowly, building up its destructive potential, and lasted for several months. As one man said, "The [Mississippi River] is relentless. It doesn't hit you hard and fast, it just keeps coming and coming."

2 "Hurricanes are devastating, but at least they're over with quickly," said Ronald Van of the Federal Emergency Management Agency. "This is cruel. It just sits around."

3 To the people of the Midwest, floods are a fact of life. Midwesterners accept floods the same way they accept blizzards—they know that sooner or later these disasters are going to happen. Every year, spring rains and melting snows swell the Mississippi as well as the many rivers and streams that flow into it. Sometimes the rivers overflow their banks or break through the dams or levees, flooding the surrounding areas. And sometimes the

A group of pigs takes refuge from the floodwaters of the Mississippi River on the roof of a submerged barn.

flooding is truly disastrous. That was the case in 1937, 1965, and 1973. But the Great Flood of 1993 was something else again. It was, as many people said, "the mother of all floods."

4 The causes for the Great Flood of 1993 can be traced back to the previous fall. Unusually heavy rains hit the Midwest, saturating the soil. The land never had a chance to dry out before the winter cold froze the ground and the snows came. That by itself would have been enough to cause some minor flooding in many places the following year. But in the spring of 1993, the Midwest got hit with a series of very heavy downpours. Ordinarily, this part of the country doesn't get a lot of rain in the spring. Unusual weather patterns, however, brought record amounts of rainfall to the region.

5 In early March, the National Weather Service was not predicting any major flooding in the Midwest. But it warned that things could worsen if more heavy rains came. By April 1, after weeks of steady rain and melting snow, the situation had become grim. The Weather Service then predicted that sections of Iowa could expect moderate to severe flooding. That was a classic understatement. By May 10, Mother's Day, many parts of the Midwest were underwater. "Mother's Day was not all spring flowers, cake, and sunshine," wrote Tom Meersman of the Minneapolis Star Tribune. "It was a Sunday of floodwaters, mud, washed-out roads, cleanup—and worry."

6 There was ample reason to worry. The Great Flood of 1993 was just getting warmed up. By early June, the floods had arrived in earnest. Warm, moist air feeding up from the Gulf of Mexico collided with cool, dry air from Canada. That combination produced severe thunderstorms and torrential rains throughout the region. Several inches of rain fell in many places. For example, New London, Iowa, got an unbelievable 6½ inches of rain in 15 minutes. All that water had no place to go but into the local streams and rivers.

7 By June 30th, the Mississippi River, which drains the entire Midwest, had reached all-time record crests at Burlington, Iowa, and Keithsburg, Illinois. The flooding was so bad that barge traffic was closed from St. Louis, Missouri, north to St. Paul, Minnesota. "This is like watching a disaster movie like *The Towering Inferno*," said Emmett Hahn, an official at the Emergency Operations Center in St. Louis. "You leave the movie thinking, 'That was exciting, but it would never happen in real life because you couldn't have all those events at one time.' But that's what's happened."

8 In July, the Great Flood of 1993 turned really nasty. Again, just when people thought it couldn't get any worse, it did. Heavy downpours continued to soak the Midwest as a stalled high-pressure system off the East Coast kept pumping warm tropical air into the upper Mississippi Valley. Nearly all of the levees between Hannibal, Missouri, and St. Louis broke, inundating the countryside. Eight inches of rain fell on Kansas City, Missouri. That

McDonald's famous golden arches are submerged in the Mississippi floodwaters near St. Louis, Missouri.

downpour produced seven feet of water in some parts of the city. By mid-July, the death toll from the flood had reached 20. The crops on millions of acres of prime farmland were underwater. Also, thousands of Midwesterners were left homeless or without potable water or electricity.

9 At the same time, the courageous people of the Midwest did their best to hold back the waters. Day after day, night after night, they piled sandbag on top of sandbag in an often hopeless attempt to save their farms and homes. Inmates from local jails joined in the fight to hold off the water, winning the deep thanks of many residents. Allan Church, a convicted burglar, said after a day of sandbagging, "That was the best thing I ever did. Those people were really happy to have me around."

10 It's hard to imagine just how heart-breaking a flood like this can be unless you have lived through one. But the images provided by news photographs can help—friends comforting those who have lost their homes, parents holding priceless photo albums over their heads, people rowing boats down streets to rescue neighbors stuck on rooftops. No photograph, however, can convey the noxious smell of the mud. Pam Christian of Iowa said, "It smelled so bad I was choking."

11 The Great Flood of 1993 had its share of heroes. One was Bob Scott, a 48-year-old truck driver. He worked with more than 300 volunteers in a futile effort to keep open the Bayview Bridge near Quincy, Illinois. When the protecting levees gave way, the river submerged the town under 20 feet of water. The Mississippi also swept away cars lying in its path. Scott saved one woman by pulling her off her car's roof; he also grabbed a man who was hanging halfway out of the driver's window of his car.

12 By the end of July, nearly three quarters of the more than 1,300 levees had been breached. The federal government declared nine Midwestern states disaster areas. The flood finally crested at Cairo, Illinois, in early August. Fortunately, the Mississippi River at this point widens and deepens, allowing it to flow south without causing further mayhem.

13 Still, the death and destruction between St. Paul in the north and Cairo in the south was impressive enough. The Great Flood of 1993 lasted more than three months. The official death toll stood at 50. The merciless flood left more than 70,000 people homeless and more than 20 million areas of farmland underwater. Officials estimated the total damage at $12 billion. Those totals put the disaster in second place, behind the $17-billion Hurricane Andrew, as the most costly natural calamity in American history.

If you have been timed while reading this article, enter your reading time below. Then turn to the Words-per-Minute Table on page 195 and look up your reading speed (words per minute). Enter your reading speed on the graph on page 196.

Reading Time: Lesson 18

_______ : _______

Minutes *Seconds*

A Finding the Main Idea

One statement below expresses the main idea of the article. One statement is too general, or too broad. The other statement explains only part of the article; it is too narrow. Label the statements using the following key:

M—Main Idea **B—Too Broad** **N—Too Narrow**

_______ 1. In 1993, record rainfall caused terrible floods throughout the Midwest for several months.

_______ 2. The people of the Midwest accept floods as a fact of life.

_______ 3. Many Midwesterners used sandbags to try to hold back the flood waters.

_______ Score 15 points for a correct M answer.

_______ Score 5 points for each correct B or N answer.

_______ **Total Score:** Finding the Main Idea

B Recalling Facts

How well do you remember the facts in the article? Put an X in the box next to the answer that correctly completes each statement about the article.

1. Every year, spring rains and melting snows swell
- ☐ a. New England.
- ☐ b. the Mississippi River.
- ☐ c. the Gulf of Mexico.

2. By April 1, the National Weather Service predicted
- ☐ a. moderate to severe flooding in parts of Iowa.
- ☐ b. severe flooding all over the Midwest.
- ☐ c. light rains throughout the summer in the Midwest.

3. The Great Flood of 1993 turned especially nasty in
- ☐ a. May.
- ☐ b. June.
- ☐ c. July.

4. Allan Church, who helped in the sandbagging effort, was
- ☐ a. a truck driver.
- ☐ b. an official at the Emergency Operations Center in St. Louis.
- ☐ c. a convicted burglar.

5. In early August, the flood finally crested in
- ☐ a. Cairo, Illinois.
- ☐ b. St. Paul, Minnesota.
- ☐ c. Quincy, Illinois.

Score 5 points for each correct answer.

_______ **Total Score:** Recalling Facts

C Making Inferences

When you combine your own experience and information from a text to draw a conclusion that is not directly stated in that text, you are making an inference. Below are five statements that may or may not be inferences based on information in the article. Label the statements using the following key:

C—Correct Inference **F—Faulty Inference**

_______ 1. People of the Midwest welcomed any help they could get to fight the flood waters.

_______ 2. Many people lost their homes and possessions in the Great Flood of 1993.

_______ 3. Most Midwesterners just gave up and watched helplessly as the flood waters rose.

_______ 4. The prisoners who were enlisted to help stop the flood waters resented having to do the work.

_______ 5. It took a long time to clean up and rebuild the areas most affected by the flood.

Score 5 points for each correct answer.

_______ **Total Score:** Making Inferences

D Using Words Precisely

Each numbered sentence below contains an underlined word or phrase from the article. Following the sentence are three definitions. One definition is closest to the meaning of the underlined word. One definition is opposite or nearly opposite. Label those two definitions using the following key. Do not label the remaining definition.

C—Closest **O—Opposite or Nearly Opposite**

1. Unusually heavy rains hit the Midwest, <u>saturating</u> the soil.

_______ a. polluting

_______ b. drenching

_______ c. drying out

2. Also, thousands of Midwesterners were left homeless or without <u>potable</u> water or electricity.

_______ a. impure

_______ b. bottled

_______ c. drinkable

3. No photograph, however, can convey the <u>noxious</u> smell of the mud.

_______ a. foul

_______ b. sweet

_______ c. actual

4. He worked with more than 300 volunteers in a <u>futile</u> effort to keep open the Bayview Bridge near Quincy, Illinois.

_______ a. emotional

_______ b. vain

_______ c. effective

5. Fortunately, the Mississippi River at this point widens and deepens, allowing it to flow south without causing further <u>mayhem</u>.

_______ a. needless damage

_______ b. great concern

_______ c. great improvement

_______ Score 3 points for each correct C answer.

_______ Score 2 points for each correct O answer.

_______ **Total Score:** Using Words Precisely

Enter the four total scores in the spaces below, and add them together to find your Reading Comprehension Score. Then record your score on the graph on page 197.

Score	Question Type	Lesson 18
_______	Finding the Main Idea	
_______	Recalling Facts	
_______	Making Inferences	
_______	Using Words Precisely	
_______	**Reading Comprehension Score**	

Author's Approach

Put an X in the box next to the correct answer.

1. What does the author mean by the statement "It was, as many people said, 'the mother of all floods'"?

☐ a. It was the oldest flood of all.
☐ b. It created other floods.
☐ c. It was the worst flood of all.

2. What is the author's purpose in writing "The Great Mississippi Flood of 1993"?

☐ a. To compare floods to other natural disasters
☐ b. To inform the reader about the causes and effects of the Great Flood of 1993
☐ c. To describe the weather in the Midwest

3. From the statement "Allan Church, a convicted burglar, said after a day of sandbagging, 'That was the best thing I ever did,'" you can conclude that the author wants the reader to think that Church

☐ a. was proud of the work he had done.
☐ b. was a hardened criminal.
☐ c. gave up his life of crime after the flood.

4. How is the author's purpose for writing the article expressed in paragraph 3?

☐ a. The author compares the floods to blizzards.
☐ b. The author explains what causes floods that occur from time to time in the Midwest.
☐ c. The author tells the reader about springtime weather patterns in the Midwest.

_______ Number of correct answers

Record your personal assessment of your work on the Critical Thinking Chart on page 198.

Summarizing and Paraphrasing

Follow the directions provided for question 1. Put an X in the box next to the correct answer for question 2.

1. Look for the important ideas and events in paragraphs 4 and 5. Summarize those paragraphs in one or two sentences.

____

____

____

2. Choose the sentence that correctly restates the following sentence from the article:

   "Heavy downpours continued soaking the Midwest as a stalled high-pressure system off the East Coast kept pumping warm tropical air into the upper Mississippi Valley."

☐ a. Heavy rainfall pounded the Midwest, while the East Coast enjoyed warm, tropical weather.

☐ b. A weather pattern in the East pumped warm air into the Mississippi Valley and ended the rainfall in the Midwest.

☐ c. A weather pattern in the East brought warm, wet air to the upper Mississippi Valley, causing heavy rains in the Midwest.

_______ Number of correct answers

Record your personal assessment of your work on the Critical Thinking Chart on page 198.

Critical Thinking

Follow the directions provided for questions 1, 3, and 4. Put an X in the box next to the correct answer for the other questions.

1. For each statement below, write O if it expresses an opinion and write F if it expresses a fact.

_______ a. A flood is a more devastating disaster than a tornado or plane crash.

_______ b. Midwesterners are more courageous than people who live in other climates.

_______ c. In June 1993, New London, Iowa, received $6\frac{1}{2}$ inches of rain in 15 minutes.

2. From what the article told about the Mississippi River, you can predict that

☐ a. it will never flood again.

☐ b. it will probably dry up in a few years.

☐ c. heavy rains will cause the river to flood again in the future.

3. Choose from the letters below to correctly complete the following statement. Write the letters on the lines.

   In the article, _______ and _______ are alike.

   a. the flooding in Hannibal, Missouri

   b. the flooding in Quincy, Illinois

   c. the flooding in Chicago, Illinois

4. Choose from the letters below to correctly complete the following statement. Write the letters on the lines.

   According to the article, heavy rainfall caused _________ to _________, and the effect was _________.

   a. millions of acres of farmland were submerged
   b. the levees between Hannibal and St. Louis
   c. break

5. What did you have to do to answer question 2?

☐ a. find an opinion (what someone thinks about something)
☐ b. make a prediction (what might happen next)
☐ c. find a comparison (how things are the same)

_________ Number of correct answers

Record your personal assessment of your work on the Critical Thinking Chart on page 198.

Personal Response

Describe a time when you had to deal with the effects of bad or unusual weather.

____

____

____

____

Self-Assessment

From reading this article, I have learned

____

____

____

____

LESSON 19

DANGER BEHIND LOCKED DOORS

The morning shift had just started at Imperial Food Products in Hamlet, North Carolina. Machines were turned on, and workers were taking their places along the assembly lines.

2 Most of the 200 workers at the plant were women. And most didn't like their jobs. The work was hot, greasy, and monotonous. But jobs were scarce in their small town, so the women were glad they at least had one.

3 Imperial Food Products was a factory that processed chicken. In September 1991 it was the biggest employer in Hamlet. Workers were hired to cut up, weigh, bread, fry, and package chickens. Then the packaged chicken was sent to fast-food restaurants. Over the past 10 years, chicken had become very popular in the United States. And poultry plants had ordered their assembly lines to move twice as fast to keep up with the demand. At Imperial Food Products, the conveyor belts moved briskly. Workers' rest breaks were strictly timed. Anyone who took long breaks or complained about the work could be fired.

4 Most people who lived in Hamlet were poor. The town's business was bad, and many of the stores and shops were closed or boarded up. Those people who did work often had to take low-paying jobs. For many residents, it was hard to make enough money to feed and clothe their families.

Workers from the Imperial Food Products plant sit outside after fire claimed the lives of 25 of their co-workers.

5 Mary Alice Quick, age 38, worked at the Imperial plant. She used her salary to support her children and grandchildren. Another worker was Cynthia Marie Ratliff. She was 20 years old and just out of high school.

6 On September 3, 1991, Quick and Ratliff reported to work at the usual time. At first the assembly lines ran smoothly. Then, at about 8:00 A.M., a fuel line running a conveyor belt suddenly ruptured. Instantly the fuel inside the line turned to vapor. Flames under a chicken fryer ignited the vapor, and fire broke out in the plant.

7 This fire wasn't the first one ever to start at Imperial Food Products. Workers were used to putting out grease fires near the frying vats. But this one immediately got out of control.

8 Thick yellow smoke began to fill the series of brick buildings. Flames spread throughout the plant. Frightened workers left their places and raced for the exits.

9 But the exit doors were padlocked.

10 People in the plant panicked. "I thought I was gone, until a man broke the lock off," said Letha Terry. Unfortunately, many people were not so lucky.

11 Sam Breeden was passing by on the road outside the processing plant that morning. He heard victims inside crying for help. "They were screaming 'Let me

This locked door was kicked several times by workers who were trying to escape the fire.

out!'" said Breeden. "They were beating on the door."

12 Anxious townspeople gathered around the plant. Some worked in the factory at other times of the day. All had friends or family members inside.

13 One woman who lives near the plant saw at least three bodies wrapped in sheets and lying on the grass. And injured workers were sprawled on the ground in need of help. "It was pitiful, it was sad, it was terrible," she said. "I used to work on the line breading chicken and it was awfully dangerous...."

14 When firefighters finally broke into the plant, they found bodies clustered around locked doorways. Black footprints marked the inside of the doors. They found others inside the freezer, where some workers had gone to escape the fire's heat and smoke. One firefighter even discovered the body of his own father.

15 Twenty-five people were killed in the blaze at Imperial Food Products. More than 50 were injured. Among the dead were Mary Alice Quick and Cynthia Marie Ratliff. Many of their friends stood weeping outside the plant as the firefighters brought out the bodies.

16 Terrelle Quick, Mary Alice's 12-year-old son, watched the firefighters carry bodies from the factory. He had been called into the principal's office and sent home after the school had learned about the fire. His sister told him what happened. Terrelle said, "I thought I was going to get my school shoes like she promised me...." Instead, he heard that his mother had been killed.

17 But if the exit doors had been open, her life might have been saved. Firefighters could have put out the fire sooner, and workers could have escaped. Why were the doors locked?

18 Brad Roe, son of the owner of Imperial Food Products, was the manager of the Hamlet plant. When asked why the doors were locked, he said, "I can't tell you right now. But there were plenty of doors that were open. Certain doors are locked at certain times. I can't tell you which doors were locked, if any were locked."

19 In fact, only one door was open when the fire broke out.

20 Some people have speculated that the doors were locked to keep workers from stealing chicken. Other people think that the locked doors helped keep flies and rats away from the chicken. In any case, locked exits made a dangerous situation even worse.

21 Employee Brenda McDougald said, "That fryer was so dangerous and there were no fire alarms.... It was so hot in there that you cooked while you worked and those doors in the back stayed locked."

22 Every year, thousands of people are injured in on-the-job accidents. The Occupational Safety and Health Administration (OSHA) is a government agency that is supposed to make sure that workplaces are safe for employees. But in 1991 North Carolina had only 27 inspectors to oversee more than 150,000 workplaces. Because OSHA was understaffed, Imperial Food Products had never been inspected in 11 years of operation.

23 Since the fire, the Imperial Food Products plant has remained closed. The company's owner, Emmett J. Roe, has been fined more than $800,000 for violating safety codes. On September 13, 1992, he pleaded guilty to the crime of involuntary manslaughter. He has been sentenced to 20 years in prison.

If you have been timed while reading this article, enter your reading time below. Then turn to the Words-per-Minute Table on page 195 and look up your reading speed (words per minute). Enter your reading speed on the graph on page 196.

Reading Time: Lesson 19

_______ : _______

Minutes *Seconds*

A Finding the Main Idea

One statement below expresses the main idea of the article. One statement is too general, or too broad. The other statement explains only part of the article; it is too narrow. Label the statements using the following key:

M—Main Idea **B—Too Broad** **N—Too Narrow**

_______ 1. Dangerous working conditions contributed to the deaths at Imperial Food Products.

_______ 2. OSHA inspectors never visited the Imperial Food Products factory.

_______ 3. Every year, thousands of people are injured in on-the-job accidents.

_______ Score 15 points for a correct M answer.

_______ Score 5 points for each correct B or N answer.

_______ **Total Score:** Finding the Main Idea

B Recalling Facts

How well do you remember the facts in the article? Put an X in the box next to the answer that correctly completes each statement about the article.

1. Hamlet is a small town in
- ☐ a. Georgia.
- ☐ b. South Carolina.
- ☐ c. North Carolina.

2. Imperial Food Products processed
- ☐ a. chicken to be sold in supermarkets.
- ☐ b. chicken to be sold to fast-food restaurants.
- ☐ c. many different kinds of poultry.

3. The fire started because
- ☐ a. a machine on the assembly line exploded.
- ☐ b. part of a chicken fryer began to melt.
- ☐ c. vapor from a fuel line caught fire.

4. When Terrelle Quick was called out of class, he thought that his mother
- ☐ a. was going to get him school shoes.
- ☐ b. had been killed.
- ☐ c. had lost her job.

5. OSHA is supposed to make sure that workplaces
- ☐ a. are safe for employees.
- ☐ b. use modern equipment.
- ☐ c. are run inexpensively.

Score 5 points for each correct answer.

_______ **Total Score:** Recalling Facts

C Making Inferences

When you combine your own experience and information from a text to draw a conclusion that is not directly stated in that text, you are making an inference. Below are five statements that may or may not be inferences based on information in the article. Label the statements using the following key:

C—Correct Inference **F—Faulty Inference**

_______ 1. Most people in Hamlet could not afford to lose their jobs.

_______ 2. The tragedy at the processing plant was caused by careless workers.

_______ 3. Brad Roe could not explain why the exit doors were locked.

_______ 4. OSHA needs more inspectors.

_______ 5. The fire at Imperial Food Products did not have much effect on the town.

Score 5 points for each correct answer.

_______ **Total Score:** Making Inferences

D Using Words Precisely

Each numbered sentence below contains an underlined word or phrase from the article. Following the sentence are three definitions. One definition is closest to the meaning of the underlined word. One definition is opposite or nearly opposite. Label those two definitions using the following key. Do not label the remaining definition.

C—Closest **O—Opposite or Nearly Opposite**

1. The work was hot, greasy, and monotonous.

_______ a. repetitious and boring

_______ b. dangerous

_______ c. always new and exciting

2. Instantly the fuel inside the line turned to vapor.

_______ a. fire

_______ b. a gas

_______ c. a solid

3. Anxious townspeople gathered around the plant.

_______ a. carefree

_______ b. worried

_______ c. angry

4. Some people have speculated that the doors were locked to keep workers from stealing chickens.

_______ a. been certain of

_______ b. questioned the police about

_______ c. made guesses about

5. On September 13, 1992, he pleaded guilty to the crime of <u>involuntary</u> manslaughter.

_______ a. intentional

_______ b. accidental

_______ c. occasional

_______ Score 3 points for each correct C answer.

_______ Score 2 points for each correct O answer.

_______ **Total Score:** Using Words Precisely

Enter the four total scores in the spaces below, and add them together to find your Reading Comprehension Score. Then record your score on the graph on page 197.

Score	Question Type	Lesson 19
_______	Finding the Main Idea	
_______	Recalling Facts	
_______	Making Inferences	
_______	Using Words Precisely	
_______	**Reading Comprehension Score**	

Author's Approach

Put an X in the box next to the correct answer.

1. The author uses the first sentence of the article to

☐ a. inform the reader about the story's setting.

☐ b. tell the reader about working conditions at Imperial Food Products.

☐ c. compare Imperial Food Products to other plants.

2. Which of the following statements from the article best describes working conditions at Imperial Food Products?

☐ a. "The work was hot, greasy, and monotonous."

☐ b. "At Imperial Food Products, the conveyor belts moved briskly."

☐ c. "Workers were hired to cut up, weigh, bread, fry, and package chicken."

3. What does the author imply by saying "Black footprints marked the inside of the doors"?

☐ a. The Hamlet plant was not kept very clean.

☐ b. Desperate workers had tried to kick the locked doors down during the fire.

☐ c. During the fire, workers had marked the doors to help others find their way out of the plant.

4. The author probably wrote this article in order to

☐ a. discourage the reader from eating chicken at fast-food restaurants.

☐ b. convey the terror that the trapped workers felt.

☐ c. tell the reader about a deadly fire at a chicken processing plant.

_______ Number of correct answers

Record your personal assessment of your work on the Critical Thinking Chart on page 198.

Summarizing and Paraphrasing

Put an X in the box next to the correct answer.

1. Below are summaries of the article. Choose the summary that says all the most important things about the article but in the fewest words.

☐ a. When a fire erupted at the Imperial Food Products plant in Hamlet, North Carolina, many people died because they were locked inside. Since the fire, the company has remained closed, and the owner has been fined and imprisoned.

☐ b. The fire at a chicken processing plant in North Carolina killed 25 people and injured more than 50 others.

☐ c. On September 3, 1991, a fire broke out in Imperial Food Products when a fuel line running a conveyor belt ruptured. Panicked workers raced for the exits but found most of the doors padlocked. Twenty-five workers died in the fire. The plant has remained closed since the fire, and the company's owner, Emmett J. Roe, has been fined for violating safety codes. He has also been sentenced to 20 years in prison for involuntary manslaughter.

2. Read the statement about the article below. Then read the paraphrase of that statement. Choose the reason that best tells why the paraphrase does not say the same thing as the statement.

Statement: Although Brad Roe, manager of the Hamlet plant, couldn't explain why most of the doors were locked, some people have suggested that they were locked to prevent stealing or to keep flies and rats away from the chicken.

Paraphrase: Brad Roe said that the doors at the Hamlet plant were locked to keep rats from stealing the chicken.

☐ a. Paraphrase says too much.

☐ b. Paraphrase doesn't say enough.

☐ c. Paraphrase doesn't agree with the statement about the article.

CRITICAL THINKING

_________ Number of correct answers

Record your personal assessment of your work on the Critical Thinking Chart on page 198.

Critical Thinking

Put an X in the box next to the correct answer for questions 1, 2, and 5. Follow the directions provided for the other questions.

1. Which of the following statements from the article is an opinion rather than a fact?

☐ a. "Because OSHA was understaffed, Imperial Food Products had never been inspected in 11 years of operation."

☐ b. "'It was pitiful, it was sad, it was terrible,' [one woman] said."

☐ c. "Most of the 200 workers at the plant were women."

2. From what Brenda McDougald said, you can predict that she will

☐ a. be happy to work at the Imperial Food Products plant if it opens again.

☐ b. never apply for a job at a plant like Imperial again.

☐ c. quickly forgive the management of Imperial Food Products plant.

3. Choose from the letters below to correctly complete the following statement. Write the letters on the lines.

In the article, _________ and _________ are alike.

a. Mary Alice Quick's fate in the fire

b. Sam Breeden's fate in the fire

c. Cynthia Marie Ratliff's fate in the fire

4. Read paragraph 10. Then choose from the letters below to correctly complete the following statement. Write the letters on the lines.

   According to paragraph 10, _________ because _________.

   a. a man broke the lock off a door
   b. people in the plant panicked
   c. Letha Terry escaped from the plant

5. What did you have to do to answer question 3?

☐ a. find an opinion (what someone thinks about something)
☐ b. find a comparison (how things are the same)
☐ c. draw a conclusion (a sensible statement based on the text and your experience)

_________ Number of correct answers

Record your personal assessment of your work on the Critical Thinking Chart on page 198.

Personal Response

If I were the author, I would add

____

____

____

____

because

____

____

____

____

Self-Assessment

While reading the article, I found it easiest to

____

____

____

____

LESSON 20

THE WORLD'S WORST ACCIDENT
Massacre at Bhopal

In Bhopal, India, it was a quiet December night. The air was cool and still, and the winds were calm. Some city residents were asleep in their homes, but many poor families were sleeping together in tiny hovels or out in the open air. At the train station, homeless families slept in corners and under benches. No one suspected that the night would be different from any other.

2 No one, that is, except for the workers on duty at Bhopal's Union Carbide chemical plant—who listened in horror to a deadly hissing sound that signaled Bhopal's doom.

3 Bhopal is the capital city of Madhya Pradesh (MAHD-yuh pruh-DESH), a state in central India. About 700,000 people live in Bhopal, and most suffer from overwhelming poverty. Some try to make a living by selling cigarettes or repairing bicycles, but many are beggars who depend on scant handfuls of coins to buy food for their families.

4 In 1969 Union Carbide opened a pesticide factory on a five-acre plot of land just outside Bhopal city limits.

The Union Carbide pesticide plant in Bhopal, India, was built in a heavily populated area. Poor maintenance of safety devices at the facility contributed to the disaster that claimed more than 2,500 lives.

Pesticides are poisons that are meant to kill pests such as weeds and insects. The company had the blessings of India's government, which welcomed foreign factories. Factory profits help the country financially, and corporations also hire Indians to work in the plants.

5 By 1984 the Union Carbide plant had grown into a huge, expensive facility that spread over 80 acres of the city. The factory was producing and packaging a pesticide called Sevin. Some people began to worry that the residents near the plant might be in danger. One official asked that the plant be moved out of city limits. The government fired that official, and the plant remained.

6 Around the plant were hundreds of tiny dwellings—shacks and huts put up by the poor people of Bhopal. Few of these people worked in the factory. Instead, they sold goods to factory workers, did minor repair work, or ran errands.

7 On the evening of December 3, 1984, about 120 employees were still working inside the Union Carbide plant. Some were monitoring the chemical storage tank that contained 45 tons of methyl isocyanate (METH-uhl eye-so-SYE-uh-nate), one of the chemicals used to make Sevin.

8 Methyl isocyanate, usually called MIC, is an extremely dangerous chemical. Because it can react with many different substances, it should be handled and stored very carefully. But the Union Carbide plant was not enforcing safety standards. For example, MIC should be kept under refrigeration, but the refrigeration unit at the factory was not

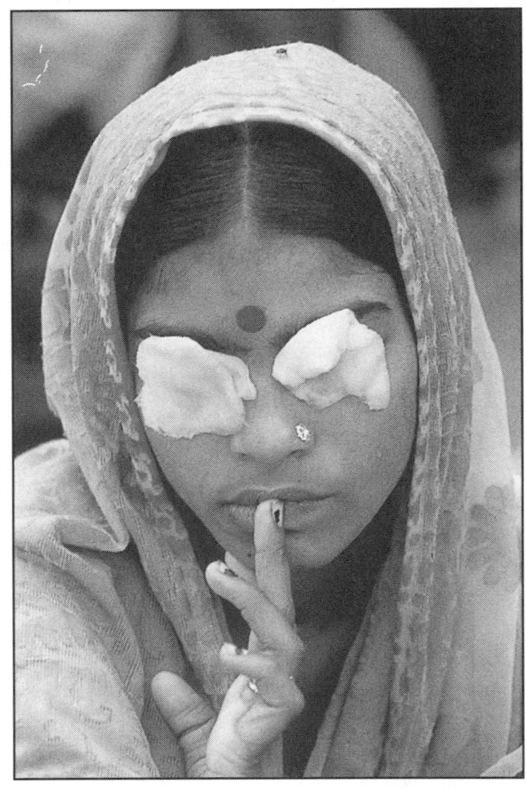

This woman's eyes are bandaged after she was exposed to the poison gas that escaped from a storage tank at the Union Carbide plant.

turned on. Even though the tank had a gauge that measured temperature and pressure, employees didn't pay attention to it because it rarely worked right. Safety devices had been installed to neutralize the gas, but none were operating correctly.

9 At 11:00 P.M., workers noticed that their eyes had begun to water and burn. The tank was leaking! At first they saw drops of liquid, but eventually the liquid became a heavy yellow gas. The workers were concerned, but they decided to deal with the problem after their tea break. When they returned to the tank more than an hour later, they saw that the pressure inside had cracked a concrete slab six inches thick. A few minutes before 1:00 A.M., they heard a loud hissing sound. The deadly gas was escaping through a smokestack into the night air.

10 Panic broke out at the plant. Workers began running for their lives. Finally, nearly an hour after the gas started to leak, engineers from another company sealed the broken tank. By that time, however, all the gas had escaped.

11 The heavy gas formed a dense fog that floated close to the ground. It passed over the shacks and huts surrounding the factory and over the railway station. Then it spread through the city, hovering over shops, temples, and streets.

12 Wherever the cloud passed, it left devastation. Entire families died in their sleep, while cattle and dogs dropped to the ground and died where they lay.

13 M. A. Kahn, a farmer who lived close to the plant, was lying in bed when he heard thumping sounds. He went outside and found two cows dead on the ground. A third groaned and collapsed as Kahn watched. When the farmer's eyes started to burn, he ran inside in fear.

14 Many people in Bhopal thought that an enemy nation had dropped a nuclear bomb. Others thought the poisonous yellow cloud was a sign that the world was ending. Thousands of people thronged the streets—some in cars or carts, a few on the backs of cattle, but most on foot. Many were already blinded by the gas, and they groped and stumbled their way along crowded roads. Every street was littered with the bodies of people and animals. Some people were lying in gutters in agonized, frozen positions.

15 Hundreds of injured citizens began filling the local hospital and makeshift clinics, their eyes swollen shut, their lungs filled with fluid. Most of the patients died within a few hours. The disaster struck hardest at children and the elderly. Their lungs were either too small or too weak to withstand the poison.

16 By dawn the death toll was enormous. And by the end of the week, more than 2,500 people had died, and at least 200,000 had been injured. The city of Bhopal was paralyzed, and India was in shock. The accident was the worst industrial disaster in the history of the world.

17 Union Carbide tried to defend its safety policies, but in the end, company officials admitted that plant safety was not adequate. One plant employee said he sounded an alarm to warn the city of the accident. But few residents recall hearing it.

18 The company is still involved in billion-dollar lawsuits related to the Bhopal disaster. Still, very little money has actually gone to the victims. Of those injured, 17,000 still suffer from the effects of MIC gas. Many have been permanently blinded or have suffered serious lung damage. Hundreds of women have given birth to babies with deformities. These people hope that someday they will be compensated for their suffering, but they know that money will not bring back their health.

19 "We never understood why they [Union Carbide] would build a factory containing poison gas close to where people live," one survivor said. "They could have gone out in the jungle where no one lives. Now we are mourning our dead."

If you have been timed while reading this article, enter your reading time below. Then turn to the Words-per-Minute Table on page 195 and look up your reading speed (words per minute). Enter your reading speed on the graph on page 196.

Reading Time: Lesson 20

________ : ________

Minutes *Seconds*

A Finding the Main Idea

One statement below expresses the main idea of the article. One statement is too general, or too broad. The other statement explains only part of the article; it is too narrow. Label the statements using the following key:

M—Main Idea **B—Too Broad** **N—Too Narrow**

_______ 1. The Indian government has encouraged foreign corporations to set up factories in India.

_______ 2. Methyl isocyanate is an extremely dangerous chemical used in making Sevin.

_______ 3. The gas leak in Bhopal was the worst chemical accident in history.

_______ Score 15 points for a correct M answer.

_______ Score 5 points for each correct B or N answer.

_______ **Total Score:** Finding the Main Idea

B Recalling Facts

How well do you remember the facts in the article? Put an X in the box next to the answer that correctly completes each statement about the article.

1. Madhya Pradesh is

☐ a. the capital of Bhopal.
☐ b. a large chemical plant.
☐ c. a state in central India.

2. Most people in Bhopal live in

☐ a. overwhelming poverty.
☐ b. luxury.
☐ c. housing provided by the factory.

3. The factory in Bhopal

☐ a. produced and packaged pesticides.
☐ b. employed most of the people who lived near the plant.
☐ c. did minor bicycle repair work.

4. The workers first noticed the leaking tank when

☐ a. they smelled a sour, musty odor.
☐ b. a supervisor looked at the pressure gauge.
☐ c. their eyes began to water and burn.

5. The gas cloud

☐ a. hovered high in the air.
☐ b. floated close to the ground.
☐ c. exploded in flames.

Score 5 points for each correct answer.

_______ **Total Score:** Recalling Facts

C Making Inferences

When you combine your own experience and information from a text to draw a conclusion that is not directly stated in that text, you are making an inference. Below are five statements that may or may not be inferences based on information in the article. Label the statements using the following key:

C—Correct Inference **F—Faulty Inference**

_______ 1. Union Carbide helped India's economy for a while.

_______ 2. Most people in Bhopal earn enough money to live comfortably.

_______ 3. The workers made a mistake when they left for their tea break without trying to stop the MIC leak.

_______ 4. MIC gas does not affect animals.

_______ 5. The gas leak did no permanent damage to the people of Bhopal.

Score 5 points for each correct answer.

_______ **Total Score:** Making Inferences

D Using Words Precisely

Each numbered sentence below contains an underlined word or phrase from the article. Following the sentence are three definitions. One definition is closest to the meaning of the underlined word. One definition is opposite or nearly opposite. Label those two definitions using the following key. Do not label the remaining definition.

C—Closest **O—Opposite or Nearly Opposite**

1. Some city residents were asleep in their homes, but many poor families were sleeping together in tiny hovels or out in the open air.

_______ a. underground caves

_______ b. mansions

_______ c. shacks or huts

2. Then it [the gas] spread through the city, hovering over shops, temples, and streets.

_______ a. moving away

_______ b. hanging in the air

_______ c. burning rapidly

3. Thousands of people thronged the streets—some in cars or carts, a few on the backs of cattle, but most on foot.

_______ a. crowded

_______ b. cleaned

_______ c. deserted

4. Many were already blinded by the gas, and they groped and stumbled their way along the crowded roads.

_______ a. hitchhiked

_______ b. felt their way uncertainly

_______ c. moved with confidence

5. These people hope that someday they will be compensated for their suffering….

_______ a. rewarded

_______ b. punished

_______ c. interviewed

_______ Score 3 points for each correct C answer.

_______ Score 2 points for each correct O answer.

_______ **Total Score:** Using Words Precisely

Enter the four total scores in the spaces below, and add them together to find your Reading Comprehension Score. Then record your score on the graph on page 197.

Score	Question Type	Lesson 20
_______	Finding the Main Idea	
_______	Recalling Facts	
_______	Making Inferences	
_______	Using Words Precisely	
_______	**Reading Comprehension Score**	

Author's Approach

Put an X in the box next to the correct answer.

1. The main purpose of the first paragraph is to

☐ a. describe the weather in Bhopal in December.

☐ b. tell the reader that there was much poverty in Bhopal.

☐ c. compare that night in December to other nights in Bhopal.

2. From the statements below, choose those that you believe the author would agree with.

☐ a. Union Carbide should have built their plant in the jungle where no one lives.

☐ b. The workers who did not deal immediately with the gas leak are solely to blame for the accident at the plant in Bhopal.

☐ c. Union Carbide can never really compensate the people of Bhopal for the accident.

3. Choose the statement below that is the weakest argument for building an insecticide plant within city limits.

☐ a. Profits from the plant would help the area financially.

☐ b. The plant would hire local residents.

☐ c. An accident at the plant would endanger the city's inhabitants.

4. In this article, "Some people were lying in gutters in agonized, frozen positions" means

☐ a. people lay frozen with terror in the gutters.

☐ b. some people in Bhopal were so poor that they slept in gutters.

☐ c. some people had died in great pain in the gutters.

_______ Number of correct answers

Record your personal assessment of your work on the Critical Thinking Chart on page 198.

Summarizing and Paraphrasing

Follow the directions provided for questions 1 and 2. Put an X in the box next to the correct answer for question 3.

1. Look for the important ideas and events in paragraphs 10 and 11. Summarize those paragraphs in one or two sentences.

____

____

____

2. Reread paragraph 15 in the article. Below, write a summary of the paragraph in no more than 25 words.

____

____

____

____

Reread your summary and decide whether it covers the important ideas in the paragraph. Next, decide how to shorten the summary to 15 words or less without leaving out any essential information. Write this summary below.

____

____

____

3. Choose the sentence that correctly restates the following sentence from the article:

   "Some try to make a living by selling cigarettes or repairing bicycles, but many are beggars who depend on scant handfuls of coins to buy food for their families."

☐ a. Some work, but others steal in order to buy food.

☐ b. Some beg coins from those who try to make a living by selling cigarettes or repairing bicycles.

☐ c. Some try to work for their living, while others support their families by begging for money.

_______ Number of correct answers

Record your personal assessment of your work on the Critical Thinking Chart on page 198.

Critical Thinking

Put an X in the box next to the correct answer for questions 1 and 4. Follow the directions provided for the other questions.

1. From the article, you can predict that if the workers from the nearby plant had sealed the broken tank as soon as the gas started to leak,

☐ a. lives would have been saved.

☐ b. no one would have been harmed at all.

☐ c. the workers would have been fired.

2. Choose from the letters below to correctly complete the following statement. Write the letters on the lines.

   In the article, ________ and ________ are different.

   a. Madhya Pradesh

   b. MIC

   c. methyl isocyanate

3. Choose from the letters below to correctly complete the following statement. Write the letters on the lines.

   According to the article, ________ caused deadly gas to ________, and the effect was ________.

   a. a leak in a gas tank

   b. thousands of people were killed

   c. escape through a smokestack

4. How is the accident at Bhopal an example of a calamity?

☐ a. The event was unexpected.

☐ b. The accident killed or injured thousands of people.

☐ c. The accident focused attention on the inadequate safety policies at the plant.

________ Number of correct answers

Record your personal assessment of your work on the Critical Thinking Chart on page 198.

Personal Response

If you could ask the author of the article one question, what would it be?

____

____

____

____

Self-Assessment

A word or phrase in the article that I do not understand is

____

____

____

____

THE OKLAHOMA CITY BOMBING

Sometimes survival is a matter of blind luck. That was clearly true for at least a few people who were in the Alfred P. Murrah Federal Building in Oklahoma City one fateful day. They just happened to be in the right spot at the precise moment when a bomb went off in the building at 9:02 A.M. on April 19, 1995. Some people survived because they went to the bathroom or strolled over to the coffee machine or visited a friend down the hall.

2 Brian Espe couldn't believe his good fortune. At first, thinking the noise was an earthquake, he dove under his desk. When he got up to look around, everyone else was gone. The adjacent offices had crashed through the floor and landed several floors below. "My surviving," Espe later said, "was nothing short of a miracle."

3 The monstrous explosion sliced the top of the federal building in half. People on one side lived while most of those on the other side tumbled several stories to their deaths in the rubble below. A secretary lived because she happened to be away from her desk. One man's life was saved because he had gone to the bath-

Rescue workers at the Alfred P. Murrah Federal Building survey the damage caused by a truck bomb carrying 4,000 pounds of explosives.

room. Nobody else in his office was so lucky. Another man was spared because he left his office moments before the blast.

4 Other people survived only through the heroic efforts of firefighters, nurses, doctors, off-duty police officers, and paramedics who rushed to the scene to help. One person they saved was a 20-year-old woman named Dana Bradley. Rescuers found her crying in the rubble with the lower half of her leg pinned under tons of steel-reinforced concrete. She was trapped in a space so small doctors couldn't reach her. For two hours the doctors tried to figure out a way to save Bradley. Twice they had to flee the area for fear of another explosion or collapsing debris. "Please don't leave me!" she pleaded each time.

5 As time passed, it was clear something had to be done. Bradley was in bad shape: her blood pressure was dropping, and she was in the early stages of shock. Finally, the doctors decided to risk cutting away some of the steel-reinforcing rods that trapped her. That attempt could have caused a further collapse, perhaps killing Bradley and the doctors. Luckily, though, the cuts were made without mishap.

6 Even with the cut rods, however, there was still only enough room for one doctor, crawling on his hands and knees in about a foot of water, to reach Bradley. It was then that Bradley heard the doctors' grim assessment of her situation. They would have to cut off her lower leg if they were going to save her life. Bradley begged them to think of something else. But there were no other options. She screamed as the doctor removed her leg with a surgical saw and scissors. But, at last, the doctors were able to pull her out of the building.

7 Later, Dana Bradley received more tragic news. Not only had she lost a leg in the explosion, she had also lost her mother and two children. They were among the 168 people who died in the

Timothy McVeigh, who drove the truck and set off the bomb, was convicted and sentenced to death.

bombing. Another 500 people were injured by falling glass, concrete, and other debris. One man was pierced in one hundred places by shards of glass. Doctor Richard Crook treated several people suffering from slashed throats and punctured lungs. “We saw ruptured eyeballs and rib fractures,” he said. “One man was driving by the building when the bomb went off and had his windows open. It ruptured his eardrums.”

8 The bomb did not discriminate between rich and poor, white and black, or young and old. The dead ranged in age from four months to 73 years old. The tales of individual grief, like that of Dana Bradley, pulled at the nation’s heartstrings.

9 There was one image that truly captured the horror of this catastrophe. It was the photograph of firefighter Chris Fields emerging from the smoldering ruins with the lifeless body of one-year-old Baylee Almon in his arms. The little girl had just celebrated her birthday the day before. Her mother, Aren Almon, had dropped Baylee off at the second-floor day care center. When she first heard the blast, Aren thought it might be a clap of thunder. But then she saw it was the federal building. “We heard that they had found a baby with yellow booties,” she said, “and I knew it was her.”

10 The day care center took the full force of the explosion. Nineteen children in the nursery died. A few children, who somehow lived through the bombing, were found dazed and wandering about, crying frantically for their parents. Rescuers found severed limbs scattered among the toys and dolls. Some rescuers couldn’t bear to look down at the children they cradled in their arms. One of the young victims had been decapitated; others were burned beyond recognition.

11 The sight of those children stunned everyone. Robert Buckner, a paramedic, expressed the outrage that most Americans felt. “It’s all a nightmare,” he said. “But the kids? Why anyone would want to do this to a place with a day care center is beyond comprehension.”

12 One of the rescuers spotted Oklahoma Governor Frank Keating, who had rushed to the scene to offer his support. “Find out who did this,” the rescuer begged Keating. That desire was shared by all Americans. Along with the devastating grief, there was blind rage. Who could do such a thing?

13 The basic facts of the bombing soon became apparent. Somebody had parked a Ryder rental truck next to the Murrah Building. The innocent-looking truck contained 4,000 pounds of high explosives. The blast from these explosives was so powerful that it was felt 30 miles away. Some people in outlying towns such as Guthrie and Chandler thought it was a sonic boom. The bomb blew a crater 30 feet across and 8 feet deep in Northwest Fifth Street and sent a red-orange fireball into the sky. Cars parked along the street exploded. The explosion was so powerful that it killed two people in a building across the street.

14 At first, many people assumed that the bombing was the work of foreign terrorists. But it wasn’t. In this case, the terrorists were homegrown Americans. The man who actually drove the Ryder truck and set off the bomb was Timothy McVeigh, a bitter loner with a grudge against the U.S. government. Apparently he thought killing innocent men, women, and children was a good way to create a better world. McVeigh was later arrested, convicted, and sentenced to death. Another man, Terry Nichols, was also arrested and convicted for his part in planning the bombing.

15 The Oklahoma City bombing was the worst case of domestic terrorism in the history of the United States. The senseless death of 168 people will not soon be forgotten. And people were outraged by the number of orphans created by the bombing. Ten children lost both their parents in the blast. More than 150 young people under the age of 23 lost a parent. Such wounds never really heal.

If you have been timed while reading this article, enter your reading time below. Then turn to the Words-per-Minute Table on page 195 and look up your reading speed (words per minute). Enter your reading speed on the graph on page 196.

Reading Time: Lesson 21

________ : ________

Minutes *Seconds*

A Finding the Main Idea

One statement below expresses the main idea of the article. One statement is too general, or too broad. The other statement explains only part of the article; it is too narrow. Label the statements using the following key:

M—Main Idea **B—Too Broad** **N—Too Narrow**

_____ 1. A firefighter carrying the lifeless body of one-year-old Baylee Almon symbolized the tragic bombing.

_____ 2. The Oklahoma City bombing was one of the worst disasters in American history.

_____ 3. The bombing of the federal building in Oklahoma City, which killed 168 people and caused tremendous suffering, was carried out by two men who bore a grudge against the U.S. government.

_____ Score 15 points for a correct M answer.

_____ Score 5 points for each correct B or N answer.

_____ **Total Score:** Finding the Main Idea

B Recalling Facts

How well do you remember the facts in the article? Put an X in the box next to the answer that correctly completes each statement about the article.

1. On April 19, 1995, the Murrah Federal Building in Oklahoma City was destroyed by
   - ☐ a. a bomb.
   - ☐ b. an earthquake.
   - ☐ c. a sonic boom.
2. Rescuers found Dana Bradley
   - ☐ a. wandering around the rubble in a daze.
   - ☐ b. crouching unharmed under her desk.
   - ☐ c. pinned under tons of concrete.
3. A man driving by the building at the time of the blast
   - ☐ a. had his eardrums ruptured.
   - ☐ b. was pierced by bits of glass.
   - ☐ c. suffered a slashed throat.
4. The day care center on the building's second floor
   - ☐ a. was, fortunately, spared by the blast.
   - ☐ b. took the full force of the explosion.
   - ☐ c. was closed that day.
5. The explosives used in the blast were set off in
   - ☐ a. the building across the street from the Murrah Building.
   - ☐ b. a Ryder rental truck.
   - ☐ c. the nearby town of Guthrie.

Score 5 points for each correct answer.

_____ **Total Score:** Recalling Facts

C Making Inferences

When you combine your own experience and information from a text to draw a conclusion that is not directly stated in that text, you are making an inference. Below are five statements that may or may not be inferences based on information in the article. Label the statements using the following key:

C—Correct Inference **F—Faulty Inference**

_______ 1. Most people couldn't understand why Timothy McVeigh bombed the Murrah Building.

_______ 2. The freedom to bomb places you don't like is guaranteed by the U.S. Constitution.

_______ 3. Americans were shocked and horrified by the Oklahoma City bombing.

_______ 4. McVeigh bombed the Murrah Building because it represented the U.S. government.

_______ 5. McVeigh and Nichols hadn't intended to kill anyone in the explosion.

Score 5 points for each correct answer.

_______ **Total Score:** Making Inferences

D Using Words Precisely

Each numbered sentence below contains an underlined word or phrase from the article. Following the sentence are three definitions. One definition is closest to the meaning of the underlined word. One definition is opposite or nearly opposite. Label those two definitions using the following key. Do not label the remaining definition.

C—Closest **O—Opposite or Nearly Opposite**

1. The <u>adjacent</u> offices had crashed through the floor and landed several floors below.

_______ a. separated

_______ b. neighboring

_______ c. larger

2. Luckily, though, the cuts were made without <u>mishap</u>.

_______ a. good luck

_______ b. good lighting

_______ c. misfortune

3. One man was pierced in one hundred places by <u>shards</u> of glass.

_______ a. frames

_______ b. fragments

_______ c. complete panes

4. The bomb did not <u>discriminate between</u> rich and poor, white and black, or young and old.

_______ a. communicate to

_______ b. treat in a similar way

_______ c. see the difference between

5. It was the photograph of firefighter Chris Fields emerging from the smoldering ruins with the lifeless body of one-year-old Baylee Almon in his arms.

_______ a. burning slowly, usually without flames

_______ b. almost collapsing

_______ c. blazing wildly

_______ Score 3 points for each correct C answer.

_______ Score 2 points for each correct O answer.

_______ **Total Score:** Using Words Precisely

Enter the four total scores in the spaces below, and add them together to find your Reading Comprehension Score. Then record your score on the graph on page 197.

Score	Question Type	Lesson 21
_______	Finding the Main Idea	
_______	Recalling Facts	
_______	Making Inferences	
_______	Using Words Precisely	
_______	**Reading Comprehension Score**	

Author's Approach

Put an X in the box next to the correct answer.

1. From the statements below, choose those that you believe the author would agree with.

☐ a. The bombing would have been of minor importance if 19 children hadn't been killed.

☐ b. The bomb in Oklahoma City shattered the lives of the victims and their families.

☐ c. The police and medical help acted heroically to try to save lives after the bombing.

2. From the statement "'Find out who did this,' the rescuer begged Keating," you can conclude that the author wants the reader to think that

☐ a. the rescuer wanted the person responsible to be tried and punished for the crime.

☐ b. Keating was reluctant to find the criminals responsible.

☐ c. the rescuer had a pretty good idea who was responsible.

3. Choose the statement below that best describes the author's position in paragraph 14.

☐ a. Timothy McVeigh's actions were understandable.

☐ b. McVeigh and Nichols should be put to death for their crime.

☐ c. McVeigh killed innocent people to demonstrate his grudge against the U.S. government.

4. The author tells this story mainly by

☐ a. retelling Dana Bradley's personal experiences of the Murrah Building bombing.

☐ b. comparing the Oklahoma City bombing to an act of foreign terrorism.

☐ c. telling different people's experiences of the bombing.

_________ Number of correct answers

Record your personal assessment of your work on the Critical Thinking Chart on page 198.

Summarizing and Paraphrasing

Put an X in the box next to the correct answer.

1. Below are summaries of the article. Choose the summary that says all the most important things about the article but in the fewest words.

☐ a. On April 19, 1995, a bomb exploded in the federal building in Oklahoma City, killing 168 people and injuring hundreds more. Two Americans were convicted for their roles in the bombing.

☐ b. A bomb exploded in a Ryder rental truck and killed 168 people in Oklahoma City.

☐ c. The bombing of the Alfred P. Murrah Federal Building in Oklahoma City on April 19, 1995, killed 168 people. A day care center took the full force of the explosion; 19 children from the center died. Timothy McVeigh, a loner who disagreed with U.S. policies, was convicted and sentenced to death for the bombing. Terry Nichols was also convicted for his part in the crime.

2. Read the statement about the article below. Then read the paraphrase of that statement. Choose the reason that best tells why the paraphrase does not say the same thing as the statement.

Statement: The rescuers worked hard to find the children but then couldn't bear looking at them because the young victims' bodies were so badly mutilated.

Paraphrase: The rescuers didn't bother looking for the children because they knew that all of the young victims were dead.

☐ a. Paraphrase says too much.

☐ b. Paraphrase doesn't say enough.

☐ c. Paraphrase doesn't agree with the statement about the article.

_________ Number of correct answers

Record your personal assessment of your work on the Critical Thinking Chart on page 198.

Critical Thinking

Put an X in the box next to the correct answer for questions 1, 3, and 4. Follow the directions provided for the other questions.

1. From the information in paragraph 14, you can predict that

☐ a. the Ryder rental company knew what McVeigh and Nichols planned to do with the truck.

☐ b. Terry Nichols tried to persuade Timothy McVeigh to halt the bombing.

☐ c. many people will protest Terry Nichols's requests for an early release.

2. Choose from the letters below to correctly complete the following statement. Write the letters on the lines.

   In the article, ________ and ________ are alike.

   a. Richard Crook's role following the bombing
   b. Robert Buckner's role following the bombing
   c. Frank Keating's role following the bombing

3. What was the effect of one man's decision to walk to the washroom just before the blast?

   ☐ a. He died in the explosion.
   ☐ b. His life was saved.
   ☐ c. He lost a leg.

4. How is the Oklahoma City bombing an example of a calamity?

   ☐ a. Two Americans—not foreign terrorists—were responsible for the bombing.
   ☐ b. The motive of the bomber was unclear.
   ☐ c. Many innocent men, women, and children were needlessly and violently killed.

5. Which paragraphs from the article provide evidence that supports your answer to question 2?

   ____

________ Number of correct answers

Record your personal assessment of your work on the Critical Thinking Chart on page 198.

Personal Response

A question I would like answered by Timothy McVeigh is

____

____

____

____

Self-Assessment

What concepts or ideas from the article were difficult to understand?

____

____

____

____

Which were easy to understand?

____

____

____

____

Compare and Contrast

Think about the articles you have read in Unit Three. Choose the four calamities that you feel were the saddest. Write the titles of the articles in the first column of the chart below. Use information from the articles to fill in the empty boxes in the chart.

Title	Who were the victims of this calamity?	How did this calamity affect the lives of those who survived it?	What part of this calamity was most difficult to understand or accept?

If you could send a message to the victims or the survivors of this calamity, what would you say? ______________________

____

____

Words-per-Minute Table

Unit Three

Directions: If you were timed while reading an article, refer to the Reading Time you recorded in the box at the end of the article. Use this words-per-minute table to determine your reading speed for that article. Then plot your reading speed on the graph on page 196.

Lesson	15	16	17	18	19	20	21	
No. of Words	1289	1097	1104	1127	987	1063	1184	
Minutes and Seconds								*Seconds*
1:30	859	731	736	751	658	709	789	**90**
1:40	773	658	662	676	592	638	710	**100**
1:50	703	598	602	615	538	580	646	**110**
2:00	645	549	552	564	494	532	592	**120**
2:10	595	506	510	520	456	491	546	**130**
2:20	552	470	473	483	423	456	507	**140**
2:30	516	439	442	451	395	425	474	**150**
2:40	483	411	414	423	370	399	444	**160**
2:50	455	387	390	398	348	375	418	**170**
3:00	430	366	368	376	329	354	395	**180**
3:10	407	346	349	356	312	336	374	**190**
3:20	387	329	331	338	296	319	355	**200**
3:30	368	313	315	322	282	304	338	**210**
3:40	352	299	301	307	269	290	323	**220**
3:50	336	286	288	294	257	277	309	**230**
4:00	322	274	276	282	247	266	296	**240**
4:10	309	263	265	270	237	255	284	**250**
4:20	297	253	255	260	228	245	273	**260**
4:30	286	244	245	250	219	236	263	**270**
4:40	276	235	237	242	212	228	254	**280**
4:50	267	227	228	233	204	220	245	**290**
5:00	258	219	221	225	197	213	237	**300**
5:10	249	212	214	218	191	206	229	**310**
5:20	242	206	207	211	185	199	222	**320**
5:30	234	199	201	205	179	193	215	**330**
5:40	227	194	195	199	174	188	209	**340**
5:50	221	188	189	193	169	182	203	**350**
6:00	215	183	184	188	165	177	197	**360**
6:10	209	178	179	183	160	172	192	**370**
6:20	204	173	174	178	156	168	187	**380**
6:30	198	169	170	173	152	164	182	**390**
6:40	193	165	166	169	148	159	178	**400**
6:50	189	161	162	165	144	156	173	**410**
7:00	184	157	158	161	141	152	169	**420**
7:10	180	153	154	157	138	148	165	**430**
7:20	176	150	151	154	135	145	161	**440**
7:30	172	146	147	150	132	142	158	**450**
7:40	168	143	144	147	129	139	154	**460**
7:50	165	140	141	144	126	136	151	**470**
8:00	161	137	138	141	123	133	148	**480**

Plotting Your Progress: Reading Speed

Unit Three

Directions: If you were timed while reading an article, write your words-per-minute rate for that in the box under the number of the lesson. Then plot your reading speed on the graph by putting a small X on the line directly above the number of the lesson, across from the number of words per minute you read. As you mark your speed for each lesson, graph your progress by drawing a line to connect the X's.

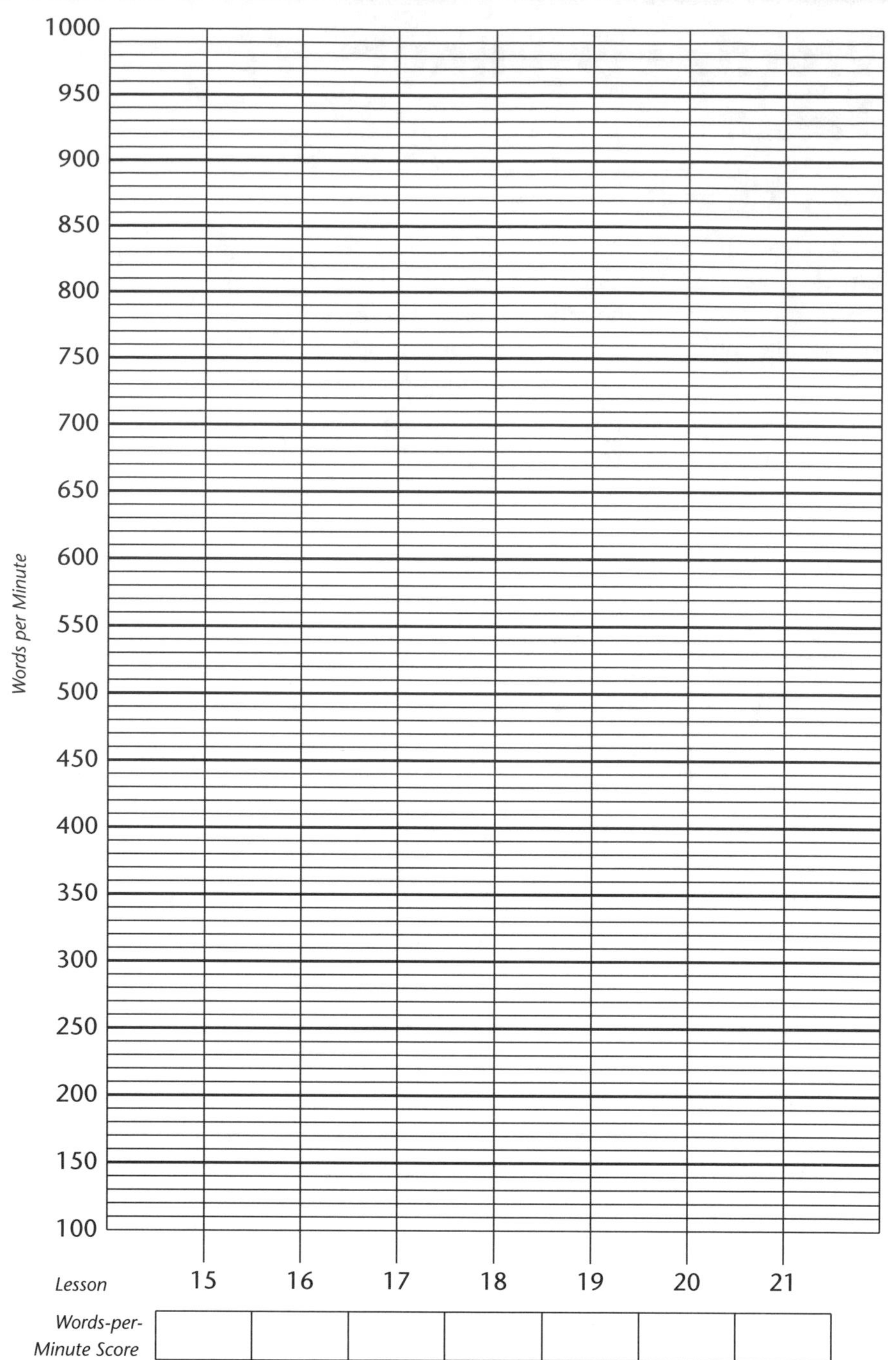

Plotting Your Progress: Reading Comprehension

Unit Three

Directions: Write your Reading Comprehension score for each lesson in the box under the number of the lesson. Then plot your score on the graph by putting a small X on the line directly above the number of the lesson and across from the score you earned. As you mark your score for each lesson, graph your progress by drawing a line to connect the X's.

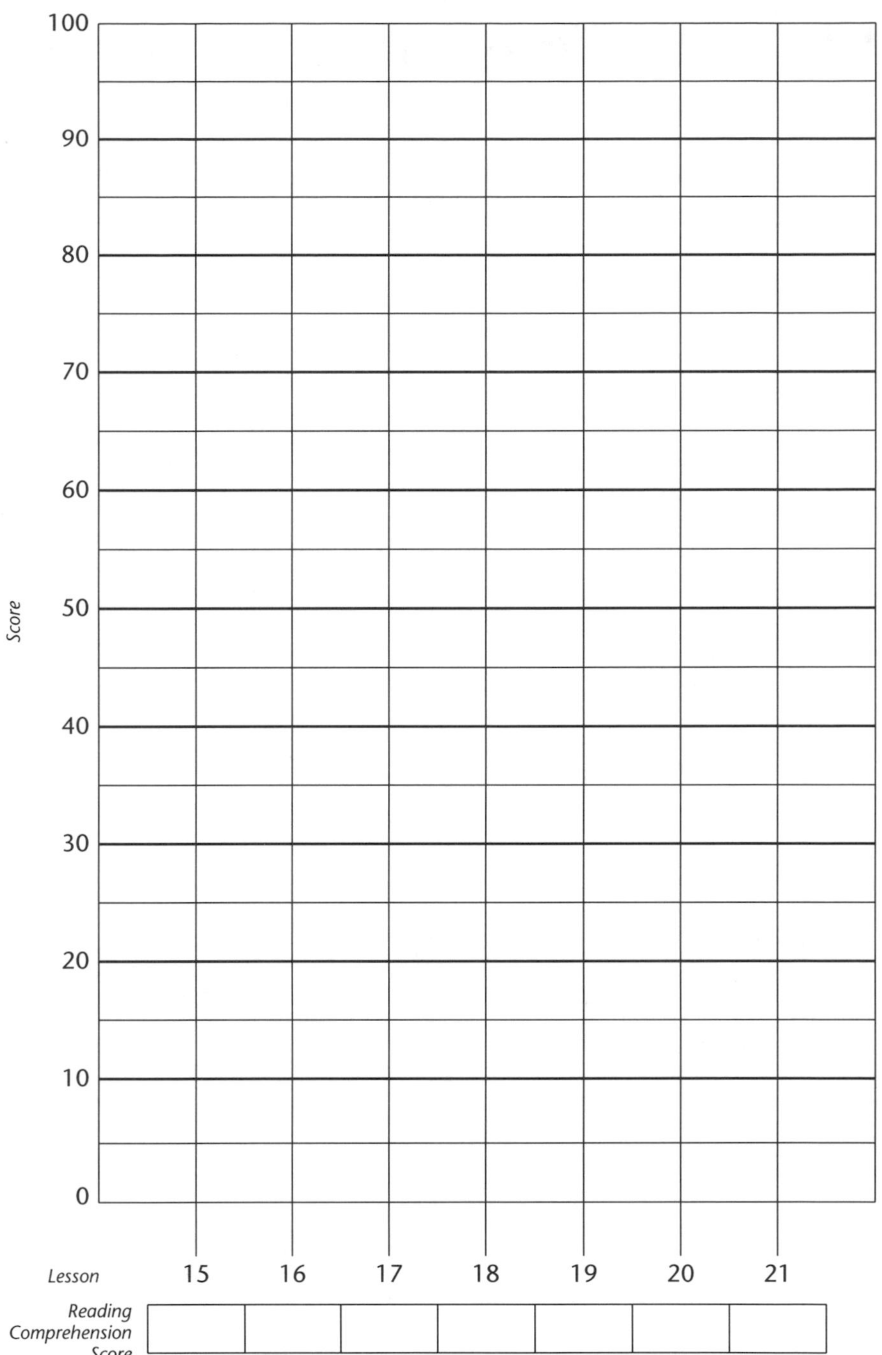

Plotting Your Progress: Critical Thinking

Unit Three

Directions: Work with your teacher to evaluate your responses to the Critical Thinking questions for each lesson. Then fill in the appropriate spaces in the chart below. For each lesson and each type of Critical Thinking question, do the following: Mark a minus sign (–) in the box to indicate areas in which you feel you could improve. Mark a plus sign (+) to indicate areas in which you feel you did well. Mark a minus-slash-plus sign (–/+) to indicate areas in which you had mixed success. Then write any comments you have about your performance, including ideas for improvement.

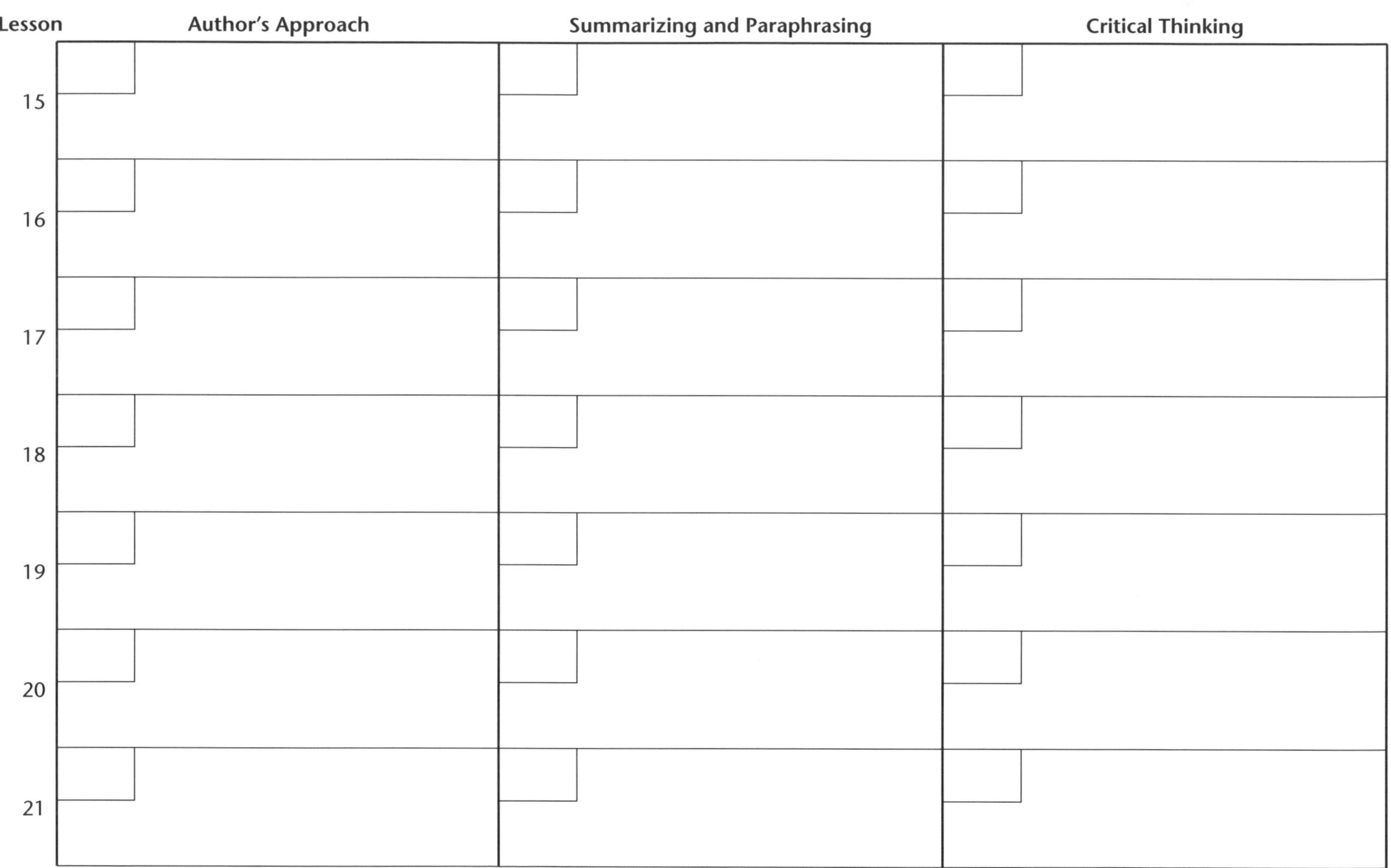

Lesson	Author's Approach	Summarizing and Paraphrasing	Critical Thinking
15			
16			
17			
18			
19			
20			
21			

Picture Credits

Cover: E. R. Degginger/Photo Researchers, Inc.

Sample Lesson: pp. 3, 4 CDC/Science Source/Photo Researchers; p. 5 AP/Wide World Photos

Unit 1 Opener: p. 13 AP/Wide World Photos

Lesson 1 pp. 14, 15 Corbis-Bettmann

Lesson 2 pp. 22, 23 Brown Brothers

Lesson 3 p. 30 Ted S. Warren, Austin *American-Statesman*/Gamma-Liaison; p. 31 AP/Wide World Photos

Lesson 4 p. 38 UPI/Corbis-Bettmann; p. 39 Dave Williams/The Photo Library Wales

Lesson 5 p. 46 AP/Wide World Photos; p. 47 Whitehead/Gamma-Liaison

Lesson 6 p. 54 AP/Wide World Photos; p. 55 Jan Housewerth, Kansas City *Star*/AP/Wide World Photos

Lesson 7 p. 54 Remsberg/Gamma-Liaison; p. 55 AP/Wide World Photos

Unit 2 Opener p. 75 AP/Wide World Photos

Lesson 8 p. 76, 77 AP/Wide World Photos

Lesson 9 p. 84 AP/Wide World Photos; p. 85 UPI/Corbis-Bettmann

Lesson 10 p. 92 PA News Photo Libary; p. 93 AP/Wide World Photos

Lesson 11 p. 100 Sygma; p. 101 Corbis-Bettmann

Lesson 12 pp. 108, 109 Mark Crosse/Gamma-Liaison

Lesson 13 p. 116 Frank Spooner/Gamma-Liaison; p. 117 Tampyx/Gamma-Liaison

Lesson 14 p. 124 AP/Wide World Photos; p. 125 Pam Francis; Inset: David Woo, Dallas *Morning Star*/Sygma

Unit 3 Opener p. 137 Reuters/Corbis-Bettmann

Lesson 15 p. 138 AP/Wide World Photos; p. 139 Sygma

Lesson 16 p. 146 AP/Wide World Photos; 147 Bob Thomas/Gamma-Liaison

Lesson 17 pp. 154, 155 NASA

Lesson 18 pp. 162, 163 Reuters/Corbis-Bettmann

Lesson 19 p. 170 AP/Wide World Photos; p. 171 Jerry Wolford/Sipa-Press

Lesson 20 p. 178 Baldev/Sygma; p. 179 Pablo Bartholomew/Gamma-Liaison

Lesson 21 pp. 186, 187 Agence France Presse/Corbis-Bettmann